Making Se

Palgrave Study Guides

Authoring a PhD	Presentation Skills for Students
Career Skills	The Principles of Writing in Psychology
Critical Thinking Skills	Professional Writing (2nd edn)
e-Learning Skills	Research Using IT
Effective Communication for Arts and Humanities Students	Skills for Success
Effective Communication for Science and Technology	The Study Abroad Handbook
The Exam Skills Handbook	The Student's Guide to Writing (2nd edn)
The Foundations of Research	The Student Life Handbook
The Good Supervisor	The Study Skills Handbook (2nd edn)
How to Manage your Arts, Humanities and Social Science Degree	Study Skills for Speakers of English as a Second Language
How to Manage your Distance and Open Learning Course	Studying the Built Environment
How to Manage your Postgraduate Course	Studying Business at MBA and Masters Level
How to Manage your Science and Technology Degree	Studying Economics
How to Study Foreign Languages	Studying History (3rd edn)
How to Write Better Essays	Studying Law
IT Skills for Successful Study	Studying Mathematics and its Applications
Making Sense of Statistics	Studying Modern Drama (2nd edn)
The Mature Student's Guide to Writing (2nd edn	Studying Physics
The Palgrave Student Planner	Studying Programming
The Personal Tutor's Handbook	Studying Psychology (2nd edn)
The Postgraduate Research Handbook	Teaching Study Skills and Supporting Learning

Palgrave Study Guides: Literature

General Editors: John Peck and Martin Coyle

How to Begin Studying English Literature (3rd edn)	How to Study Modern Poetry
How to Study a Jane Austen Novel (2nd edn)	How to Study a Novel (2nd edn)
How to Study a Charles Dickens Novel	How to Study a Poet
How to Study Chaucer (2nd edn)	How to Study a Renaissance Play
How to Study an E. M. Forster Novel	How to Study Romantic Poetry (2nd edn)
How to Study James Joyce	How to Study a Shakespeare Play (2nd edn)
How to Study Linguistics (2nd edn)	How to Study Television
	Practical Criticism

Making Sense of Statistics

A Non-mathematical Approach

Michael Wood

palgrave
macmillan

First published 2003 by
PALGRAVE MACMILLAN
Houndmills, Basingstoke, Hampshire RG21 6XS and
175 Fifth Avenue, New York, N.Y. 10010
Companies and representatives throughout the world

PALGRAVE MACMILLAN is the global academic imprint of the Palgrave Macmillan division of St. Martin's Press, LLC and of Palgrave Macmillan Ltd. Macmillan® is a registered trademark in the United States, United Kingdom and other countries. Palgrave is a registered trademark in the European Union and other countries.

ISBN-13: 978-1-4039-0107-1 paperback

Logging, pulping and manufacturing processes are expected to conform to the environmental regulations of the country of origin. This book is printed on paper suitable for recycling and made from fully managed and sustained forest sources.

A catalogue record for this book is available from the British Library.

10   9   8   7   6   5   4
12   11   10   09   08   07

Printed and bound in China

for Annette

Contents

List of Figures

List of Tables

Preface

There are a great many books on statistics, ranging from advanced mathematical works to simple introductions to the subject. The problem with books in the latter category is that statistics *is* a difficult subject: it is not that simple. This means that introductory books either cover only the very beginnings of the subject, or they leave a lot unmentioned or unexplained.

This book takes an unusual approach to statistics – a non-mathematical approach – which is designed to tackle this problem. The idea is to present a view of statistics which clarifies what the subject is really about, without getting bogged down in mathematics. There are only two mathematical equations in this book, and both are optional diversions from the main argument. Instead, the book focuses on concepts which are simple enough to describe in words and on computer simulations.

The book is intended for anyone who wants an introduction to probability and statistics which concentrates on the underlying concepts, rather than the mathematical formulae. This includes students studying statistics at college or university, readers who use statistics in research, or who want to be able to follow the ins and outs of the statistical results described in research reports, as well as readers with a general interest in statistics.

The book has a website at www.palgrave.com/studyguides/wood, from where you can download data files, interactive Excel spreadsheets and a program for 'resampling'.

I am grateful to many people for their comments, suggestions, reactions and encouragement, especially Arief Daynes, Andreas Hoecht, David Preece, Alan Rutter, Alan Stockdale, Annette Wood, and several reviewers of earlier drafts of the book.

Michael Wood
Emsworth, 2003

1 Introduction: Statistics, Non-mathematical Methods and How to Use this Book

This chapter introduces statistics and the approach taken in this book. Statistics is an important subject, but many aspects of it are difficult and misconceptions common. To try to get round some of the difficulties, this book takes a non-mathematical approach to the subject, which draws on various ideas, including computer simulation, and the random choice of balls from a bucket as a metaphor for probability and other statistical concepts. This chapter also outlines the (minimal) arithmetical expertise you will need, and makes some suggestions about computer software, and how to approach statistics and this book.

▶ 1.1 Statistics

The word *statistics* comes from the same root as the word for state, which reflects the fact that statistics originally referred to the use of data by the state. The scope of statistics has now spread far wider than this, and the term itself is commonly used in three senses. Statistics on earnings, sport, or the weather, are simply lists of numbers telling us such things as how much we earn, how many goals have been scored, or how much the earth is warming up. Statisticians refer to these numbers as 'data'. Secondly, we may refer to something calculated from this data as a statistic, for example the average earnings of teachers in the UK in 2001. The third meaning of statistics is to refer to the science which helps to analyse data,[1] and draw inferences from it, often with the help of the idea of probability. This is the subject of this book.

The methods of statistics and probability are useful when you're not quite sure what's going on. When things are certain and completely predictable, you don't need statistics; whenever there are uncertainties, or things you can't predict, statistics may have a role to play. There are three, interlinked, things you can do with statistics.

The first is that you can make predictions about what will happen. For example, the following predictions have been made with the help of statistics:

- The earth is heating up and average temperatures are likely to rise by three degrees Celsius by the 2080s.[2]
- My life expectancy is another 33 years: this is a statistically based 'best guess' about how many more years I will live.[3]
- There is 1 chance in 14 000 000 of a UK national lottery ticket winning the jackpot, but being killed by an asteroid crashing into the earth is, apparently, more likely than this: according to one estimate, 750 times more likely.[4]

None of these predictions is exact. A probabilistic prediction, like the last of these, only aims to say how probable things are, not to make definite predictions; this is, however, often the best we can do. My life expectancy is an average figure – it is the average we would expect over lots of different men of my age – so there is no implication that I will survive exactly 33 years, indeed this would be most improbable. I may drop dead tomorrow, and I may live another 60 years: both are unlikely, but experts could attach a probability to them.

The second thing you can do with statistics is build a statistical 'model': this is just a description of how a situation works in probabilistic or 'averaging' terms. (The use of the word 'model' in this context may strike you as odd, I'll return to this in Section 1.4.) For example, there is very clear evidence for a link between smoking and lung cancer: other things being equal, a person smoking 20 cigarettes a day has about a 20 times greater chance of developing lung cancer than a non-smoker.[5] A more detailed model would incorporate other factors, such as age, gender, extent of passive smoking and so on, and arrive at a more realistic assessment of the risks.

Models like this could be used to predict the number of smokers who will develop lung cancer, and the predictions above are all based on models. However, that is not really the purpose of this particular model. The main value of this model is the insight it gives us into the relationship between smoking and lung cancer and the folly of smoking. This insight might be used to estimate the savings to the health service, or the increased cost of pensions, if the number of smokers were to be reduced by a given amount (see Chapter 9 for this type of model).

The third role of statistics is to answer questions about the strength of evidence and how much certainty can be attached to both predictions and models. This can be done in several ways, of which the most useful is often to express estimates as intervals. Instead of citing a prediction from an opinion poll (based on a sample of 1000 electors) that 38% of electors will vote Labour, we can use statistics to derive the less precise, but more realistic, prediction that we can be 95%[6] confident that the number of Labour voters will be somewhere between 35% and 41%. The extent of the imprecision in this prediction is the width of this interval: 6%. If we wanted a more precise prediction with a narrower interval, we would need a larger sample for the opinion poll. Statistical methods can tell us what size we need (see Chapter 7).

It is difficult to overstate the importance of statistics. Economics, education, health care, business, weather forecasting, running a football club, getting elected to run a government, gambling or analysing a survey or an experiment all benefit from the thoughtful use of statistical methods. The modern view of the subatomic world is based on the theory of quantum mechanics, which cannot predict accurately what will happen to individual particles, but only what will *probably* happen or what will happen on *average*. Statistical ideas are an integral part of most academic disciplines: you need to know what statistics is about to do useful research in just about anything.

The same applies to everyday life. Whenever we're not quite sure what's going on, or exactly what the important influences or trends are, then the best approach, often the only approach, may be to use averages and probabilities: we need the statistical approach. Despite this, there are other ways of dealing with uncertainty that don't come under the umbrella of statistics: 'fuzzy logic' and the idea of 'chaos', for example. We'll look briefly at these in Chapter 4.

Statistics is not the most popular subject on the curriculum, and errors and misconceptions are common. In the next section, I'll look briefly at some of the difficulties of statistics, which leads into the rationale behind the non-mathematical approach taken in this book.

▶ 1.2 The difficulties of statistics

Statistics has a bad press for a variety of reasons. At an elementary level, the suspicion tends to be that results are meaningless or misleading because the data on which they are based is distorted in some way, sometimes deliberately so.[7] There are, after all, 'lies, damned lies, and statistics'.[8] When we are told that men think about sex every six seconds, or that 86% of married women committed adultery in the last year, it's natural to wonder where the information comes from, and how it could be obtained without a serious danger of distortion.

Even when data comes from a supposedly respectable source, you should be cautious. The 33-year estimate of my life expectancy is based on tables used by actuarial students in the year 2000, but they are based 'on the mortality of the male population of England and Wales in the years 1960–62'.[9] The data is based on mortality rates 40 years in the past, rather than the coming century, which is when the events responsible for my death will occur.

A different sort of difficulty arises from the statement that you are 750 times more likely to die as a result of an asteroid crashing into the earth, than to win the jackpot on the UK national lottery. There must be several thousand jackpot winners alive in the UK today; does this mean that there were 750 times this number of deaths from asteroid collisions in the last few years, and that it is far more sensible to take precautions against asteroids than it is to enter the national lottery?

It is not hard to see where the difficulties lie here.[10] Common sense and a determination to think clearly is all that is really required. At a more advanced level, however, this may not be good enough, because the statistical concepts and methods are often too convoluted and complex. For example, according to an article in the *Guardian*, 30 years ago there was a cancer cluster around the town of Aldermaston with a 'probability of chance occurrence' of 1 in 10 000 000.[11] Aldermaston was the site of a nuclear installation; the suspicion being, of course, that this was responsible for the abnormally high level of cancers in the surrounding neighbourhood. The article gives a layman's account of a common type of statistical analysis, a 'null hypothesis test'. The research raises lots of obvious questions, the most obvious being how clusters are defined, but what I want to concentrate on here is what the statistical result, a probability of 1 in 10 000 000, actually means? There are two obvious interpretations, both wrong:

1. Does it refer to the chance of getting cancer, as most people to whom I have shown the article assume? No, it does not. The probability of 1 in 10 000 000 has no relation whatsoever to the chances of contracting cancer (which is far higher than this).
2. Does it refer to the probability of the cluster being an accident and having nothing to do with the nuclear installation? This would imply that there is a 99.9999% chance of the nuclear installation being responsible for the cluster. This sounds plausible, but is again wrong.

The correct interpretation is the third, which, in my experience occurs to few, if any, statistically unsophisticated readers of the original article:

3. The probability actually refers to the chance of the cluster occurring *on the assumption that cancer cases occur at random*: that is, on the assumption that the nuclear installation had no impact. This probability differs from interpretation 2 in the same way that the probability that a successful bank robber is rich – presumably close to 100% – differs from the probability that a rich person is a successful bank robber – presumably close to 0% (Section 2.2).

Interpretations 1 and 2 both correspond to information which would be very useful to have. This is probably the reason for people assuming that one of these interpretations is correct. The correct interpretation, on the other hand, is difficult to get one's mind round, and does not tell us anything we really want to know. To the mind untutored in statistics, if we are interested in the possibility that the nuclear installation has got something to do with the cancer clusters, why mess about with probabilities based on the assumption that it hasn't? On top of that, the mathematical details of how it works are far too complex for the article to explain. These have to be taken on trust, and cannot serve to clarify the meaning of the conclusion. (We'll return to this example in Chapter 8.)

A very similar difficulty arose in the trial of Sally Clark who was accused of murdering two of her children.[12] One of the alternative explanations for the children's deaths was sudden infant death syndrome (SIDS or 'cot death'). At her original trial, a figure of 1 in 73 000 000 was quoted for the probability of having two SIDS cases in a single family. This was part of the evidence that led to her conviction, which was later overturned, but not until she had spent several years in prison.

There are three problems with this 1 in 73 000 000. First, it's wrong (see Section 5.2). Second, it's irrelevant: the defence case was the deaths were natural, but not that they were due to SIDS.[13] And third, despite its incorrectness and irrelevance, the 1 in 73 000 000 is liable to be misinterpreted as the chance that the deaths were natural, which seems to imply that the children almost certainly were murdered. This logic is completely wrong, in just the same way that the second interpretation of the Aldermaston data is wrong. In the legal context, it's known as the 'prosecutor's fallacy' (see also Exercise 6.7.3).

Unfortunately, these are not isolated examples.[14] Many statistical ideas are difficult and misconceptions are common. The idea of this book is to present a non-mathematical approach to statistics which will, I hope, make things a bit clearer. The next two sections introduce the basic elements of this approach.

▶ 1.3 Non-mathematical methods

Statistics is usually seen as a branch of mathematics. This makes non-mathematical statistics seem as sensible a concept as inedible food or illogical logic. However, I intend to prise the two domains apart by taking a particular perspective on statistics, and what some might regard as a rather restricted interpretation of mathematics. But the first question is, why bother? Mathematical statistics seems to work OK, so what's the point in non-mathematical statistics?

There are two answers to this. The first is that mathematical statistics does not work satisfactorily, except for the experts. At anything beyond an elementary level, the conceptual and mathematical difficulties are substantial, as we have just seen. This leads to incomprehension on the part of novices trying to master the subject, and to techniques being misapplied and their results misinterpreted, even by people who think they know what they are doing.

The second advantage of the non-mathematical approach in this book is that aspects of it are sometimes superior to the conventional approach by criteria that a mathematician would appreciate: generality and the ability to solve difficult problems (for example some of the methods in Chapters 7 and 8). So what do I mean by the non-mathematical approach?

The non-mathematical[15] version of statistics presented here has *no* algebra or mathematical formulae or equations, and does not rely on mathematical proofs and computer packages doing mysterious things in mysterious ways. All arithmetical relations used are simple enough to be described in words or by means of a graph. This book makes *no* assumptions about the reader's mathematical understanding beyond elementary arithmetic and the use of simple graphs. I am assuming some familiarity with the four rules of arithmetic, fractions, decimals, percentages, negative numbers and simple graphs, but that's about it (see Section 1.5).

This is *not* the same as providing you with a gentle approach to the standard mathematical formulae of statistics. These formulae do not come into the story. They are bypassed; we get the answer without them, by using concepts and methods that are simpler and more direct than the conventional ones. For example, one problem in statistics is finding a line on a graph which gives the 'best fit' to some data (Section 9.2). There is a formula, but in this book we will use trial and error, which, when assisted by a computer, is surprisingly efficient. That way we avoid the formula, and all the hidden assumptions which you need to make but never realise you are making. This does not mean that you have to take what I say on trust. You should be able to see exactly how, and why, the non-mathematical methods work, and what the answers mean. The rationale behind the methods should be transparent. This means that the mathematical difficulties – in the sense of difficulties with equations and formulae – are eliminated. However, the other difficulties discussed above remain; problems of interpretation can then be faced without the distractions of mathematics.

You may, however, want to relate these non-mathematical methods to the formulae and concepts in other statistics books and in computer packages. To help you do this, most chapters include a section called Similar concepts:

these are described in terms of the non-mathematical methods developed in the chapter. For example, the method known as 'bootstrapping' described in Chapter 7 is a non-mathematical approach to a statistical concept known as a 'confidence interval'. The usual approach to confidence intervals develops them by means of the mathematical theory of probability: this leads to formulae for deriving confidence intervals. The Similar concepts section in Chapter 7 mentions these formulae. It does not, however, explain the use or rationale of these formulae in detail, as this would take us too far from our non-mathematical approach. The important thing is to understand what a confidence interval means, so that, for example, you know whether or not it is a sensible quantity to ask a computer package to calculate.

As the language of mathematics isn't being used to help make sense of statistics, we'll need some alternatives. One metaphor that is very useful is the idea of a bucket with some balls in it. This is introduced in the next section.

▶ 1.4 Bucket and ball models and computer simulation

The usual way of approaching statistics is to set up an abstract 'model' in which words are used in special ways. Probability, for example, is described in terms of 'experiments' with 'outcomes', despite the fact that most situations involving probability are not experiments, and many of the outcomes aren't really outcomes. You then consider a 'sample space', which, of course, isn't a space, write down the rules (called axioms) which probability is supposed to obey, and then use these rules to deduce more complicated rules, in other words to use the methods of mathematics to see where they lead. The final model is typically a set of mathematical equations.

My approach here is different. We start with a *physical* model – balls in a bucket – and then relate things to this as directly as possible, without using mathematics as an intermediary. Then you can see the concepts and methods of statistics in terms of something definite and visualisable. This means we can manage without any mathematics more advanced than simple arithmetic. I mean a model in the ordinary sense of the word, like a model train or a child's doll. By playing with the model you can learn about trains or people. In just the same way, by playing with the balls in a bucket, you can, for example, estimate probabilities and understand how they can be interpreted and used. Does this mean that you will need to invest in a bucket and a lot of balls before you can proceed further? Well, no, not really, although it might be helpful. It is enough to be able to *imagine* the balls in a bucket.

So why buckets and balls? When introducing ideas of probability, textbooks often illustrate concepts by references to examples about balls in urns, because they are easy to visualise and make the necessary points in a simple way. For example:

> There are two green balls and two black balls in an urn. What is the probability that a ball drawn *at random* will be black?

The phrase 'at random' here means that we choose a ball without checking its colour in such a way that all four balls are *equally likely* to be chosen. This could be achieved if all the balls were the same size, shape, weight and texture, they are thoroughly mixed beforehand and the choice is made with a blindfold on. The answer to the question, of course, is two out of four, or 1/2 or 50%, because two of the four balls are black. I will use buckets instead of urns because they are likely to be more familiar to you. An alternative image would be to think of a lottery.

We can use the model of balls in a bucket, or a lottery, for more complicated examples. A standard demonstration in lectures on simple probability is to ask members of the audience for their estimate of the probability of two members of the audience sharing the same birthday. This turns out to be more than most people think: for example in a group of 50 there is a 97% chance that there will be at least two people with the same birthday, so the lecturer can afford a substantial bet on it. Even in a group of 23 the chance is still as much as 51%. This is according to the mathematical theory of probability. How can we do it non-mathematically?

The answer is to build a model of the situation. Imagine that the lecture room is the bucket, and each member of the audience is represented by a ball. We could imagine a portrait on each ball, but as all we are interested in is birthdays, it is simpler to imagine a birthday stamped on each ball. Where do these people in the audience come from? We could imagine a second bucket, much bigger, containing balls representing people in the local community from which the members of the audience come. If we assume the audience are effectively drawn at random from this bigger bucket, we now have a model of the audience and where it comes from.

We can now run the model, or at least the important bits of it, on a computer. Imagine drawing the balls for the audience bucket from the bigger, local community, bucket. We're interested in birthdays, and it's reasonable to assume that each person's birthday is equally likely to be any of the 365 days of the year (ignoring leap years). This means we can *simulate* this process on a computer by generating 50 numbers, each chosen randomly from the range 1–365 representing each possible birthday. Computer programs (like Excel) have built-in functions for generating random numbers like this – for behaving as though they were blindfolded and drawing balls from a bucket. If you have a computer and Excel, it would be a good idea to try it yourself to get a feel for how it works.[16]

When I did this the result was: 337 7 285 244 98 313 329 138 94 182 242 129 333 140 323 24 222 110 76 306 146 250 17 263 332 189 122 227 93 118 25 360 155 135 124 30 66 9 143 243 134 345 324 215 78 181 151 239 9 220. As you can see, there are two 'people' with the same birthday, the two 9s representing 9 January, in this 'audience'.

This, of course, is not a real audience. It's a hypothetical audience which we made by playing with our bucket and ball model. But if we now generate, say, 100 hypothetical audiences like this, we'll be in a position to say something about the real audience. To do this, a third bucket is helpful. Take one of the 100 hypothetical audiences, get a ball and put a tick on it if two people in this hypothetical audience share a birthday, otherwise put a cross on it. Repeat for each of the 100 hypothetical audiences. Put the resulting 100 balls in the third bucket.

When I generated 100 hypothetical audiences in this way, I found that 96 of the 100 balls in the third bucket were ticked. Ninety six per cent of the 100 hypothetical audiences had at least two people who shared a birthday. This suggests that about 96% of *real* audiences of 50 people will include at least two people who have the same birthday, assuming that real audiences are drawn in much the same way as the hypothetical audiences in the model. The estimate of the probability for two people sharing a birthday was 96%, not quite the 97% produced by the mathematical theory, but close enough to be useful. If I wanted a better answer, I would have to generate more 'audiences' and put more balls in the third bucket.

We don't *need* the image of buckets and balls here. We could imagine audiences of people without thinking of them as balls in a bucket. However, the idea of balls in a bucket is useful to remind us that we are dealing with a model, not with reality itself. (The 100 computer-generated audiences are imaginary, not real.) And when we come on to models which apply to a wide variety of different situations – such as the two bucket model in Chapter 5, or the pruned ball method in Chapter 6 – the bucket and ball image gives us a very useful way of describing what's going on. (The two bucket model will, in fact, simulate the birthday problem – see Section 5.4.)

The underlying metaphor may use buckets and balls, but the practical method involves 'computer simulation'. This is a very crude way of working out probabilities. All we do is run the process through on a computer lots of times and see what pattern emerges. This is, however, good enough for most purposes. Methods like this are often preferable in some ways to those obtained from the mathematical formulae: they tend to be of more general applicability and depend on fewer assumptions. Even professional statisticians tend to use simulation methods when they are faced with a very difficult problem and cannot see a suitable mathematical formula. Very similar comments apply to the trial and error method I mentioned in Section 1.3. Like simulation, this is crude and longwinded, but very effective and it's obvious what's going on. I've called methods such as this 'crunchy methods'.[17]

▶ 1.5 Numbers, calculators and computers

The approach I am following in this book may be non-mathematical, but it does use numbers! I am assuming you are familiar with the four operations of addition, subtraction, multiplication and division. This includes negative numbers,[18] fractions, percentages, and the idea of squares and square roots.[19] Calculators are helpful for working out answers, but a computer and, in particular, a spreadsheet such as Microsoft Excel is far more useful. It is much more flexible, and all the numbers and calculations you enter are stored and displayed so that you can check them and change them as necessary. Whenever, possible, I would suggest using a computer for arithmetical calculations. A spreadsheet such as Excel is the most useful piece of computer software for studying statistics. There are some Excel files on the web (see Appendix C) to accompany this book, and there is a brief introduction to the use of the package in Appendix A.

For more serious work there are a range of computer packages specifically designed for statistical analysis. One such package is SPSS (Statistical Package for the Social Sciences). I have included a brief introduction to this package in Appendix B, and I have also explained how SPSS procedures relate to the topics covered in many of the chapters of this book. The purpose of this is to assist readers using SPSS for research purposes. You do not need SPSS to study statistics. To use the Excel files you will need to have Excel installed on your computer. Similarly, SPSS is a package which must be installed on your computer. If you have neither of these, you will still be able to use a program on the web – *resample.exe* – which works independently of any other software. This program is a computer version of what is introduced in Chapter 5 as the 'two bucket model'. It is also useful for quite a lot of the material in later chapters.

Computers are useful for studying statistics. You can key in some data, ask a question about it and get an almost immediate response, often in the form of a graph. Playing with a computer in this way is very helpful for building up intuitions about how concepts and methods work. The files on the web are designed to encourage this sort of interaction (for example you could have a look at `reg2way.xls` for a preview of Chapter 9 – try adjusting the numbers in the green cells).

However, it is not essential to use a computer. I have written this book on the assumption that some readers will have a computer, but others won't. Despite this, some of the methods in this book depend on a computer; they would not be possible without one. In these cases, I have described what the software does in the text. If you have a computer, you can try it for yourself; otherwise you can simply follow the account in the text. At other points, the computer is not essential to the explanation. To avoid cluttering up the text, I have put details of how to use computer software in the notes which you will find at the end of the book.

I'll finish this section with a couple of reminders about numbers. You obviously don't need a spreadsheet to understand numbers, but if do have Excel available, you may find it clarifies even these simple points. It is often useful to write fractional numbers as percentages. For example, a third can be written as 1/3 or 0.3333 or 33.33%, and two-sevenths as 2/7, or 0.2857, or 28.57%. The first of these you can probably work out in your head, but you may need a calculator or computer for the second. Two-sevenths means 2 divided by 7. This is simple with a calculator. With Excel use the formula = 2/7 and you can then (if you want) format the cell (Format – Cells) as a percentage. If you do this, you should see 0.2857. . . change into the equivalent 28.57%.

If you write two-sevenths, or a third, as a decimal or a percentage, the sequence of digits goes on for ever, but Excel or your calculator will cut if off after about a dozen digits. In practice a long list of digits after the decimal point only confuses matters. You will find it much easier to see any patterns if you *round* numbers off so that you don't see too much detail. For example, two-sevenths rounded off to the nearest per cent (0 decimal places) is 29%, since 28.57% is a bit closer to 29% than to 28%. Don't forget to do this: it makes a big difference to how easy it is to spot patterns. Excel will round numbers for you (see Appendix A). Where appropriate, I have rounded off the results of calculations in the text of this book, so if you think I've got something slightly wrong, it may just be the rounding.

▶ 1.6 Suggestions for studying statistics and using this book

The non-mathematical approach adopted in this book means that you don't need to be a proficient mathematician to follow the argument. However, this is not the same as saying that you don't need to think. Many of the arguments are subtle and you will need to concentrate to follow them. To help you, I have included a selection of exercises at the end of most chapters to give you the opportunity to practise using statistical ideas. I have also used a bold question mark at the end of a paragraph as an invitation for you to consider your answer to the question posed before reading mine. So, whenever a paragraph ends in a bold **?**, pause to think of your own answer. You may have no idea, or you may just have a rough idea, but you are more likely to understand the answer having asked yourself the question. Sometimes I will ask something so easy that it may seem patronising (for example working out the average of a small group of numbers); the point of this is to make sure you realise how easy it is. So, when reading this book, please concentrate hard on all the details, pause to ask yourself the questions posed at the end of paragraphs ending with a bold question mark, and make sure that you have a go at the exercises. Are you likely to follow this advice**?**

When I started drafting this book, my initial assumption was that you would follow this advice and read and consider every sentence, number, table and diagram, and do all the exercises. Then I gave a draft of a few chapters to a couple of friends for their comments. There were no comments on any numbers, tables, diagrams or exercises, which raised my suspicions that none of these had been studied in any detail. Then I thought of my own approach to reading mathematical arguments: I usually skip the details and try and take in the gist of the argument, and then return to the details if I want to see how to 'do' it. To be honest, unless I do return to the details, I usually end up with a slightly vague understanding: I'm not fully confident that I see just how it works, and sometimes I do get it a bit wrong. So my advice would be to find time to look at the details, pause when you see **?**, and have a go at the exercises. This advice, however, glosses over the fact that things can be understood in different ways. And some ways are more useful than others.

1.6.1 What does it mean to understand statistics?

In Section 1.4 we saw how to solve the 'birthday' problem by simulation. I explained how the probability could be worked out by simulating lots of audiences on a computer. Alternatively, I could have told you that it is possible to use a 'formula', which is equivalent to this rule: multiply 364/365 by 363/365 by 362/365 and so on all the way to 316/365, and then subtract the answer from 1. This will give you 97%, which is the probability that at least two people in an audience of 50 share a birthday. Two different ways of getting to much the same answer. Which do you prefer**?**

If you could see *why* the rule works, my guess would be that you prefer the rule. It's (probably) easier to do than the simulation, and the fact that you know why it works should mean that you have confidence that it's right, and you should be able to adjust it for different circumstances (for example audiences of 20). You'll know exactly what the answer means, and the assumptions on which it's based.

But, it's more likely (I suspect) that you don't see why the rule works. It's just an arbitrary set of instructions: you don't know what the rationale is, so you can't adjust it, or check the assumptions on which it's based. It's a pretty useless form of understanding. In these circumstances, I hope you would prefer the simulation, because you should be able to understand *how* this works, so it should be obvious *why* it gives you the answer. This is based on the conviction that it's important to understand as much as possible of how statistical methods work and how conclusions should be interpreted. With a computer, it's often easy to get the answer, but without a deeper appreciation of how and why methods work, it is very easy to misinterpret what's going on, and very difficult to spot any snags or adapt the method to a new situation. The Aldermaston example in Section 1.2 should have alerted you to just how slippery some statistical ideas can be. The non-mathematical methods in this book are designed to be understood in this deeper sense. You should be able appreciate the rationale behind the method, as well as just seeing how to do it.

Despite this, you might feel that the simulation method is, in some sense, cheating. You just build a model of lots of audiences and look at the pattern. There is some truth in this view. If you stick to simulation, you will miss some of the insights provided by the mathematical theory of probability. But using the rule above, without any of the background understanding, would be no better. You need to understand why the rule works and where it comes from in order to get these insights. In this particular problem, this is not too difficult (you may be able to work it out after reading Section 5.2), but for more advanced problems, it would be out of reach for most people. On the other hand, the simulation method, and other similar methods, will get you answers in ways which are transparent enough to see what's going on. And they are often more flexible than most formula-based methods. That's why I'm focusing on them in this book.

1.6.2 Why are you reading this book? Advice for different readers

You may be reading this book because you have a general interest in statistics. You may want to know what statistics can offer, what the hazards are and so on, but have no specific purpose in mind. In this case the advice above applies, and that's about it. However, you may have a more specific reason for studying statistics. Does this apply to you?

There are three possibilities I can envisage. First, you may be enroled on a course in statistics. The Similar concepts section in each chapter should be helpful for relating the non-mathematical methods in this book to other methods covered in your course. Use the index. The second possibility is that you may need to use statistics for a specific purpose. Perhaps you are doing a research project that requires some statistical analysis? Your interest in statistics is as a 'producer' of statistical information. The third possibility is that you may need to interpret research reports which include statistical jargon. In this case your interest is as a 'consumer' of statistics. For example, suppose you are reading a research paper which includes an 'analysis of variance'. If you look up 'analysis of variance' in the index, you will be referred to the Similar concepts section in Chapter 8. This will tell you that analysis of variance is similar to a method explained in Chapter 8, and also relates to some of the ideas in Chapter 9. These chapters should help you understand the basic idea of analysis of variance (although not the detail).

I have tried to cater for producers and consumers in the text and the exercises at the end of each chapter. However, even if you see yourself primarily as a consumer, getting stuck in and doing some analysis yourself may be the best way of getting to grips with what it means. Conversely, even if you see yourself as a producer, interpretation is obviously important. One way in which both producers and consumers of statistics are likely to differ from the general student of statistics is that their interests are likely to be more focused. If you want to do some statistical modelling (Chapter 9), you may want to dive in here and ignore the earlier chapters. As you will see in the next section, I have tried, as far as possible, to help you do this.

1.6.3 The organisation of this book

Like most books, this book is designed to be read in the order in which it appears: Chapter 1 before Chapter 2, Chapter 2 before Chapter 3 and so on. I have, however, tried to keep individual chapters as self-contained as possible, so that readers who are interested in a particular chapter can start by reading that chapter. Dipping into later chapters before reading the preceding chapters is much easier with the approach taken in this book than the more conventional approach. The chapter on confidence intervals (Chapter 7) does not, for example, build on the chapter on probability distributions (part of Chapter 5), as it would in the conventional approach. Obviously, you will miss a few specific points, and some of the background philosophy of the book, by dipping into it like this, but you should be able to see the gist of the argument. (I have included cross-references to earlier sections to help readers who may not have read these sections.)

But which chapter is relevant to your problems? I'll finish this chapter by previewing each of the remaining chapters. You will also find a slightly longer preview at the start of each chapter. (Any terms you don't understand should become clearer after you've read the chapter in question.)

Chapter 2 defines probability via the metaphor of balls in buckets, and the ignoramus who cannot distinguish one ball from the next. Statistics is viewed as a way of treating life as a lottery. This chapter also looks at the use of samples.

Chapter 3 introduces diagrams and summary statistics: bar charts, histograms, scatter plots, averages, measures of spread and correlation. If you've got some data from a survey, or something similar, this chapter will show the main ways you can break the data down to show patterns and relationships.

Chapter 4 builds on the ideas introduced in Chapters 2 and 3, and analyses the key features of the statistical approach to life, and its strengths and weaknesses. It also gives a very brief review of related and alternative ideas, for example fuzzy logic and the idea of chaos.

Chapter 5 explains how probabilities can be estimated and interpreted by means of thought experiments with bucket models and computer simulation. It also looks at the Poisson and normal distributions.

Chapter 6 considers the problem of using evidence to decide what can be inferred about the actual world. Three approaches are introduced: the bucket and ball equivalent of Bayes theorem, null hypothesis testing, and confidence intervals.

Chapter 7 explains confidence intervals in more detail. The idea is to assess, in probabilistic terms, the size of the error when using a sample to guess what the general picture is like.

Chapter 8 explains how probabilities can be calculated to see how plausible a null hypothesis is.

Chapter 9 looks at regression modelling: a way of making predictions from a sample of data, and understanding the relationships between the variables in the data.

Chapter 10 concerns strategies for empirical research: the differences between surveys and experiments, and the practicalities of collecting data. It also (in Section 10.3) makes some suggestions about what to do if you meet some concepts or techniques which you have not seen before, and which are not covered in this book.

The website at www.palgrave.com/studyguides/wood has some data files and interactive Excel spreadsheets which you can download. All the computer files mentioned are on this website. (You will recognise a computer file as a word ending in one of: *.exe .htm .txt .xla .xls*.)

2 Probability, Samples, Buckets and Balls

This chapter looks at two interlinked areas of statistics using the bucket and ball metaphor introduced in Chapter 1: the meaning, origin and use of 'probabilities'; and 'sampling' – the process of basing probabilities, and other statistics, on a small sample rather than everything of interest. The best samples are generally 'random samples', chosen so that each individual has the same probability of being selected.

▶ 2.1 Probability

Probability is a very general idea. You can talk about the probability that it'll rain tomorrow, the probability of winning the lottery, the probability that mankind will become extinct in the next century, the probability that telepathy is possible and so on. As explained in Section 1.4, I am going to visualise probability in terms of bucket and ball models. The probability of a possibility is simply the proportion of balls in a bucket exhibiting that possibility (for example being black). For example, the probability of picking a black ball from a bucket containing two green and two black balls is 50%, because two of the four balls, or 50%, are black. Imagine that you pick a ball from this bucket and it turns out to be green. There are now three balls left, two black and one green. What's the probability now of picking a black ball?

The contents of the bucket have changed. The new probability is 2/3 or 67%. Now suppose we had put the black ball back, so we are back at the starting point with two green and two black balls in the bucket. What would the probability of a black ball be for the next draw?

The probability is 50% because there are two black and two green balls. The probability only depends on what's in the bucket, not on what's happened earlier, of course. (This distinction between replacing balls in the bucket, and not replacing them, is important. We'll return to it in Section 5.4.) What is the probability of picking a pink ball from this bucket? What about a ball which is either green or black?

The probability of picking a pink ball is zero because there aren't any in the bucket. The probability of picking a ball which is either green or black is one, because all the balls are one of these two colours. A probability of *zero* represents something that *cannot* happen, and a probability of *one* represents something that *will definitely* happen.

Most probabilities don't, of course, concern buckets and balls at all, but you can *imagine* such a model to interpret *any* probability. Obviously you won't always need to use the model explicitly. The idea is simply to use a concrete image on which to hang the abstract idea of probability. For example, what about a probability of 15% for the probability of rain falling tomorrow in a particular place? How many balls would you put in the bucket, and what would the balls represent?

You could have 100 balls with 15 labelled *rain* and the other 85 labelled *fine*. Alternatively you could have 20 balls with *rain* stamped on 3 of them. The probability is obviously the same in either case,[20] so it doesn't matter which model you choose.

The word 'possibility' is important. Probabilities are only really interesting when something is possible, but not definite or definitely impossible. For a God who knows everything, probabilities would be of no interest. Probabilities are an assessment of ignorance and must depend on the nature of the ignorance. This ignorance is represented in a bucket and ball model by the act of drawing a ball at *random*, with your eyes shut so that you can't distinguish one ball from another, and they are all *equally likely* to be chosen. The person who constructs, or imagines, a bucket and ball model is a crucial part of the situation, deserving a special name – an 'ignoramus'. Whenever you see a probability, imagine a bucket, with some suitably labelled balls in it and a blindfolded ignoramus drawing one of the balls out of the bucket.

In Chapter 1 we looked at the problem of estimating the probability that two or more people in a room have the same birthday. Here are a few more examples of probabilities.

The organiser of a fete wants to estimate the probability of rain on the day of the fete, Friday 13 June. As the fete is in June she consults the weather records for June in the last ten years. Each of these 300 days is labelled R (for rain) or D (for dry). She then decides that 13 June is likely to be similar to one of these 300 days and there's no reason to suppose one of them is any more likely than any other, so they must all be equally likely. The bucket she constructs in her mind contains balls representing these 300 days, and the probability of the possibility of rain can be estimated as the proportion of balls labelled R in this bucket. Let's say there are 96 balls labelled R, so this proportion is 96/300 or 32%.

This obviously depends on the 300 days somehow representing 'equally likely weather patterns' for the *next* 13 June. A judgement has to be made – by our ignoramus, the fete organiser – about whether this is reasonable, taking account of the fact that a sample of ten Junes might be considered small, the possibility of climate change and so on.

This is, of course, a very crude model, corresponding to a high degree of ignorance about the weather on 13 June. Imagine now that our fete organiser has access to a weather forecast which says the chance of rain is only one in ten. This makes a 300 ball model redundant: she can now simply imagine 10 balls, of which only one has R stamped on it. Is this second model better?

It's better in two senses. It uses the expertise of the weather forecaster, and it gives a more definite prediction: the closer probabilities are to 0% or 100%, the less the uncertainty, so the better the model in this sense. The greater the degree of certainty the better, provided our faith in this certainty is not misplaced.[21] The question of whether the 32% and 10% are 'true' probabilities is more difficult. The best test would be to get lots of 10% predictions and check to see if 10% of them are accurate.

Different ignoramuses may, of course, come to different decisions about the appropriate probability model. In this sense many probabilities are subjective: part of the point of talking about bucket and ball models is to emphasise the fact that probability models are just models, built according to the judgement of the ignoramus.

> A public opinion pollster asks a carefully chosen sample of 1000 electors which party they will vote for in an election. The bucket here contains 1000 balls representing the 1000 electors: 380 of them say they will vote for the Labour Party. This means that 38% of voters are likely to vote Labour or, to put it another way, the probability of a randomly chosen elector being a Labour voter is 38%.

This doesn't seem at all subjective. However, it depends on the representativeness of the sample (see Section 2.5) and whether those polled tell the truth: deciding whether these criteria are satisfied requires judgement. Some polls are more believable than others.

Some probabilities require rather more imagination to interpret. If you want the probability that telepathy – communication between people by senses which are not known to science – is possible, then you might let the balls represent worlds in which telepathy is possible and worlds in which telepathy is impossible. Furthermore, you will need to produce a set of 'equally likely' such possible worlds (see Chapter 6, especially Section 6.4).

▶ 2.2 What do the balls and buckets represent?

The balls in a bucket may represent people with birthdays (see Section 1.4), electors, possible future June days or different possible worlds. There are many possibilities: I am using the balls as a neutral model to cover any of these, as well as others we haven't thought of yet. Similarly, the bucket can represent many things: a sample of electors, a whole population, an audience at a lecture, a group of possible weather patterns or something else.[22] However, it's important to be careful. There are always different buckets containing different sets of balls corresponding to a different starting point for the probability. Consider this example:

A survey of 1000 men found that 100 of them were rich (according to some clear definition), and the other 900 were not rich. Ten of the 100 rich men were bank robbers, but only one of the 900 who were not rich was a bank robber. This is summarised in Table 2.1.

What is the probability that a bank robber is a rich man? And what about the probability that a rich man is a bank robber?

For the first probability, the relevant bucket contains balls representing all the bank robbers in the sample. This bucket contains 11 balls representing 11 bank robbers. Ten of these 11 are rich, so the probability of a bank robber being a rich man is 10/11 or 91%. For the second probability, the relevant bucket contains balls representing all the rich men in the sample. This bucket contains 100 balls of which 10 represent bank robbers, so the probability of a rich man being a bank robber is 10/100 or 10%. The two buckets represents completely different groups. Not surprisingly, the two probabilities are also completely different, but it is easy to confuse them.

This sort of confusion is at the heart of some serious problems of interpreting and using statistics. We've met two examples already in Section 1.2: the probability of 1 in 10 000 000 of an Aldermaston-style cancer cluster occurring by chance is easily confused with the probability that chance is the right explanation; and the 1 in 73 000 000 chance of two cot deaths occurring

Table 2.1 Numbers of men in different categories

	Bank robber	Not bank robber	Total
Rich	10	90	100
Not rich	1	899	900
Total	11	989	1000

in the same family is liable to be confused with the probability that cot death is the right explanation. In both cases, the problem is what the bucket represents. There are a few difficulties here: we'll return to this issue in Chapters 6 and 8.

▶ **2.3 Where do probabilities come from?**

Probabilities express our beliefs about the world. This means they need to incorporate information about this world. There are three forms which this information might take: assumptions about several possibilities being equally likely, data from a survey or similar source, or subjective opinion.

1. *Equally likely assumptions*   Sometimes it is just obvious, without doing any experiments or making any difficult judgements, that there are a number of possibilities and they are all equally likely. The probability of a dice[23] landing with six uppermost is 1/6 simply because there are six equally likely possibilities. The bucket would contain six balls, of which one is labelled 6. If I were to enter the UK national lottery, I could list two possibilities, either I win the jackpot or I don't. Can we conclude from this that my probability of winning the jackpot is 1/2 or 50%?

    Obviously not! The problem is that the two possibilities are *not* equally likely. To model the UK national lottery in terms of *equally likely* possibilities, we would need a bucket with balls representing all the possible combinations of numbers which could be drawn. There are about 14 000 000 of these, and as they are all *equally likely* (assuming the draw is fair), the probability of my winning the jackpot is about 1 in 14 000 000.

2. *Empirical data*   Probabilities can also be worked out from empirical data from surveys, experiments, weather records and so on. Such data are usually based on 'samples' which are the subject of the next section. For example, in the next chapter, I will use some data from a sample of students on their drinking habits – some of this data is in Table 3.1.

3. *Subjective opinion*   Finally, probabilities can be based on subjective opinion. It is difficult to envisage any other source for the probability that telepathy is possible. Similarly, when probabilities are used to help make business decisions, the source of information is often subjective opinion. This does not mean that the probability estimates are arbitrary: it is worth helping your experts to provide good estimates.[24]

These sources of information may, of course, be combined. The proportion of Labour voters according to our sample (or the probability of a given person voting Labour) may be 38%, but we may believe that the Labour Party has lost support since the poll, so we may decide that our best assessment is 30%. This answer is based on empirical data *and* subjective opinion.

▶ 2.4 What can you do with probabilities?

All the remaining chapters of this book bring in probability in one way or another, so the first answer to this question is that you can do statistics. Probabilities are one of the key building blocks of statistical analysis. There are also some more direct answers. The probability of an individual winning a £10 prize in the UK national lottery is 1 in 57 (1/57) (see Section 5.4). This also represents the approximate proportion of players who win £10. Proportions and probabilities are often different ways of saying the same thing. We can also estimate the number of winners. Suppose 10 000 000 tickets were sold. How many £10 prizes would you expect to be won, and how much will this cost the lottery organisers?

One fifty-seventh of 10 000 000 (10 000 000/57) is 175 483. This is the estimate of the number of winners. The cost of these prizes is £1 754 830. Would you expect these answers to be *exactly* right?

No, of course not. They'll be roughly right but not exactly. Estimates worked out from probabilities like these are called 'expected values': they are what you expect, in the long run, on average.

This illustrates how probabilities can be used for estimating totals over the whole populations. They are also useful for one-off events. Suppose you have to travel across North America. The alternatives are to fly or drive, and you know that the probability of being killed in an accident on the way is 1 in 1 000 000 if you fly, and 1 in 100 000 if you drive.[25] Other things being equal, which would you choose?

If you are sensible, you should fly. Of course, there are other important differences, but if your main concern is to avoid the remote chance of being killed, you should definitely fly. Similar points apply to many other risks and probabilities of positive events. If you want a holiday in the sun, and you have to choose between two destinations, one with a 50% probability of sunny weather and the other with a 90% record, you would obviously choose the second destination. It is sensible to look at the probabilities when making decisions about what to do.

▶ 2.5 Sampling

Probabilities, and the other statistics we'll look at in later chapters, are usually based on empirical data, and this usually comes from samples. It is often not practical to get data from *all* the people, places, times or whatever 'units of analysis', are of interest. We can't, for example, ask all 40 000 000 voters in an election how they will vote (because there are too many), or find out what the weather will be like in the future. This means we are forced to use samples. How these samples are chosen is crucial. How should the sample of 1000 electors in the example above have been selected? Obviously we want the pattern of the sample to reflect the pattern of the whole electorate as closely as possible.

It is tempting to think that the best way of achieving this is to pick a sample with the right proportions of males and females, young and old, rich and poor and so on. The problem with this is that there are too many possible factors and we cannot know which ones are closely linked to political preferences. Paradoxically, the best strategy turns out to be the exact opposite of this: ignore all information and pick the sample *at random*. We can visualise this in terms of buckets and balls:

> Imagine a bucket for the electorate, with one ball for each voter, say, 40 000 000 of them. Now choose 1000 of these at random and put these in a second bucket, labelled Sample.

Obviously, we can't be sure that we've got exactly the right proportion of, for example, males and females. But with a large sample, we can be confident that we are close. So instead of 500 males and 500 females we might have, say, 520 to 480, but it is very unlikely to be 600 to 400, or 400 to 600. (If you want to know *how* unlikely this is, you could use the computer simulation method in Section 5.4.) This trick of choosing samples at random is actually even more powerful than it may seem, because it will work for the rich or poor distinction, for the proportions in different age groups, and for *any* other distinction. Random sampling ensures that the sample will be roughly representative of *any* subcategory, *including those you haven't thought of*.

Random sampling also provides a defence against the possibility of bias. If you choose respondents on the basis of some of their characteristics, you might, perhaps unwittingly, be prone to choosing one sort of person rather than another. Perhaps you think scruffily dressed people are not typical voters and so exclude them from your sample. If you do this to any substantial extent, your sample will not give an accurate picture of the whole electorate. And even if you aren't biased in any way, people might suspect you are. Random sampling gets round this problem: everything is the luck of the draw. The only thing we have to check is that the sample is large enough for randomness to work its magic. I'll return to this in Chapter 7.

The standard way of selecting a random sample is very simple:

Table 2.2 Random numbers

6556	9146	2468	2136	8966	5931	2425	3971	2909	8219
3186	1189	5635	1226	6559	1238	8837	1589	6860	9902
8609	2032	9809	3992	6813	4927	0900	7927	7705	6682
7497	9545	3854	9673	0871	0283	9886	3974	403	2898
1646	8348	4534	7652	7209	2320	2328	8516	9548	5382

1. Make a list of voters (or whatever else you are sampling) and number them 1, 2, 3, 4 and so on. This list is often referred to as the 'sampling frame'.
2. Use random numbers to draw the sample.

If there are, say, 40 000 000 voters on your list, then you will need random numbers between 1 and 40 000 000. You can get these either from a table of random numbers (Table 2.2), or from a spreadsheet.

The number 40 000 000 is an eight-digit number, so we will need to take the random numbers in Table 2.2 in groups of eight digits. The first group of eight digits in the table gives us the number 65 569 146. As there are only 40 000 000 electors on our list, this does not correspond to a voter. What do you think we do?

Ignore it and go on to next number. This is 24 682 136 which is on the list. This is the number of the first elector in the random sample. All we have to do now is to repeat this procedure until we have a sample of the required size. If one number comes up twice, it is simply ignored on the second occasion, because the member of the sample it represents has already been selected. Alternatively, you can generate the random numbers from a spreadsheet using the randbetween or rand function.[26] If you have the sampling frame as a list on a spreadsheet, it may be easier to sort the list at random.[27]

Random sampling ensures that every member of the electorate has an equal probability of being selected, and so any suggestion of deliberate or unwitting bias is avoided. It also ensures that the members of the sample are chosen independently. If, on the other hand, they were chosen as a block, they may all come from the same district and so be too homogeneous a group to tell us about patterns in the whole electorate.

Unfortunately, random sampling is often more difficult than it may seem. First we need a list of all the electors, then we've got to number this list, and then we've got to track down all the randomly selected people to ask about their voting intentions. For a small area, like the town where I live, which has 7801 voters, it would be possible to this. But with 40 000 000 electors, even compiling the list would be hard work. This means that, in practice, corners are often cut, such as restricting the sample to a small number of geographical areas (electoral constituencies, for example). And then, what if a chosen member of the sample is out when we call, or he or she refuses to answer our questions? There may be a tendency to bias the sample towards people who are available or prepared to answer questions.

If, for practical reasons, samples are not selected randomly, the question then arises of whether they can reasonably be regarded *as if* they were selected randomly. This is a matter of judgement and, unfortunately, the reasonable judgement is often 'not really'. This is a big problem with many surveys. If you want to check the credibility of any statistical conclusions, the approach to sampling should be one of the first thing you look at. For example, if a magazine asks its readers to respond to a questionnaire about adultery, can it assume that the people who respond paint a fair picture of the readership in general? If, say, 86% of married women who respond say they have committed adultery in the last year, can we assume that this is also true of the other readers who have not responded?

The likely answer is no: committing adultery may prompt an interest in responding to the questionnaire (or it may prompt respondents not to tell the truth). It is impossible to tell: the sample is likely to be biased in ways that cannot easily be predicted, so it does not make a good basis for coming to conclusions about the readership in general.

The sample of 300 June days (see Section 2.1) was obviously not a random one. Is it good enough?

The main reason for doubt is that the data comes from only 10 years, which is a fairly small sample. It's true that there are 300 days, but the restriction to 10 years means that the data is likely to be less varied than it would be if it came from, say, 1000 years. The problem is just the same as the problem of taking the sample of electors from a small number of geographical areas: the resulting sample is unlikely to be as varied as the whole population. On the other hand, going back 1000 years is not practical, and the results may be unrepresentative of the present if the world's climate has changed appreciably over this period.

The terms 'population', 'target population' and 'universe' are often used for the whole group from which a sample is drawn and which it is intended to represent. These are natural terms when the sample represents all the electors in an election or something similar. The population is then clearly defined and can be visualised in terms of balls in a bucket and the idea of random sampling is quite clear. In other contexts, like the problem of the weather in June, the term is a less natural one, so I have avoided using it here. (The population here would be all possible June days given present climate patterns.) Samples are useful because they tell us something about a *wider context*, something beyond the sample itself. This may be the whole electorate in an election, or it may be the next 13 June. It's important to be as clear as possible about what this wider context is.

Sampling is not, of course, just relevant to estimating probabilities. We might want to estimate averages or some measure of the relationship between two variables (see Chapter 3), or build a model of some real-world phenomenon (see Chapter 9). Sampling is important whenever we are using empirical data to come to statistical conclusions. It's always worth careful consideration.

▶ 2.6 Similar concepts

- Probabilities can also be expressed in terms of ratios. If the probability of rain tomorrow is 20%, the probability of dry weather is 80%, which is *four times as likely* as rain. The 'odds' of rain are one to four.
- Mathematical probability theory defines probability in terms of a series of 'axioms' (or assumptions). In practice, this is equivalent to our definition in terms of buckets and balls, except in a few situations of little practical importance (for example according to the axiomatic treatment, it is – just – possible for events with a probability of zero to occur).
- According to the standard approach to probability, some probabilities are *conditional* on something else. For example, we might talk of the probability of a man being rich, conditional on his being a bank robber (see Section 2.2). The bucket and balls approach avoids this distinction by viewing all probabilities as conditional, the condition being defined by the bucket.
- You will find many methods of sampling besides random sampling in books on statistics or research methods. The main distinction is between 'probability sampling', where you can specify a probability of individual cases being chosen, and 'non-probability sampling', where this isn't possible. The first category includes random sampling and also 'stratified' sampling (see Section 9.1 and Table 9.1) and 'cluster' sampling. The second category includes 'opportunity' or 'convenience' sampling (taking the sample you can get easily). However, the standard by which all these methods are judged is random sampling. Stratified sampling is capable of producing slightly more reliably representative samples than random ones, but the other methods generally produce worse samples, often much worse ones.

▶ 2.7 Exercises

2.7.1 Estimating probabilities

How would you estimate the following probabilities? If you can, give the answer, although in some cases the answer may depend on information you don't have.

(a) The probability of a card from a well-shuffled pack being an ace.
(b) The probability of a two-digit, even number being exactly divisible by four (like 12, but not 10).
(c) The probability of a two-digit number which is exactly divisible by four being an even number.
(d) The probability of rain falling tomorrow in the place you are reading this.
(e) The probability of a 150-year-old human being alive in the year 2050.

If somebody else, as wise and knowledgeable as you are, were to answer these questions, would they get the same answers? In other words, which of the answers might be, to some extent, subjective?

2.7.2 Measuring the average length of words in this chapter

Word length is an important factor in assessing how easy to follow books are, so the average word length is an important piece of information for assessing readability. Suppose you wanted to estimate the average length of words in this chapter, but were too lazy to count the whole lot. The obvious thing to do is to take a sample and then assume that the sample average will be more or less the same as the average of all the words in the chapter. Use the following method to take a sample of 10 words:

> number the pages of this chapter from one upwards, then use random numbers to choose a page. Now choose a word from the page by closing your eyes, sticking a pin in the page and then taking the word you hit with the pin as the first word in your sample (open your eyes at this point). If you hit blank paper, try again until you hit a word. Then repeat the whole procedure 10 times, and work out the average length (in letters) of the 10 words.

Do you think the sampling method is truly random or biased in some way? Can you rely on your average for a reasonable estimate? The actual average length, according to my word processor, is 4.5. Your estimate is likely to be higher. Can you see why? Biases like this are often difficult to spot.

2.7.3 Choosing a sample for a TV audience research

Suppose you were to carry out a survey to find out what proportion of the population of a town watched the last episode of a popular TV soap. To do this, you take a random sample of 50 private subscribers from the local phone book, ring them up and ask the person who answers the phone. If nobody answers, you take another random name from the book. And so on, until you have interviewed 50 local residents. How would you take 50 names at random from the phone book?

This is far from an acceptable random sampling procedure. What are the main difficulties and what would you do about them? Remember that a random method of sampling gives everybody the same chance of being selected. Is this true of somebody who is always in and someone who is never in? Is it true of someone who lives by themselves and someone who lives with 19 other people? What about people who always refuse to answer phone surveys? Can you see some of the likely biases in this sample?

2.7.4 Is it worth the risk?

Data on the risks of various methods of travel[28] shows 4.40 deaths per 1 000 000 000 km by car, and 70.0 per 1 000 000 000 km on foot. My return journey to work is 5 km and I go to work on 200 days in a year. Estimate my probability of being killed in a year if I drive, and if I walk. Any comments? Should I drive because it's safer?

▶ 2.8 Summary of main points

- Probability is useful both in statistics, and for helping make sensible decisions in everyday life.
- You can always interpret a probability in terms of the random choice of a ball from a bucket.
- There are three basic sources of information for probabilities: equally likely arguments, data from surveys and other sources, and subjective opinion.
- Statistical conclusions, such as probabilities, are often based on samples of data. Random sampling is a good way of ensuring that samples give a fair picture of what they are intended to represent.

3 Summing Things up: Graphs, Averages, Standard Deviations, Correlations and so on

The starting point for a statistical analysis is typically data on a number of 'variables' (for example sex, weight, age) relating to a sample of 'cases' (for example people). This chapter looks at how we can summarise the pattern of a single variable, and the relationship between pairs of variables, by means of a few well-chosen numbers or graphs, and how these summaries can be interpreted.

▶ 3.1 Introduction

A few years ago (in 1993) I wanted to find out how much students drank. Is the stereotype of the drunken student accurate? To get some information on this, I asked a short series of questions to all the students in three groups: a full-time business course (FB in Table 3.1), a full-time course on personnel management (FP) and a part-time course on personnel management (PP). These included: How many units of alcohol did you drink last Saturday? There were similar questions for Sunday and Monday. A unit of alcohol is the amount in one glass of wine, or half a pint of beer. (UK government guidelines suggest that the maximum alcohol consumption, from a health point of view, should be 14 units a week for women, and 21 for men.) I also asked each student for their estimate of the average number of cigarettes they smoked each day.

There were 92 students in the three groups. This is too many to show you here, so I have taken a random sample of 20 of the 92, and put this data in Table 3.1. The data from all 92 students is on the web as `drink.xls`, and the group of 20 as `drink20.xls`. The data in Table 3.1 seems to confirm a few stereotypes. The figures for units drunk on Saturday night have an overall average of 5.4, well above the 2 or 3 units a night implied by the government guidelines. The average consumption for males was 13.4 units, and for females 3.3 units: males seem to drink much more than females. Similarly, the average Saturday consumption among the full-time students (7.6 units) is more than the consumption of the part-time students (5.7 units), most of

Table 3.1 Drink data from 20 students

Sex	Age	Course	Satunits	Sununits	Monunits	Daycigs
F	24	FP	0	0	0	0
M	20	FB	26	18	26	20
F	32	FP	1	3	1	0
F	32	PP	5	2	0	25
F	21	FP	3	2	0	0
M	20	FB	3	2	0	5
F	19	FB	1	2	0	5
F	21	FB	2	2	6	0
M	21	FB	6	8	8	0
M	19	FB	4	10	6	0
M	22	FB	19	0	15	7
M	23	FB	15	0	18	0
F	21	FP	5	5	0	0
F	21	FP	0	0	0	0
M	19	FB	24	6	24	0
F	21	FP	4	2	0	0
F	38	PP	0	0	0	0
F	32	PP	12	3	0	0
M	22	FB	10	8	20	0
F	19	FB	7	1	7	0

Satunits refers to the number of units of alcohol drunk on the Saturday, Sununits to the number on Sunday, and Monunits to the number on Monday. Daycigs refers to the average daily number of cigarettes smoked. This format, with short variable names, is convenient for exporting data to SPSS. The data is in `drink20.xls`.

whom had full-time jobs as well as their studies, and so were not 'proper' students. However, this difference is not as much as I had expected.

▶ 3.2 What can a sample tell us about?

As we saw in Section 2.5, samples are useful because they tell you about some wider context. I am not just interested in how much the students in three of my classes drank on three days in 1993. I am also interested in the drinking habits of other students at other times. We can visualise this in terms of buckets and balls. Imagine a bucket with balls in it to represent all 'student-days' which were lived in 1993. We need to define 'student', so let's take all full-time and part-time students in UK higher education in 1993. If there were, say, a million of these, this would mean a total of 365 million student-days. My data file from 92 students includes data on 276 (92 × 3) of these student-days, of which 60 appear in Table 3.1. How accurate a picture of the whole population of 365 million student-days will this data provide?

The picture is obviously unlikely to be fully accurate. One problem is the size of the sample. The figures in Section 3.1 about units drunk on Saturday are based on a sample of 20 student-days. The corresponding figures from all 92 students in the sample were slightly different. For example, the sample of 20 gives an average number of units drunk by full-time students of 7.6, whereas the full sample of 92 gives a figure of 5.9. Obviously, if we could get data on *all* full-time student-days in the UK in 1993, the answer would almost certainly be slightly different. We'll look at how we can estimate the likely size of these differences in Chapter 7.

A more serious problem is that I chose the sample in a haphazard way that makes it difficult to feel confident that the pattern in the sample will reflect the wider population. I had one part-time and two full-time classes, but does this reflect the general pattern? Probably not. And as I only had three classes, the sample is likely to be less varied than the whole population. I asked about a Saturday, Sunday and Monday, but perhaps students drink less on other days? And I chose just one week; if this were just before Christmas, for example, the results might be higher than they would otherwise have been. (The best way to choose a sample like this would be to choose randomly from the whole population – see Section 2.5 – but this was impractical, as it often is.)

There are yet more problems. The students who answered my questions may not have been telling the truth; one 19-year-old girl in the sample of 92 said she drank a total of 140 units (70 pints of beer) over the three days! And there is the time problem: to what extent can data gathered in the past tell us about the future? All this means that you should be very cautious about reading too much into this data. All we can do is make a judgement about the extent to which patterns found in the sample can be extrapolated to a wider context. The same problem applies to many other samples which are used as the basis of statistical analysis.

However, having said all this, for the purposes of the rest of this chapter, I'll assume that we can extrapolate the results from the sample of 92 to a wider context. I'll use the word 'students' for this slightly vague, wider context.

▶ 3.3 Variables, cases and units of analysis

The columns in Table 3.1, Sex, Age, Course and so on, represent 'variables'. These are characteristics which *vary* from person to person in the sample.

The first row in Table 3.1 gives the *values* of all the variables for the first person in the sample (F, 24, FP and so on), the second row gives the values for the second person and so on.

There are two important types of variable: 'category' and 'number'. Sex and Course are category variables: the values are categories like Male or Female. Age and the rest of the variables are number variables: their values are numbers. This is a very obvious, but very important distinction. (There are further distinctions mentioned in the Similar concepts section.)

The 'unit of analysis' in this survey is the student. Each student in the survey, represented by a row in Table 3.1, is known as a 'case'. In this survey the cases are people, but in other surveys they could be countries, accidents or days.

Sections 3.4–3.8 are organised according to the number and type of the variables whose values you want to summarise.

▶ 3.4 Summarising a single variable

The information in Table 3.1 is a bit of a mess. It is not easy to see any patterns. In this section I'll look at ways of summing up the pattern of a single variable. This pattern is often referred to as a 'distribution'. If the variable is a category variable, then all you can do is count up the number of people in each category and present the results in a table, bar chart or pie diagram. You can also use this data to estimate probabilities as described in the last chapter. This is too obvious to bother with an example, but we will look at the two variable equivalent in Section 3.5. If the variable is a number variable, there are more possibilities.

3.4.1 Histograms
A histogram is a bar chart to show the frequencies of different values of a number variable. This is a very useful sort of diagram, often overlooked by beginners. Figures 3.1 and 3.2, both based on the sample of 92, illustrate two histograms.

In Figure 3.1, the bars represent the number of students who drank no units, one unit, two units and so on. The word 'frequency' in this context means simply how frequently something happened, in other words, how many of the students each bar applies to. One 20-year-old girl in the sample claimed to have drunk 40 units (20 pints of beer) on the Saturday. This is far more than the rest of the students in the sample and is excluded from Figure 3.1 because I think it isn't true. Drinking this much would be dangerous. Obviously you should consider such 'outliers' carefully, and only exclude them if there is good reason.

Figure 3.1 Histogram of units drunk on Saturday based on sample of 92 (one outlier excluded)

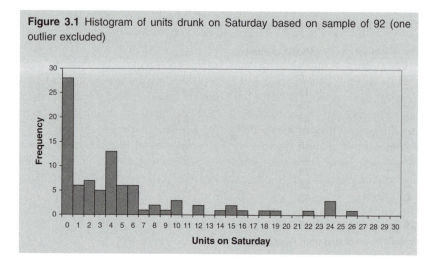

Figure 3.2 Histogram of estimated total weekly units drunk based on sample of 92 (three outliers excluded)

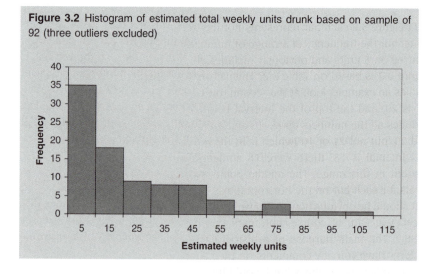

Figure 3.2 shows the estimated weekly consumption based on this sample. For each student the average over the three days is calculated, and then multiplied by seven to give an estimate for the week; this is easy with Excel.[29] Do you think this is likely to be an accurate estimate, or is it likely to be too high or too low?

I think it may be too high if students drink more at the weekends than during the rest of the week. But it's the best we can do with this data.

Table 3.2 Frequencies for Figure 3.2

Top of interval	Middle of interval	Frequency
10	5	35
20	15	18
30	25	9
40	35	8
50	45	8
60	55	4
70	65	1
80	75	3
90	85	1
100	95	1
110	105	1
120	115	0
Above 120 (excluded from Figure 3.2)		3

In Figure 3.2 each bar represents not the frequency of a single number of units, but the frequency of a range of numbers. The first bar, for example, is centred on 5 units and obviously includes all quantities from zero up to 10. Figure 3.2 is based on Table 3.2. This shows the frequencies in each 'interval'. As an example, look at the second row of this table. The top of the interval is 20, and the top of the interval below is 10. The interval in question includes all the numbers above 10 and up to and including 20: eg 11.7, 18.7 and 20, but not 21 or 10 (which is in the interval below). The frequency for this interval is 18: there were 18 students in the sample who drank an amount in this range. The middle points of each interval are used as the labels for each bar on the horizontal axis.

It should be obvious how to draw histograms like Figure 3.2 by hand. Using Excel, you can, of course, automate this process.[30] It's even easier with SPSS.[31] The main purpose of a histogram is to get a feel for the general pattern. Have you any comments on the general pattern of Figure 3.2**?**

The pattern is roughly what I would have expected: more than 50% drink modestly – less than 20 units a week – but there is a 'tail' of bigger drinkers. It is often useful to compare histograms for different groups, for example males versus females or full timers versus part timers. Histograms like Figure 3.2 are far more useful than those which show frequencies of individual values like Figure 3.1 whenever there are a large number of different possible values. The scale in Figure 3.2 goes up to 120, and fractions are also possible. A diagram like Figure 3.1, with a bar for each value, would be messy and uninformative. If you don't believe me, draw it!

3.4.2 Averages: the mean and the median of a number variable

Sometimes it is helpful to sum up a distribution as a single number to show where the centre or 'average' is. There are two commonly used, and useful, measures: the mean and the median. The 'mean' is simply the ordinary average of everyday life. To work it out you simply add up all the values in the sample and divide by the number of values. In the case of the data on units drunk on Saturday night in Table 3.1, these values are the number of units drunk by each individual student, and the number of values is, of course, 20. What is the mean number of units drunk on Saturday night by the sample in Table 3.1?

The mean is 7.4 units of alcohol. The mean of the whole sample of 92 students is 5.4 units. In ordinary English, of course, this is simply the average. Excel follows this usage: the function for the mean is average.

The 'median' is simply the middle value when the values are arranged in order of size. What is the median number of units drunk on Saturday night by the sample in Table 3.1?

To work this out you need to put the values in order of size. There are three zeros, so they come first: 0, 0, 0, 1, 1, 2, 3, 3, 4, 4, 5, 5 and so on. The median is the middle value in this list. There are, however, an even number of values, 20, so there is no middle value. The middle is between the 10th (4) and the 11th (5), so we take the value midway between these two: the median is 4.5 units of alcohol. Half the values (ten of them) are below 4.5 and the other half (the other ten) are above 4.5, so 4.5 is squarely in the middle.

As with the mean, this is not quite the same as the median of the whole sample of 92, which comes to 3.5 units. Which do you think is the more useful measure, the mean or the median?

It depends on the situation and on what you want to know. If you were buying the drinks for a group of students on Saturday night, the mean is a useful measure if you want an idea of how much the drinks will cost. The mean is obtained by adding up all the units drunk and then imagining them shared out equally between the students, each student then gets the mean number of units. If you were buying drinks for a group of 20 students, you would expect them – assuming they are average students – to drink about 20 times this mean, or 108 units of alcohol (using the mean of 5.4 from the whole sample of 92 students, as this is more likely to be representative of students in general). You could then estimate how much this will cost. This won't be exact, but the best sort of average you can use here is the mean.

If, on the other hand, you want some idea of the state of inebriation of a typical student, then the median is more use. The median of 3.5 means that half the students you meet on a Saturday night are likely to have more to drink than 3.5 units and the other half less. (In our sample of 92 students, 46 drank less than 3.5 units on Saturday and 46 more than 3.5.) The idea of quartiles and percentiles (see below) extends this idea further. In practice, the median is an underused measure. It is often more meaningful than the mean. Don't forget it.

In our sample, the median is less than the mean. Why is this?

Figures 3.1 and 3.2 show that the distribution is not symmetrical. The values tail off more gradually at the top end than they do at the bottom. The distribution is said to be 'skewed', which is the reason for the difference between the mean and the median. It may be obvious to you why this should be, but if not, imagine working out the mean by taking the numbers in pairs – first the biggest and the smallest: 26 and 0 which have a mean of 13, second the next biggest and next smallest: 24 and 0 (there are two 0s in the data) which have a mean of 12 and so on. You will end up with 10 numbers, none of which are less than 4.5 (the median of the 20 values in Table 3.1), so the overall mean must be more than 4.5.

With some data, only whole numbers make sense. Imagine a country where the mean number of offspring people have is 2.7. Any particular person might have 2 children or 3, but 2.7 children is obviously impossible. Is it meaningful and sensible to talk about a mean of 2.7 here?

Yes. If there were a million people, the mean of 2.7 enables you to predict that they will have about 1.35 million children, which helps to predict population trends (remembering that children have two parents). Means are helpful because they enable you to estimate totals, and if the total is useful, then so is the mean. However, the mean obviously does *not* represent a typical family. Needless to say, Excel and SPSS can be used to work out means and medians.[32]

3.4.3 Maximum and minimum, quartiles and percentiles of a number variable

These concepts provide another way of summing up the pattern. The idea is very simple: arrange the numbers in order of size – just as we did for the median – and then read off

- the maximum and minimum
- the value halfway up the list (the median)
- the values a quarter and three-quarters of the way up the list (the 'first quartile' and the 'third quartile')
- the value 10% of the way up the list (the '10th percentile'). Similarly the value 80% of the way up the list is the 80th percentile. The first quartile is the same as the 25th percentile. And so on.

What are the quartiles of the number of units drunk on Saturday night by the sample whose alcohol consumption is shown in Table 3.1? What is the 80th percentile? What is the maximum?

The first step is the arrange the data in order of size, just as we did for the median (0, 0, 0, 1, 1, 2, 3, 3, 4, 4, 5, 5, 6, 7, 10, 12, 15, 19, 24, 26). There are 20 numbers in the list, so a quarter of the 20 is 5 and the other 15, starting from the sixth in the list, are the remaining three-quarters. The fifth number is 1 and the sixth is 2. The obvious thing then is, just like the median, to say that the first quartile is midway between these two, that is, 1.5 units of alcohol. Similarly the third quartile is 11 (midway between the 15th and 16th numbers: 10 and 12), and the 80th percentile is midway between the 16th and the 17th number (12 and 15), that is, 13.5.

You may wonder what happens if we want the 78th percentile, 78% of the way up the list. Where exactly is this? Presumably a bit less than 13.5, but how much less? You may also be a bit confused about why I chose midway between the fifth and the sixth number for the first quartile; I've explained above, but you may not be convinced. If so, please don't worry. These points are not very important. Quartiles and percentiles are particularly useful with large samples, and with large samples it usually makes little difference if you choose one number, or the next, or something between them. Imagine a sample of 1000 students. Strictly, the first quartile is midway between the 250th and 251st number in the list of 1000, but these are very likely to be the same or only very slightly different. So it really doesn't matter much.

Excel[33] and SPSS[34] have exact definitions of quartiles and percentiles built in; you could try analysing the data in Table 3.1 with these packages to see what answers they give. You will probably find that you get *three* different answers, because these packages use more subtle methods than the midway method above.

Quartiles and percentiles are useful because they are easy to interpret. The first quartile is 1.5 units: this means that 25% of students drank less than 1.5 units, and the other 75% drank more. Similarly the 80th percentile consumption (13.5 units) is the level of consumption that is exceeded by 20% of students. And from another survey, it was found that the 95th percentile of the heights of 17-year-old men in the UK in the 1990s was about 190 cm;[35] this is the height of a man towards the top of the spectrum of heights, 95% of the way up, to be precise. Only 5% of 17-year-old men were taller than this.

3.4.4 Measures of the spread of a number variable: range, interquartile range, mean deviation and standard deviation

Histograms are a good way of showing the overall pattern of a distribution. Quartiles and percentiles can also be used to similar effect. Averages, however, just focus on one aspect, the middle, either in the sense of the mean or the median. Whether the values spread out far from this average, above it, below it or in both directions, is impossible to say from the average alone.

Table 3.3 Weights in grams of apples in two bags

Bag 1	130	124	124	120	121	124	128	129
Bag 2	173	192	36	166	119	31	178	129

We often need a measure of 'spread' as well as an average. Let's consider another example. The weights (in grams) of the apples in two bags are in Table 3.3.

The apples in Bag 1 are produced on a factory farm with industrial-style controls: the result is that the apples are all very similar in weight. The 'range' (biggest minus smallest) is only 10 g. By contrast, the apples in Bag 2 are organically grown and very variable: their weights are much more spread out. Some are much bigger than others. The range in this case is 161 g (192 − 31). Note that the mean weights of apples in both bags are very similar: 125 g in Bag 1 and 128 g in Bag 2. The total weight of each bag is obviously eight times the mean: 1000 g and 1024 g. Is this obvious?

I hope so. Remember that to work out the mean you find the total weight and then divide by the number of apples. Multiplying the mean by the number of apples just undoes the last step and gets back to the total weight.

I'll explain four ways of measuring spread. We have already met the first. The 'range' is simply the difference between the biggest and smallest value, 10 g for Bag 1 and 161 g for Bag 2, as explained above. This is very simple, but it has a couple of snags. The fact that it depends on just two values in a sample means it tends to be rather erratic. All the information from values in the middle is ignored. The second snag is that the range of big samples is likely to be bigger than the range of smaller samples. Imagine, say, a thousand apples from the Bag 2 source. In this bigger bucket, there is very likely to be a bigger apple than the 192 g apple in Bag 2, and one smaller than 31 g. This means that the range is almost certain to be more. For this reason, it is difficult to generalise the range to a wider context, although you can still compare two samples like Bag 1 and Bag 2. On the other hand, it is very simple and very easy to interpret.

The 'interquartile range' is just what it says it is, the range or difference between the two quartiles. Using the method for quartiles in the last section, what are the two quartiles of the weights in the two bags? And using these, what are the two interquartile ranges?

The quartiles for Bag 1 are 122.5 and 128.5, which gives an interquartile range of 128.5–122.5 or 6 g. The corresponding figure for the second bag is 98 g. The bigger figure for Bag 2 indicates that the quartiles are much further apart, which reflects the fact that the weights are more varied.

The 'mean deviation from the mean' is also just what it says it is. Taking Bag 1 as our example, the mean is 125, so the deviation from the mean of the first (130 g) apple is 5 g. Similarly, the deviation of the second is 1 g. The mean deviation is simply the mean of all eight deviations (5, 1, 1, 5, 4, 1, 3, 4) which is 3 g. What is the corresponding mean deviation from the mean for Bag 2?

You should have found this is 49.5 g, far bigger than Bag 1's figure, because the weights are more spread out so the deviations from the mean are, on average, larger.

The 'standard deviation' (sd) is defined as the square root of the mean of the squared[36] deviations from the mean. All this means is that we square the deviations above (25, 1, 1, 25, 16, 1, 9, 16), take the mean as before (11.75), and then take the square root of the answer (3.43). This is the standard deviation for the first bag. What is the standard deviation of the weight of apples in the second bag?

The standard deviation is 59.18 g, much larger than Bag 1, as we would expect. The sd is similar to the mean deviation from the mean. The only difference is the squaring, and then the square rooting to undo the squaring. Not surprisingly, the two answers tend to be similar: the sd is normally a bit bigger but how much bigger depends on the pattern of the numbers.

You may wonder why we bother with the sd when the mean deviation from the mean seems similar, but more straightforward. The reason is that the sd is necessary for much of the mathematical development of statistics, for example we need it if we are to use the normal distribution (Section 5.6). As this is a book on *non-mathematical* statistics, my initial inclination was to leave it out and concentrate on more user-friendly measures. The reason for including the sd is that it is very widely used: it has cornered the market for measures of spread. You will find references to standard deviations all over the place, so it is essential to understand what it is.

The standard deviation is influenced strongly by outliers – values much larger or smaller than the rest of the distribution. For example, the standard deviation of the results in Figure 3.2 is 24 units of alcohol. Including the three outliers (126, 163, 327) increases the standard deviation to 43, a very substantial difference. This makes the standard deviation a rather erratic measure if there are outlying values. These outliers may be mistakes in the data, which can have a disproportionate effect on the answer. Do you think the mean deviation from the mean and the interquartile range will be as strongly influenced by outliers?

No. The mean deviation is increased from 19 to 26 by including the outliers in Figure 3.2. The interquartile range is unchanged at 33. The exact size of outliers makes no difference here: if they were even larger, the third quartile and the interquartile range would be unchanged.

In my view, the popularity of the standard deviation is undeserved. It is complicated and prone to giving odd answers in some situations. I will not use it much in the rest of this book. The mean deviation from the mean and the interquartile range are generally preferable ways of measuring spread. Or look at the percentiles, or draw a histogram.

In SPSS you will find all of this under Analyze – Descriptive statistics. There are also useful Excel functions.[37]

3.4.5 Proportion of values over a critical level

The final way of summing up the pattern of a number variable is to reduce it to a category variable. Taking three units a day as the limit for reasonable drinking, we can define anything over this as over the limit. Table 3.1 shows that the proportion of students over the limit on Saturday night was 12 out of 20, or 60%. What is the corresponding figure for the whole sample of 92 (use Figure 3.1 or Excel[38])?

The proportion in the whole sample is 46 out of 92, or exactly 50%. You can, of course, think of this as the probability of a student drinking too much.

▶ 3.5 Summarising the relation between two category variables

We are often interested not so much in a single variable but in how two variables relate to each other. Do students drink more on Saturday night than they do on Sunday nights? Do students who smoke a lot also drink a lot? Do male students drink more than female students? Are male students more likely to smoke than female students? All these questions involve two of the variables in Table 3.1, units on Saturday and units on Sunday, average cigarettes and units drunk, sex and units on Saturday and sex and smoker/non-smoker. How can we analyse these?

If we have two category variables, the obvious thing to do here is to make a table to show how frequently each combination of values (male smoker, male non-smoker, female smoker and female non-smoker) occurs. Table 3.4 presents this information as percentages because it is easier to compare males and females. It is usually a good idea to use percentages in these tables, although you will need to ensure that you choose the right percentages. The percentages in Table 3.4 are row percentages; column percentages (the percentage of non-smokers who are female and so on) are of less obvious interest here. Can you see how Table 3.4 is produced from the data in Table 3.1?

There are 12 females listed in Table 3.1, of whom 10 are listed as 0 under Daycigs. Ten out of 12 is 83% and so on. Tables like this are easy to produce

Table 3.4 Percentages of female and male smokers in Table 3.1

Sex	Non-smoker	Smoker	Total
Female	83%	17%	100% (n = 12)
Male	63%	38%	100% (n = 8)
Total	75%	25%	100% (n = 20)

n is the number of students on which the percentages are based.

with SPSS[39] or with Excel.[40] You can also illustrate this table by means of bar charts of various kinds; I'll leave you to explore this if you want to.

▶ 3.6 Summarising the relation between one category and one number variable

Tables of frequencies like Table 3.4 are not really practical if either of the variables is a number variable. (If you can't see why, try setting up a table like Table 3.4 to show the relationship between Satunits and Sex.) The number variable needs to be summarised using the mean or something similar (for example the median). Table 3.5 shows how the male data on units drunk on Saturday night can be compared with the female data.

Check that you can see how this is worked out from Table 3.1. It is good practice to include the number of people that each mean is based on. Statisticians tend to use the symbol n for this number. The table is easily produced by SPSS (Analyze – Compare means – Means) or Excel.[41] You could also include other quantities, for example median, standard deviation, in the table.

▶ 3.7 Summarising the relation between two number variables

When we have two number variables, tables like Table 3.5 are not feasible. Instead, there are four possibilities: producing a 'scatter diagram', working out the difference between values of the variables, a 'correlation coefficient' between the variables or the 'slope' in a regression model. The next three subsections deal with the first three of these. We'll leave the fourth until Chapter 9 when we look at regression.

Table 3.5 Mean units drank on Saturday night for males and females (based on Table 3.1)

Sex	Mean units on Saturday	n (number of students)
Female	3	12
Male	13	8
Overall	7	20

Figure 3.3 Scatter diagram of Satunits and Sununits

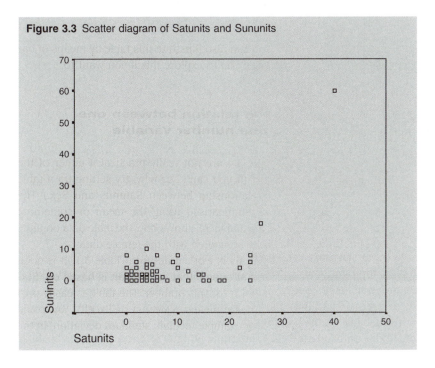

3.7.1 Scatter diagrams

Scatter diagrams are very useful for showing the detailed relationship between two number variables. Figures 3.3, 3.4 and 3.5 show three of these, all based on the full set of data from which Table 3.1 is extracted. These diagrams are all produced by SPSS (Graphs – Scatter). They could easily be produced by Excel (use the Chart Wizard), but SPSS offers some useful extras, for example if you want to see *all* the scatter diagrams showing the relation between several variables, use Graph – Scatter – Matrix.

Figure 3.4 Scatter diagram of Satunits and Monunits

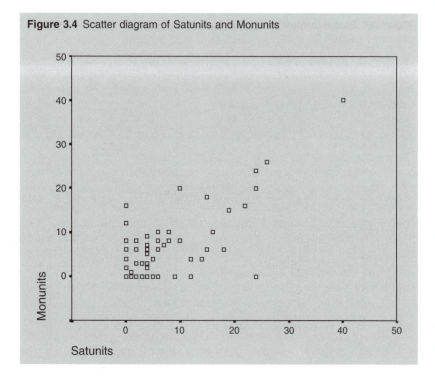

In these diagrams, each point represents a student, for example in Figure 3.3 the top right point represents a student who says she drank 40 units on Saturday and 60 on Sunday. Each diagram has a different pattern which tells its own story. Apart from the two points on the right, there seems little relationship between the amounts drunk on Saturday and Sunday. The pattern of Sunday drinking for those who drunk nothing on Saturday is fairly similar to the pattern for those who drunk 24 units on Saturday. On the other hand, Figure 3.4 shows that there is a slight tendency for students who drank more on Saturday to drink more than average on Monday as well. Why do you think there was this difference between Sunday and Monday?

I don't know. One possibility is that some of the heavy drinkers on Saturday had too much of a hangover to drink much on Sunday, but had recovered to return to heavy drinking by Monday.

Figure 3.5 shows the relationship between age and units drunk on Saturday. What do you think this diagram shows?

I think it shows that students over 30 drink less than the younger students. There is only one student over 30 who drank more than 10 units on Satur-

Figure 3.5 Scatter diagram of age and Satunits

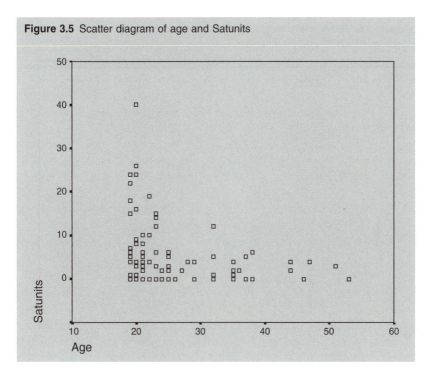

day, and the majority drank much less. On the other hand, among the younger students, there were some very heavy drinkers.

In Figure 3.5, I have put age along the horizontal axis. This is because there is a convention that says you should put the 'independent' variable along the horizontal axis. In this example, age is the independent variable and units drunk on Saturday is the 'dependent' variable, because it is natural to assume that units drunk on Saturday depend, to some extent, upon age, but not vice versa. However, this is often a hazy distinction, and this rule is only a convention. Which is the independent variable in Figure 3.4**?**

You might say that they both have the same status, so neither is the independent variable, so it doesn't matter which one goes on the horizontal axis. Or, you might think that Monday consumption depends on Saturday consumption because Monday comes after Saturday, so Saturday should go on the horizontal axis. I think either attitude is OK.

Figures 3.3, 3.4 and 3.5 are all based on a sample of 92 students. Each student is represented by one point, so there should be 92 points in each diagram. In fact, if you count up, you will find that there are considerably fewer than 92 points in all three diagrams. Why do you think this is**?**

Figure 3.6 SPSS scatter diagram with sunflowers

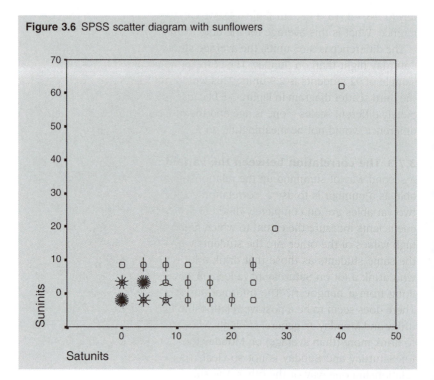

There were several students who drank nothing on Saturday and Sunday. This means that the point in the bottom left on Figure 3.3 represents not one student but a whole group of students. Similarly, some of the other points will represent several students. Figure 3.6 shows one way of getting round this problem. This is produced by SPSS.[42] What do you think the 'sunflowers' represent?

Each petal of the sunflowers represent a single student, for example a three-petalled sunflower represents three students.

3.7.2 Differences between the variables

Sometimes it is useful to summarise the relationship between two variables by means of a single number, rather like an average gives a crude summary of the pattern of a single variable. There are different ways in which this can be done. The first is to focus on the *difference* between the two variables. For example, we could subtract the units drunk on Sunday from the units drunk on Saturday to give a measure of how much more is drunk on Saturday (0, +8, −2, +3, +1 . . . in Table 3.1). We can then work out the average difference. What is this average for the data in Table 3.1**?**

The difference is 3.65 units: the average student drank this much more on Saturday night than on Sunday. The corresponding difference for the whole sample of 92 students is 2.9 units. This would not make sense in relation to the third scatter diagram in Figure 3.5 because the two variables are on completely different scales – one is age and the other alcohol consumption. The difference would not be meaningful.

3.7.3 The correlation between the variables

A second way of summing up the relationship between two numerical variable as a number is to use a 'correlation coefficient'. This works even if the two variables are on completely different scales like Figure 3.5. Correlation coefficients measure the extent to which high values of one variable go with high values of the other. Are the students who drink a lot of Saturday night the same students as those that drink a lot on Monday night. Or do those who drink a lot on Saturday have less on Monday (perhaps they are recovering from a hangover)? The informal answers can be seen in Figure 3.4. There does seem to be a positive relationship between consumption on Saturday and Monday. In general students who drink more on Saturday do seem to drink more (than average) on Monday too. On the other hand, the picture for Saturday and Sunday is not so clear. There does not seem to be much relationship one way or the other. The simplest way to measure correlation is as follows.

Imagine meeting two of the students in Table 3.1 and comparing their drink figures for Saturday and Sunday. If the two students were the first two in the list, the bigger drinker on Saturday (number two in the list with 26 units) would also be the bigger drinker on Sunday (18 units vs 0 units). I'll call this a 'same-direction' observation. This tends to confirm the idea that Saturday and Sunday drinking are correlated. On the other hand, if the two students were the next two in the list, the conclusion would be the opposite. Number four drunk more on Saturday (5 vs 1), yet number three drank more on Sunday (3 vs 2). This is a 'reversed-direction' observation. The question now is whether, if we met lots of pairs of students, we would have predominantly same-direction or reversed-direction observations. Answering this question with all 20 students in Table 3.1 is rather hard work, so I'll start by imagining that we just have the first four. The analysis is in Table 3.6.

Table 3.6 shows that there are six possible pairs of students, of which five give same-direction observations. Five-sixths of the observations are same-direction, and one-sixth are reversed-direction. This provides a crude measure of correlation. If we met any a pair of students from this group, at random, the probability of a same-direction observation would be 5/6, and

Table 3.6 Calculation of a correlation coefficient between Satunits and Sununits

	Second student			
First student	1	2	3	4
1				
2	+1			
3	+1	+1		
4	+1	+1	−1	

+1 indicates a same-direction observation, and −1 a reversed-direction one. The numbers 1, 2, 3, 4 represent the students in the first four rows of Table 3.1.

of a reversed-direction observation would be 1/6. This indicates a fairly high correlation. Can you use the first four rows of data in Table 3.1 to do a similar calculation for age and units drunk on Saturday?

You should have found two same-direction observations, and three reversed-direction observations. The sixth is inconclusive – neither one thing nor the other – because the ages of the third and fourth students are the same. This suggests a probability of a same-direction (SD) observations of 2/6 or 1/3, and 3/6 or 1/2 for reversed-direction (RD) observations. Notice that you are comparing the ages of the two students, and the amounts they drank on Saturday. You do not need to compare ages with amount drunk, which would, of course, not be a sensible thing to do.

These probabilities can be converted to a measure known as 'Kendall's correlation coefficient' (or sometimes 'Kendall's tau'):

Kendall's correlation coefficient = proportion of SDs – proportion RDs.

In the first example (Table 3.6) this would come to 5/6 − 1/6 or 0.67. What is Kendall's correlation coefficient in the second example (age and Satunits)?

One-third minus a half which is −0.17. This is negative, indicating that there are more reversed-direction observations.

Kendall's correlation coefficient is designed to range from +1 to −1. It will be +1 if all the pairs are same-direction and none are reversed, so the formula becomes simply 1 − 0. This will be the case if the scatter diagram shows an 'uphill' straight line. This is shown in the first scatter diagram in Figure 3.7. Take any two crosses you like in this diagram, and you will get a same-direction observation.

Figure 3.7 Scatter diagrams corresponding to correlations of +1, 0 and −1

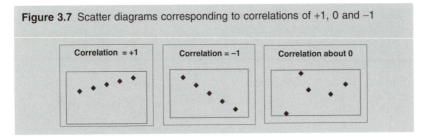

Table 3.7 Relation between Kendall's correlation coefficient and the probability of a same-direction observation

Kendall's correlation coefficient	Probability of same direction observation
+1	1
+0.5	0.75
0	0.5
−0.5	0.25
−1	0

This assumes there are no inconclusive pairs.

At the other extreme Kendall's correlation would be −1 if all the pairs were reversed (the formula would be 0 − 1). And if there are approximately equal numbers of same and reversed-direction pairs, the correlation would be about zero. Table 3.7 is intended as a reminder for interpreting correlations, for example a correlation of +0.5 means that the probability of a same-direction observation is 75%.

So far we have just used samples of four. The corresponding correlations for all 92 students (in *drink.xls*) are given in Table 3.8. Not surprisingly, the answers are rather different from the calculations based on the first four students in Table 3.1.

This table shows, for example, that the correlation between age and units drunk on Saturday is −0.22. This indicates a weak negative relationship. What do you think the probability of two students encountered at random being a same-direction pair, that is, the older one drinking more?

Using Table 3.7 the answer is obviously between 0.25 and 0.5, say about 0.4. Table 3.7 assumes there are no inconclusive pairs for which Age or Sat-units, or both, for the two students are equal. As there are inconclusive pairs

Table 3.8 Kendall's correlation coefficient between variables in Table 3.1 (data from all 92 students)

Age				
−0.22	Satunits			
−0.07	0.20	Sununits		
−0.26	0.33	0.16	Monunits	
−0.12	0.10	0.11	0.09	Daycigs

like this, Table 3.7 should be viewed as a rough guide only. The scatter diagram showing the relationship between these two variables is Figure 3.5. This shows a weakish negative relation as the correlation leads us to expect. Similarly the correlation between Satunits and Monunits is positive (0.33) as Figure 3.3 suggests.

Working out Kendall's correlation coefficient by the method of Table 3.6 is hard work for anything but very small samples. You can use SPSS[43] or Excel[44] to do the calculations for you. You will, however, find that the answers may not quite tally. SPSS uses a slightly different version of Kendall's tau. You will also find a function, correl, in Excel, which produces another correlation coefficient (Pearson's), and yet other correlation coefficient, Spearman's, produced by SPSS. I'll sort this out in Section 3.10.

▶ 3.8 Summarising the relation between three or more variables

This is obviously more complicated. Table 3.9 relates three of the variables in the drink data (Course, Sex, Satunits). This is an edited version of an SPSS table,[45] but a similar table can be produced using a Pivot Table in Excel (see Appendix A.4).

Table 3.9 shows that the pattern of males drinking more than females holds for the two full-time courses, but not for the part-time course (PP). However, there were only four males on this course, so we should obviously not be too confident that this conclusion can be safely generalised beyond this sample. It is always good practice to include the sample size on which means and other statistics are based so that readers do not jump to firm conclusions based on very small samples. You could also display the means in Table 3.9 as a clustered bar chart.[46] It is possible to include further vari-

Table 3.9 Table showing relation between three variables in drink data

| Course | Satunits for female students | | | | Satunits for male students | | | |
	Mean	Bottom q'tile	Top q'tile	n	Mean	Bottom q'tile	Top q'tile	n
FB	5.9	0.6	8.1	19	11.7	3.5	22.5	20
FP	2.7	0.0	4.3	20	4.8	1.0	12.0	10
PP	2.5	0.0	4.0	19	0.3	0.0	–	4

Edited version of SPSS output from Custom tables – Basic tables procedure. n is the number in each group. There were only four students in the male PP group who drank only one unit between them, so SPSS has refused to estimate the third quartile.

ables in tables like 3.9, but this may be at the cost of making the presentation too complex to take in. SPSS also offers three-dimensional scatter plots for three numerical variables (Graphs – Scatter), which you may wish to try.

▶ 3.9 Beyond the data: cause, effect and the wider context

My reason for going on and on about the data from the 92 students is not that I expect you to be particularly interested in this group of students. I'm sure you aren't. My intention, and hope, is that this data is helpful for learning about a wider context, in which you may be more interested. There are several different aspects of this wider context. First, I hope you will apply the methods in the sections above to situations of interest to you. Second, even if you are interested in the drinking habits of students, you would certainly want come to conclusions about a wider population of students. The extent to which this is possible and meaningful depends on a number of factors, particularly the source of the sample (see Section 3.2) and its size (see Chapter 7).

There is also a third, slightly more subtle, issue. This is the extent to which we can use the data to come to conclusions about cause and effect. As an example, consider the fact that the average number of units drunk on Saturday night by the full-time students in this sample of 92 was 6.5, whereas the corresponding figure for the part-time students was 2.1. The full-time students drank a lot more than the part-timers, who had full-time jobs to do when they were not studying. What explanation would you suggest for this difference?

There are many possible answers, but they fall into four categories. The first type of answer just says it's chance. If you took another sample of students, the answer may be different. In this case, the size of the difference, and the relatively large sample, suggests this is unlikely. But it's certainly possible: we'll look at how the chance explanation can be checked in Chapter 8.

The second category of answer focuses on suggesting a mechanism by which being a full-time student can *cause* students to drink more than they would if they were part-time. It might be excessive amounts of free time, the lack of pressure to turn up to work early in the morning, or a culture of heavy drinking. Whatever the detailed explanation, the common feature of these explanations is that they imply that if a student changes from a full-time to a part-time course, the change is likely to be accompanied by a reduction in the amount drunk. If the drinking of a full-time student is a problem, the cure may be transfer to a part-time course. Was your suggested explanation of this type?

If it wasn't, there are two further possibilities. The third is that there might be some essentially accidental feature of the samples which leads to the difference in Saturday drinking habits. The part-time sample contained a greater proportion of female students and a greater average age. Female students tended to drink less (Table 3.5), as did older students (Figure 3.5). This could be the explanation for the difference in drinking patterns between full-time and part-time students. If this explanation is right, would forcing a student from a full-time to a part-time course be likely to cure a heavy drinking problem?

No, of course not. This would not change either age or sex. The final type of explanation would involve a drinking habit somehow making people become full-time students. Does this sound plausible?

It's definitely possible. Drinkers might be attracted to the (full-time) student lifestyle, or employers might be put off by excessive drinking. To sum up, if D represents being a heavy drinker, F represents being a full-time student, the data shows a tendency for D and F to be associated: D people tend to be F people and vice versa. There are four possible types of explanation:

1. It's chance: another sample may be different.
2. F causes D.
3. Something else causes D and F.
4. D causes F.

So, when you notice a relationship between two variables, be careful about jumping to conclusions. You should always check out these four types of explanation.

▶ 3.10 Similar concepts

There are distinctions between different types of number variables: those on 'continuous' and 'discrete' scales; and 'ordinal', 'interval' and 'ratio' scales. You will find more information in more detailed texts.[47] There are many other ways of summing up data: numerous types of graph and coefficients to measure various characteristics of the data. I've been selective in this chapter and left out anything which seems too easy to be worth going on about (pie charts, simple bar charts, the mode as a type of average), or too complicated to be useful. Many things simply don't justify the effort of getting to know them. You will also find so-called short methods for calculating standard deviations and correlation coefficients. These are a complete waste of time: the best short method is a computer (or calculator). Forget them! However, there are a few other concepts which must be mentioned here because they are widely used: you will probably come across them so you need to know a bit more about them.

The standard measure of correlation – what is meant when people simply refer to the correlation – is 'Pearson's product moment correlation coefficient'. This is the quantity calculated by the Excel function correl. It is similar to Kendall's tau (Section 3.7.3), ranging from +1 for a perfect positive relation to −1 for a perfect negative relation. However, it is calculated in a different way, by means of a relatively complex formula which meshes well with mathematical probability theory, the original reason for its popularity. Obviously, in any given situation, Pearson's and Kendall's coefficients will give slightly different answers, but they are generally close enough for you to use what you have learned about Kendall's when interpreting Pearson's correlation. Figure 3.7 applies to Pearson's coefficient as well as Kendall's. Between the three values in this figure (−1, 0, +1), there is a tendency for Pearson's coefficient to be larger (in magnitude, ignoring any negative sign) than Kendall's, for example the Pearson correlation corresponding to the Kendall correlation of −0.22 in Table 3.8 is −0.29.

As well as being arithmetically awkward, the standard deviation is also a nuisance because it comes in two versions. The standard deviation defined in Section 3.4.4 corresponds to the Excel function stdevp, or σ_n on many calculators. The slight problem with this function is that if you use it with the data from a sample to estimate the standard deviation of a wider population, there will be a consistent tendency for the answer to be too small. The other version, stdev (or σ_{n-1}), has a correction built in so that, on average, the answer will be much closer. In practice, as you are usually using a sample to come to conclusions about a wider population, the version with the correction is the one you usually want. For this reason, it is the one produced by SPSS. If you are in doubt about which function is which, remember that stdev – the one you probably want – is the *larger* of the two. However, with large samples, the difference is small and certainly not worth worrying about.

In a similar vein, Kendall's tau (Section 3.7) comes in different versions. SPSS produces tau-b which incorporates a correction for inconclusive observations for which there is a tie on one or both variables. This complicates the interpretation of Kendall's tau, for example Table 3.7 won't be exactly right. Kendall's tau-b attempts to get round this, but at the cost of losing a lot of the transparency, which is the main advantage of Kendall's tau in the first place.

Another measure of the spread of the values of a number variable is the 'variance'. This is simply the square of the standard deviation. It is important for statistical modelling; we will see how in Section 9.3.1.

If you want to see some further possibilities (box and whisker plots, stem and leaf plots, measures of skewness, the variance, trimmed means and so on), explore the output produced by SPSS, especially the menu options under Analyze – Descriptive statistics. But I have tried to cover the essentials here.

▶ 3.11 Exercises

The obvious thing to do is to try out the concepts and methods in the sections above with some data of your own. Get some data on something you care about and explore it.

3.11.1 Histograms

What is the best width of interval for a histogram? If you have Excel, you could try experimenting with different interval (bar) widths for Figure 3.2. What about one unit? And what about 20? I think you will find 10 is about the best, but this is to some extent a matter of opinion. The file `words.xls` contains data on the lengths of words (number of letters) in passages from two different sources: Lewis Caroll's *Alice's Adventures in Wonderland* and an academic sociology article. Draw a histogram to show the pattern of each distribution. Have you any comments on the differences between the two distributions?

Now draw another version of the first histogram with just three intervals (bars): the first comprising one, two and three-letter words; the second only four-letter words, and the third words with five or more letters. You should find that the middle bar is the smallest, apparently suggesting that Lewis Caroll tends to avoid four-letter words. Is this right? (The lesson of this is that when you draw a histogram you should always make the intervals the same width.)

3.11.2 Quartiles, percentiles and so on

In a firm with 2000 employees, the upper quartile of the salary distribution is £25 000, the 95th percentile is £40 000, the mean salary is £19 000 and the standard deviation of the salaries is £8000. Answer as many of the following questions as you can (you may not have the information to do them all):

- How many employees earn more than £40 000?
- How many employees earn £25 000 or less?
- How many employees earn between £25 000 and £40 000?
- How many employees earn less than £19 000?
- How many employees earn less than £11 000?

3.11.3 Experiments with correlations and standard deviations

The marks for a group of four students in two examinations were:

Mathematics: Ann: 60, Bill: 75, Sue: 85, Dan: 90
English: Ann: 50, Bill: 48, Sue: 49, Dan: 46

The standard deviations (stdevp) of the marks are 11.5 for maths and 1.5 for English. Pearson's correlation coefficient between the marks in the two subjects is −0.8. Work out Kendall's correlation coefficient. Is it similar to Pearson's coefficient? Assuming that these marks are reasonably typical of all students doing the two examinations, what comments would you make about the difference between the two standard deviations, and about the correlation? Would it be fair to add the marks in the two examination to give students an overall mark?

You should be able to answer the following questions without a computer or calculator:

- What would the standard deviation of the maths marks be if the marks were halved (that is, they became 30, 37.5, 42.5, 45)?
- What if 30 was deducted from each mark?
- What effect would both of these changes have on the correlation? Would it still be −0.8 in both cases?
- Find the standard deviations of these marks: 60, 60, 75, 75, 85, 85, 90, 90 (compare with the maths marks above)
- And the standard deviation of these: 70, 70, 70, 70.

If you have a computer available you should be able to check these.

The final part of this exercise exploits one of the strengths of spreadsheets; the fact that they allow you to experiment: to change the data and see what effect this has on the answer. See if you can find six numbers whose mean is 30 and whose standard deviation is 10. Make the best guess you can, then work out the standard deviation (using the function stdevp), then try and adjust the guess and so on until the mean is 10 and the sd is 30 (both to the nearest whole number). How many steps did you need?

3.11.4 Exploring relationships between variables on the Isle of Fastmoney

The data in the file *iofm.xls* is from a random sample of 100 people on an (imaginary) island. Sexn is a numerical coding for sex, run 10 km is each person's time in minutes in a 10 km race, cycle 10 km is their time in a cycle race, and earn000E is their earnings in thousands of euros. What relationships can you find between the variables? Are they all what you would expect? (We'll return to this example in Chapter 9.)

3.11.5 Risk and return on the stock market

The file *shares.xls* contains daily share prices for three shares traded on a stock market. It also contains a calculation of the daily return: the gain you would make if you bought the share the day before and sold it on the day in question. For example, if you buy a share for £5 and sell it the next day for £4.50, you have lost £0.50 or 10% of your original investment. So the return would be −10%. Produce a histogram of the daily returns of each of the three shares over the time period. (So you need three histograms, one for each share.) Now work out the means and standard deviations of the daily returns for each of the three shares, and the (three) correlation coefficients between the returns for each of the three shares. How would you explain the interpretation of these to someone not familiar with statistics?

▶ 3.12 Summary of main points

There are many ways of summarising things statistically. In this chapter I have explained what I think are the most useful of these. Regardless of the type of summary you use, you should always consider carefully the source of the data you are using, and be cautious about generalising your results or jumping to conclusions about cause and effect.

4 Why Use Statistics? Pros, Cons and Alternatives

Chapters 2 and 3 introduced some of the basic concepts of statistics – probability, sampling, methods of summarising patterns of data – and should have given you some of the flavour of statistical reasoning. There are, however, other ways of handling the uncertainties of life. This chapter starts by reviewing some of the key features of the statistical approach, and then looks at the role of some of these alternatives. If you like, you can skip this diversion: the main account of statistics continues in the next chapter.

▶ 4.1 Introduction

Smoking causes lung cancer. The married are happier, on average, than the unmarried.[48] According to recent press reports, the A889 in the Scottish Highlands is the most dangerous road in the UK. Happy workers are more productive than unhappy workers. Patients in different areas of the UK have different survival rates after treatment for cancer. What these all have in common is that they are statistical conclusions. In each case the research works by taking large samples of people, or car journeys, counting up the numbers in various categories (the happily married, the happily unmarried, the unhappily married, the unhappily unmarried and so on) and working out average measurements in these categories or something broadly similar.

We are living in the age of statistics. Every morning the news seems to include another result of statistical analysis, with clear implications for how we should live our lives: stop smoking, get married, avoid the A889 and so on. As large-scale data collection and analysis becomes easier, this trend is perhaps inevitable. The scale is important; in earlier times, informal statistics on, say, disease would have been noted on a local level, but there would have been far too little data to see anything but the crudest patterns.

As explained in Chapter 1, my approach in this book is to use the model of a bucket with some balls in it to describe many aspects of statistics. We can think of statistical methods as bucket and ball methods. For example, we can visualise the people in a survey to investigate the relation between marriage and happiness as balls with the relevant information (marital and happiness status) stamped on them. One person may be represented by a ball stamped with the words 'married' and 'happy'; another's ball might be stamped 'unmarried', 'unhappy'. The statistician is then in a position to start counting balls to compare the various groups. There might be other bits of information stamped on the balls as well, age, for example. The bucket and ball model has the advantage of drawing attention to some of the characteristic features of the statistical approach. Let's see what these are.

▶ 4.2 Characteristic features of the statistical approach

The first feature is that all balls have the same status. If we take a group of people – each represented by a ball – and work out their average age, or the proportion who are happy, each person in the group has the same input to the answer.

The second feature is that there is only a limited amount of information stamped on each ball (values of number and category variables) which allows us to compare balls and summarise the properties of a group. We might stamp on each ball 'married' or 'unmarried' and the age of the person. However, names are irrelevant, as are all the little details that would help us to get to know these people 'as people'. Statistics treats people as if they were balls in a bucket. This is not, of course, to deny that people are people, but statistics deals with a much simplified view of reality. If, for example, we had two balls in a bucket, both stamped with 'married', 'happy', '36', these two balls are *identical* from the point of view of a statistical analysis. There is no difference between them. Obviously they represent different people with different personalities and interests, but that's another story.

The third feature is the fact that statistics then works by a mechanical process of counting the various balls in the bucket. There are rules for finding probabilities, averages or standard deviations which can be performed by a computer. Once we've decided which statistics we're going to work out, we just follow the rules. Judgement is, of course, needed to decide on the starting point – which data to use and how to build our bucket and ball model – and interpret our results. But the statistical analysis itself is a mechanical, ball-crunching process.

What's stamped on the balls is not always true. The data in the file drink.xls (Section 3.1) includes one female who apparently drank 140 units of alcohol over three days. This is difficult to believe, as anyone drinking this much would probably be seriously ill, if not dead. It is entirely possible, and in my view very likely, that the student in question just made these figures up. Or she may have been so drunk she couldn't remember how much she drank. Either way, we can't assume the data is true. The balls in the bucket are just a model of reality; this model may not correspond exactly with reality. Doing statistics with balls in a bucket, and not the people themselves, should help to remind you that statistics is a story which may not always correspond exactly with reality.

▶ 4.3 What sort of conclusions does statistics provide?

The result of this mechanical ball crunching is that we get to know about tendencies or probabilities – what is generally true, true on average or most probable. We find out that male students drink more than female students on average, or that the married are happier than the unmarried, on average. But, of course, there are some females who drink more than some males, and some unmarried people who are happier than some married people.

Care is needed when using statistical averages. Suppose the average (mean) number of children born to women in a country is 2.3. Is this a helpful piece of information for a study of population trends?

Yes, it obviously is. Would it be sensible to take it as indicating the typical family for a study of the experience of women in this country?

No, for equally obvious reasons: no woman has 2.3 children! Furthermore, the experience of women with no children is likely to be very different from the experience of women with (say) two children. And the experience of both will be very different from that of women with ten children. You need to be very careful about using statistical conclusions which 'average' over very diverse scenarios.

Sometimes we are just concerned about a single person or a single event. We then need to use statistical information about general tendencies or probabilities to come to the best conclusion we can. We might decide that the probability of fine weather on 13 June (see Section 2.1) is 68%, or that we are more likely to be happy if we get married. We can't be certain, of course. The weather and happiness are too complex to be certain. But the statistical approach still gives us useful information.

Usually, the precise causes behind these tendencies or probabilities is to some extent unknown. We may have an idea why smoking causes cancer, or why the married tend to be happier than the unmarried, but we probably do not understand the exact reasons. By taking large numbers of cases, statistics can demonstrate things whose detailed working remains mysterious, and which could never be recognised by studying individual cases. Sometimes this ability of statistics to see the general truth seems magic, surpassing what ought to be possible. We are told, on the basis of a public opinion poll, that 35% of the electorate will vote Labour, *despite the fact that we have not been asked*. How can the statistician tell without asking everyone eligible to vote? In fact there are likely to be errors but the size of these errors can be estimated with surprising accuracy (see Chapter 7).

Of course, if we have a sufficient understanding of a situation we don't usually need statistics. Jumping out of tall buildings is obviously likely to harm people. We know enough about gravity and human bodies for this to be entirely predictable, so there is no point in a statistical survey. But the health effects of eating meat or drinking red wine are less easily predicted, so a statistical analysis which enables us to spot the general tendency, despite all the other influences involved, is very helpful.

There is another side to statistics; it can be used to decide which of a number of possible hypotheses is true, or to assess the likely error in a numerical measurement. This side of statistics is introduced in Chapter 6, where we will use as an example the problem of deciding whether a volunteer in a telepathy experiment, Annette, is actually telepathic or not (see Section 6.2). There are two hypotheses here: either Annette is telepathic or she isn't. Analysing this statistically is a little more complicated (see Chapter 6). In one approach to the problem (Section 6.4), we envisage a bucket with balls representing *possible worlds*; we might conclude that balls representing worlds in which Annette is telepathic are much more numerous than those representing worlds in which she is not telepathic, so she probably is telepathic. Another approach is explained in Section 6.6. In both approaches, the conclusions depend on probabilities: we can never be 100% sure which hypothesis is true.

Statistics has a reputation, in some quarters, for being boring. There are a number of possible reasons for this. It's usually viewed as a mathematical subject and mathematics is sometimes seen as boring; I hope my approach in this book goes some way towards dealing with this. However, the perspective here may also not have immediate appeal. A simplified view of reality in which people (or whatever) are reduced to a few crude pieces of information stamped on some balls in a bucket may strike you as a rather boring attitude to the world. The advantage, of course, is that this simplification enables you to see through the fog of detail and see that, for example, smoking does cause cancer.

There is also the problem that the statistical results are sometimes not quite real. We are told that in the 1930s 'urban air pollution probably killed at least 64,000 extra people each year in the UK',[49] but we can never be sure who these people were. Some people who died of respiratory disease would have died even if the air had been less polluted, whereas others would not, but we cannot be sure which category a particular person is in. They are balls in a bucket, not real people. This makes the problem more difficult to identify with than, say, the people killed by the events of 11 September 2001. In this case, journalists can get our attention and sympathy by telling us stories of individual people, which is far more difficult with air pollution. But in the long run, air pollution is more important.

► 4.4 What are the alternatives to statistics?

Attitudes to statistics tend to be polarised. There are those who think that statistics is the answer to all problems and those who think it is never any help. The most helpful attitude falls somewhere in the middle. Statistics is very useful, but there are other ways in which we can deal with the uncertainties of life. I'll mention some of these possibilities briefly in this section, and then discuss three of them at slightly greater length in the next three sections.

Science – proper science in the sense of physics, chemistry or biology – tries to derive laws which explain exactly how things work. If it's successful, of course, then we don't need statistics. If we know enough about happiness to be able to deduce how happy people will be from their circumstances, then we have no need for a statistical analysis. Statistics is just the last resort when we don't understand things properly. So the first alternative to statistics is to try and understand things in the manner of science. If you know anything about research in management, education or the social sciences, you will probably be surprised by the idea of science as an alternative to statistics. Statistics tends to be seen as the scientific approach. It is true that natural science uses statistics to analyse measurement errors, and some theories are formulated in terms of statistics. But there is nothing statistical about $E = mc^2$, it is supposed to be exactly true everywhere, with no statistical qualifications.[50] Statistics should *not* be identified with the scientific approach: some approaches to science may be statistical but many are not.

There are several other approaches to analysing uncertainty in numerical terms besides probability (which leads on to statistical methods). These include 'surprise theory', 'certainty factors' and several others.[51] 'Fuzzy logic' is the only one of these to have made much of an impact and is the subject of Section 4.6. 'Chaos' is another term with a high profile. This refers to random behaviour in systems which are obeying explicit, deterministic (non-probabilistic) laws. You might think this is a contradiction in terms – if it's obeying laws, it's not random – but, as we'll see in Section 4.7, this is not always quite true. Finally, and perhaps most obviously, we might study particular cases, or individual people, as an alternative to statistics. Journalists do this when they want to bring, say, a famine, or the attacks on 11 September, to life for their audience. As well as reporting the statistics of the famine, they will also follow the stories of individuals to show what the famine really means. But do such anecdotes have a place in the serious business of research?

▶ 4.5 Anecdotes about specific cases

The problem with taking too much notice of special cases is that they may not be typical. They may not reflect the broader picture. It is always tempting to generalise from a few personal experiences. If you happen to know a couple of female students who drink too much, and a male student who is a teetotaller, you may well not believe that male students drink more than female students. Studies of the way people assess probabilities intuitively have found that it is very common for people to be misled into giving too much weight to personal experiences and high-profile examples.[52] This is not entirely surprising: the antidote is, of course, to collect and analyse the data systematically.

Special cases, then, should not be given too much weight, statistically speaking. But that's not to say they are of no value. For example, there are people who have a natural immunity to the HIV virus which causes AIDS.[53] From a broad statistical point of view they may be a negligible minority, but it would obviously be interesting to know why they are immune, because this may lead to possible ways of helping other patients. Similarly, total quality management is an approach to managing a business which is said by the gurus to bring tremendous benefits. The trouble is that there is widespread scepticism about whether it actually works. Now imagine that an organisation were to be found where total quality management was, indisputably, working well and bringing the anticipated benefits. Obviously, this organisation would be worth studying in depth to see exactly how total quality management had worked its wonders, in the hope that something would be learned which could be helpful to other organisations.

In both examples, the study of the particular case is worthwhile because it illustrates *possibilities* which may be of wider interest.[54] There is no guarantee of this, and certainly no statistical conclusions are possible. But the study of these particular cases may help us to learn about possibilities of which we may otherwise have been unaware. Obviously the cases should be chosen carefully; they may be of special interest like the two examples above, or they may be chosen because they seem typical in some sense. This principle is also accepted as an adjunct to standard statistical practice. You should always check data for outliers that do not fit the pattern, and then check to see if you can see what is going on. For example, the girl who said she drank 140 units in three days (Section 3.2) was probably lying, but if not, the reasons for her exceptional tolerance might be medically interesting.

Statistical process control (SPC) is a set of statistical methods used for monitoring business and industrial processes. A large part of the purpose of SPC is to identify unusual situations so that they can be investigated more fully. For example, many industrial processes are monitored statistically so that if something goes wrong the problem will be picked up by the statistics because it does not fit the normal pattern. Then the people in charge can investigate to see what happened and take appropriate action. The statistics here are used to distinguish the unusual cases so that they, and only they, can be explored further.

▶ 4.6 Fuzzy logic

Suppose you were asked to find out whether it is true that students drink too much on Saturday night. We've already looked at some data on this question in Chapter 3. Looking at the data in Table 3.1, would you say that students do drink too much on Saturday night? Yes or no?

You might say that you can't answer this because the question is too vague, in several different senses. The first type of vagueness is due to the fact that some students do undoubtedly drink too much (26 units is 13 pints of beer which cannot be healthy), whereas others drink nothing, which is obviously not too much. We could plot a histogram (Figure 3.1) to show this variation. This is what statistics is about: we can analyse this using concepts like probability, averages and measures of spread.

There are, however, other types of vagueness. The most important is *how much* does a student have to drink for it to count as too much? We could take the UK government guideline of 3 units a night, which means that we would draw a very sharp distinction between 'too much' (4 or even 3.5 units) and 'OK' (3 units). On the other hand, we might feel it makes more sense to use a continuous scale from 2 units – definitely OK – to 10 units – definitely too much. This is the idea behind fuzzy logic. Instead of treating statements as true or false (a so-called 'two valued logic'), we use a continuous scale from 0 – definitely false – to 1 – definitely true. What 'truth value' would you give to the assertion that a student who had 6 units had drunk too much?

The obvious answer is 0.5, on the grounds that 6 units is midway between 2 units (truth value of 0) and 10 units (truth value of 1). The relationship I am assuming between units drunk and truth value is shown in Figure 4.1. However, I can't really say that 0.4 or 0.6 is wrong. And why did we choose

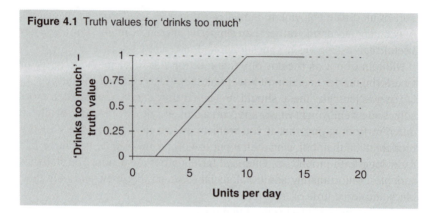

Figure 4.1 Truth values for 'drinks too much'

2 units for the zero of the truth value and 10 units for the top of the scale? Inevitably it's a bit arbitrary. It's based on my judgement and different people might have different views. Fuzzy logic is itself a bit fuzzy.

Kosko's book *Fuzzy thinking*,[55] puts the case for avoiding sharp true/false or black/white distinctions, and using a fuzzy scale wherever possible. And in many contexts he certainly has a point. I was listening to a pundit being asked on the radio whether men were now able to cook and look after themselves at home. The expected answer was yes or no. The real answer would acknowledge the fact that men vary, and that household skills need to be assessed on a fuzzy or sliding scale. It's not just a matter of competent or incompetent, but rather there are varying degrees of competence. And, of course, we need statistics to cope with the fact that men are not all the same.

In the black and white world of true and false, we might have a rule which says that *if* the student has drunk too much *and* the route home is dangerous, *then* the student should be restrained from going home. The difficulty here is that 'drunk too much' and 'dangerous' are fuzzy quantities. How much too much has the student drunk? How dangerous is the route home? Is it a moderately busy road, or does it involve a path along the top of a precipice? Obviously we need to take this into account, and fuzzy logic is one way of doing this. Fuzzy logicians would then set up a rule to relate the two truth values to the recommendations about whether we should stop the student from going home. It is an antidote to the black and white reasoning of true and false.

In practice, only logicians really need this antidote. When doing a survey, it is common practice to ask people, for example, how much they enjoy their work on a five-point scale ranging from 1 representing 'not at all enjoyable' to 5 representing 'very enjoyable'. Then a score of 3 would represent some sort of moderate enjoyment. Similarly, I asked my students (see Chapter 3) how much they drank, rather than simply whether they drank. Both are more useful than asking yes/no questions. And instead of simply asking whether it will rain or not on the day of a fete (Section 2.1), it might be more useful to ask the fuzzier question of how good the weather will be.

Fuzzy scales like these should not be confused with probability. Saying somebody's enjoyment of work is 3 on a 0 to 5 scale – or 60% – is obviously different from saying that if you were to encounter a random worker, the probability of their enjoying their work is 60%. It's important not to confuse fuzzy logic with probability. Often we have statistical questions about fuzzy variables. Unfortunately, some statisticians like to answer these questions in black and white, true or false terms. The conclusion may be that the hypothesis is false, instead of a fuzzier, but more useful conclusion about how much truth there is in it (see Chapter 8, especially Sections 8.4 and 8.6.3).

▶ 4.7 Chaos

The words 'chaos' and 'chaotic' have rather different meanings in mathematics and everyday life. In ordinary language if we talk of chaos we mean confusion, things being arranged with no apparent pattern. This is similar to the idea of randomness: a random sample is one chosen without any reference to the patterns in the data. In mathematics, chaos has a more restricted meaning: 'stochastic behaviour occurring in a deterministic system'.[56] Let's see what this means.

A 'deterministic' system is one which is determined by exact rules which can be used to predict what will happen next. For example, the movement of the earth, moon and sun are determined by mechanical forces which are described (with almost complete accuracy) by the laws of motion devised by Isaac Newton. These laws can be used to predict where the earth, moon and sun are at any given time. They were used to predict the onset of a total eclipse of the sun in Penzance, Cornwall at 37 seconds past 11.11 am on 11 August 1999. This was predicted years in advance with almost complete accuracy. This is a deterministic system; if we know where the sun, earth and moon are now, and how fast they are going and in which direction, we can predict eclipses for hundreds of years.

'Stochastic' behaviour, on the other hand, is random behaviour, or behaviour which can only be described in terms of probabilities. At first sight, there would seem to be no place for randomness in deterministic systems, because we ought to be able to use the laws of the system to work out exactly what will happen. There is, however, often a practical problem which means that this is not true.

Imagine that you have been given a rather unusual type of bank account. Instead of working out the balance in the account every day by adding up what has been paid in and what has been taken out, the balance is £1250 on 1 January, and thereafter it is worked out by a simple rule. Every day, the bank applies the rule and works out the new balance. This is a deterministic system: everything is decided by the rule, with nothing being left to chance.

Table 4.1 shows some daily balances for four of these accounts a few months after they were opened. Three of the four are based on a deterministic rule, but the bank has cheated for the fourth which is based on a rule using random numbers. Can you tell which account is based on random numbers?

It should be obvious that the first is not random and the second has an obvious cycle. This leaves the last two, both of which look fairly random. In fact, the third is deterministic, and the fourth is random. Despite the fact that

Table 4.1 Balances in four bank accounts opened on 1 January

Date	Account 1	Account 2	Account 3	Account 4
20 May	£268	£970	£1746	£1546
21 May	£268	£2	£1112	£412
22 May	£268	£1744	£25	£230
23 May	£268	£970	£1901	£325
24 May	£268	£2	£1623	£1596
25 May	£268	£1744	£775	£1286
26 May	£268	£970	£101	£38
27 May	£268	£2	£1616	£470
28 May	£268	£1744	£758	£67
29 May	£268	£970	£117	£274
30 May	£268	£32	£1559	£1885
31 May	£268	£1744	£624	£1026
01 Jun	£268	£970	£282	£1776
02 Jun	£268	£2	£1030	£1274
03 Jun	£268	£1744	£2	£1610
04 Jun	£268	£970	£1993	£24
05 Jun	£268	£2	£1972	£1850
06 Jun	£268	£1744	£1889	£60
07 Jun	£268	£970	£1581	£946
08 Jun	£268	£2	£676	£1007
09 Jun	£268	£1744	£210	£1423

All balances rounded off to the nearest whole number in the table, although the next day's balance is worked out from the *unrounded* number.

it is deterministic, it is difficult to see a pattern in Account 3: no values are repeated and there is no obvious cycle. There is some sort of weak pattern: every value of £1000 or more is followed by a lower number, which would probably not be true if the sequence were genuinely random. However, this pattern does not enable you to predict, say, five days in advance.

Imagine now that you have the option of taking the money from one of these accounts, but you have to name the day five days in advance. How would you do this for each of the accounts? Can you predict the likely balance in each account on 14 June**?**

This is easy for the first, the balance will be £268 whenever you choose to take it. In the second the predictable cycle makes it almost as easy; my prediction would be £2. The last two, however, are more or less unpredictable. According to the spreadsheet on which Table 4.1 is based, the balance in Account 3 on 14 June is £356, and in Account 4, £412. But I'm sure you did not manage to predict this! The rule the bank uses for Accounts 1–3 is actually very simple:

1. Divide yesterday's balance by 1000.
2. Subtract 1.
3. Multiply the answer by itself, remembering that if you multiply a negative number by itself the answer is positive.
4. Multiply the answer by 500 for Account 1, by 1750 for Account 2, and by 2000 for Account 3. This is the new balance.

To take an example, for Account 3 on 2 January, step 1 gives 1.25 (the balance on 1 January was £1250), step 2 gives 0.25, step 3 gives 0.0625 and step 4 gives the new balance of £125. Applying this process to this balance (0.125, −0.875, 0.765625, 1531) gives the balance for 3 January. And so on. There is no randomness involved, just explicit, arithmetical rules. It is easy to set this up on a spreadsheet, as I did to generate Table 4.1.[57]

And yet the result for Account 3 looks pretty random. A seemingly simple rule has resulted in chaos. But two slightly different rules, differing only in step 4, result in the more predictable patterns you might expect from an arithmetical rule. The clue to what is going on here is to look at what happens if we change the opening balance on 1 January slightly. Let's imagine the bank puts in an extra pound to start us off (£1251 instead of £1250). This shouldn't make too much difference, or will it? For Account 1 the change makes no difference after the first few days. The account seems destined to settle down to £268. For Account 2, the balance on 9 June (day 160) changes from £1744 to £2. There is, however, much the same cycle of three values, the balance the next day becomes £1745. The changed balance has just shifted the cycle by a day.

For Account 3, however, the balance on 9 June changes from £210 to £419. Even smaller changes have a massive impact by the time we get to 9 June. For example, a balance on 1 January of £1250.01 leads to £1975 on 9 June, £1250.02 leads to £751, and £1250.03 leads to £640. Tiny changes in the starting conditions get magnified to enormous changes later on. This leads to some oddities. For example, on 25 January the balance is £1982, on the 26th it is £1928, and it has returned to £1982 by 30 January. Does this mean that it is now starting a five-day cycle and must return to £1982 after another five days on 4 February?

No! On 31 January the balance is £1930, slightly different from the £1928 on the 26th, and by 4 February the difference has got bigger, the balance being £1961. The point is that the balance on 25 January is not *exactly* the same as on 30 January, and the difference gets magnified as the rule is applied every day.

If you have tried to reproduce the balances in Account 3 on your own computer, you will probably have obtained different answers. The spreadsheet on which Table 4.1 is based was not Excel; when I transferred the worksheet to Excel, the answers changed yet again. The balance for Account 3 on 9 June is £1917 instead of £210. Why do you think this is?

Most fractional numbers cannot be expressed exactly as decimals; they have to be rounded off to a particular number of decimal places. The difference is that each spreadsheet stores a different number of decimal places (for example 0.333 versus 0.333333); this means that the numbers stored are slightly different and these differences get magnified in the way we have just seen. Whenever the laws of a system mean that the final result is very sensitive to the initial conditions, this sort of *chaotic* behaviour may result.

One of the standard examples of chaotic behaviour is the weather. The atmosphere obeys the laws of physics so, if we were clever enough, we should be able to use information about what the atmosphere is doing now to predict what it will be doing in a second's time, and use this to work out what it will be doing in the next second, and so on, for ever. This is roughly what weather forecasters use their computer for. But it doesn't work for more than a few days, perhaps up to week. After that the inevitable inaccuracies in the data on which the computer works means that the forecasts get far less reliable. The problem is that small differences in the initial conditions may get magnified. The problem is far, far worse when predicting weather than when predicting the bank balances above, of course. With the bank balance there is just one initial condition, the initial balance. With weather forecasting, there will be millions of initial conditions, corresponding to the condition of the atmosphere all over the world. Needless to say, millions of initial conditions are likely to produce more of a headache than one.

The problem has been christened the butterfly effect.[58] A butterfly's wing produces a tiny change in the atmosphere. The atmosphere is now different from the way it would have been without the butterfly. These differences may get magnified – just like the penny extra on the balance above – and mean that the difference between the world with the butterfly and the world without it may be the difference between a hurricane on the other side of the world and no hurricane. Perhaps the hurricane which devastated southern England in 1987 would not have happened if a particular butterfly somewhere had not flapped its wings. Nobody knows if this is so; the weather is chaotic and unpredictable.

So where does this leave us? The main point to bear in mind is that understanding that something is chaotic does not solve many problems. Probabilities and statistics are still useful for weather forecasting. Chaotic events are random,[59] so statistics will probably be helpful. The mathematical theory of chaos[60] may also help. It may tell us which sort of values to expect, whether we will get chaos (like Account 3), or more predictable patterns like Accounts 1 and 2. And if we have got a chaotic situation, understanding the deterministic laws may help to some extent. For example, there is some sort of pattern in Account 3: the balance seems to go down in small steps, then suddenly jump again (but never to more than £2000), and then decline in another series of steps. This pattern could be helpful for predicting tomorrow's balance, but not next year's.

Which brings me back to that eclipse. I went to Cornwall to try to see it. The forecast of the time of the eclipse was, of course, correct. The weather, despite being a deterministic system, was chaotic and could only be forecast probabilistically. The forecast the day before was that the sky would probably be overcast, in which case the eclipse would not be visible. In the event the sky was overcast!

▶ **4.8 Exercise**

4.8.1 Experimenting with chaos
Use a spreadsheet to calculate the balance in the bank accounts described in Section 4.7. Do you get the same results as in Table 4.1? Can you see any way of forecasting the balance in Account 3? Now try experimenting with different numbers in step 4 of the rule. Which numbers give you chaotic results?

▶ **4.9 Summary of main points**

- Statistical methods enable you to see general patterns and tendencies, which provide an invaluable perspective in many walks of life. Statistics often allow you to see through a fog of detail to truths which may not otherwise be apparent.

- It is often tempting to focus on particular cases, perhaps those which are familiar, accessible or have a high profile. This has its place for demonstrating what is possible, but may lead to misjudging the overall picture.
- There are many other approaches to handling uncertainty, two of which, fuzzy logic and the idea of chaos, are briefly reviewed in this chapter.

5 Calculating Probabilities: Mental Ball Crunching and Computer Games

In this chapter, we look at how we can start from probabilities defined in the ways explained in Chapter 2, and then do some calculations, thought experiments or computer simulations to work out probabilities of a whole range of further possibilities. For example, starting from the assumption that all numbers in the UK national lottery are equally likely to be drawn, we can work out the probability of winning the jackpot or a £10 prize. This leads to the idea of a 'probability distribution' to describe how probabilities are distributed among, for example, the different possible prizes. To model these distributions, the bucket and ball metaphor is extended to the 'two bucket model'. Finally, we see how two standard distributions, the 'Poisson distribution' and the 'normal distribution', can be modelled both by simulation and Excel formulae.

▶ 5.1 Working out probabilities by listing equally likely possibilities

Informal ideas of probability arise from games of chance – dice, cards, tossing coins and so on. In these games, it is easy to list all the possibilities that can occur – the six numbers that may be uppermost on the dice, the 52 cards that may be dealt or the head on one side of a coin and the tail on the other. We can then assume that all these possibilities are *equally likely*, and that the probability of any one of them is 1/6 in the first case, 1/52 in the second and 1/2 in the third.[61] This line of argument can easily be extended. The probability of getting 5 or more on the dice is 2/6, because this is equivalent to 2 of the 6 possibilities. Similarly, the probability of getting an ace or the two of spades is 5/52, because this will happen if one of these five cards is chosen. What is the probability of getting a picture card?

Twelve of the 52 cards are picture cards, so this probability is 12/52 or 3/13.

Let's take another simple example. I toss a coin three times, and want to decide the probability of getting three heads. Can you see how to list the equally likely possibilities and use these to work out the probability? (Don't worry if you can't see how to do this, I want to use this to show you what to do when you strike difficulties.)

The answer should be 1/8 or 0.125. If you got this right, well done. If you didn't, don't worry. I'll explain another approach (and what the equally likely possibilities were) in the next section.

▶ 5.2 Working out probabilities by thought experiments: the lots of times tactic

In many situations, there is no obvious list of equally likely possibilities. Then we need to resort to some experimentation, either in our heads or with the help of a computer. I'll start with the mental variety. If you find this a bit of a headache, don't worry. In the next section we'll do it by computer which is often easier. The key idea here is what I'll call the 'lots of times' tactic. Imagine it, whatever it is, happening lots of times, and then imagine a big bucket containing lots of balls, one for each of the times 'it' happened (using the bucket and balls metaphor explained in Chapter 2). Let's see how this works with the three coin-toss problem. To build, mentally speaking, a suitable bucket and ball model, imagine doing the three coin-tosses 1000 times. Each of the 1000 results can be represented by one of 1000 balls in a bucket.

To do this, imagine stamping a sequence of Hs (heads) and Ts (tails) on each ball. Some balls, for example, might have HTT stamped on them, meaning that the first coin-toss was H, and the next two T. There are eight possible sequences (HHH, HHT, HTH, HTT, THH, THT, TTH, TTT); each ball will have one of these stamped on it. These sequences must start with H or T, and there's no reason to suppose that either is more likely than the other. So about half of these 1000 balls (500) will have a sequence starting with H, and the other half will have a sequence starting with T.

Now think about the 500 whose sequence starts with H. Half of these will also have an H in second place, this makes half of 500 or 250 balls. Now think about these 250. Half of these will have an H in third place as well. How many balls will be labelled HHH?

There are 125 balls labelled HHH. This means that 125 of the 1000 balls in the bucket represent three heads. What is the probability of three heads?

The probability is 125/1000 or 1/8. If you did this experiment for real, would you expect *exactly* 125 HHH?

No, of course not. Random events are not that predictable. We might get 120 or 129, but 300 would be very, very unlikely. It should be close to 125. We are using the bucket to represent long-term averages, not the exact numbers we would expect in practice.

It is often helpful to set out the reasoning in the form of a tree, showing

Figure 5.1 Tree diagram for three coin-tosses

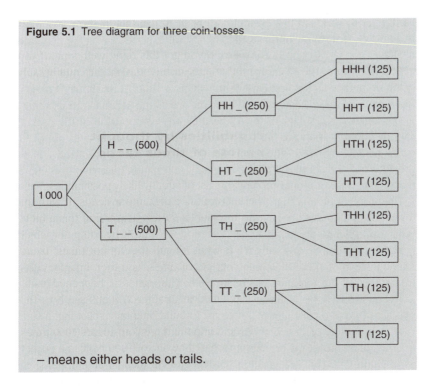

− means either heads or tails.

the successive subdivisions of the balls in the bucket, as in Figure 5.1. Alternatively, instead of imagining 1000 balls, we could simply imagine the proportions of the balls in the bucket at each stage of this argument (1/2, 1/4 and 1/8), which means we get the probabilities directly.

What if we wanted the probability of getting two or three heads? What will this come to?

All we have to do is count up these possibilities: this comes to four of the eight subcategories on the right-hand side of Figure 5.1, or 500 out of 1000 or 1/2. A more elegant argument for this problem would start with the observation that there are only two possibilities: two or more heads, or one or fewer heads, which means the same as two or more tails. As heads and tails are equally likely, this means that two or more heads, and one or fewer heads, are equally likely, so the probability in question is 1/2. (This is using the equally likely method of Section 5.1.)

As a further example, consider the problem of working out the probability that a hand of two cards are both aces. Start with an ordinary pack of 52 playing cards, shuffle them and deal two. This is the first hand. Now replace the cards, shuffle again and deal the second hand. Do this, say, 1000 times.

I will refer to hands in this example rather than using the metaphor of balls in a bucket. How many of these 1000 hands will have an ace as the first card dealt?

Because four of the 52 cards are aces, about one thirteenth of these hands will have an ace as the first card dealt, which is 1000/13 or about 77 hands. How many of these 77 hands will have an ace as the second card as well?

The answer is *not* 1/13 of the 77 because the composition of the pack is slightly different if an ace has been dealt. There will be three aces out of 51 cards, so 3/51 or 1/17 of the remainder of the pack will be aces, and 1/17 of the 77 hands or about 4.5 of the original 1000 hands have two aces. So a reasonable answer would be 4 or 5.

The problem here is that the numbers are too small. Two aces is too rare for us to get a handle on the long-term proportion starting from 1000 hands. What could we do about this?

Make the number of hands we imagine larger. Say we start with 10 000 hands instead of 1000. How many of these would you expect to be two aces (remember all the numbers will be 10 times larger)?

The answer will be 10 times 4.5, or 45. What is the overall probability for two aces in a two card hand?

The probability comes to about 45/10 000 or 0.45%. Alternatively, thinking in terms of fractions, the probability is 3/51 of 4/52, or 1/17 of 1/13, or 1/221,[62] as in Figure 5.2. This is a small probability: two aces are very unlikely to be dealt.

Notice that Figure 5.2 does not differentiate between kings, queens and jacks; all that matters is whether a card is an ace or something else. On the other hand, it does distinguish between the first card dealt and the second: 'Ace, Not Ace' is separate from 'Not Ace, Ace'. If you added up the probabilities of the four boxes on the right-hand side of Figure 5.2, what would the answer be?

The answer should be 1 or 100%. Every one of the 1000 hands must fall into one of those four categories, so the total number of hands must be 1000 so the probability is 1000 out of 1000, or 100%. If you don't believe this, add up the fractions in the four boxes. You can also read off the probability of getting one or two aces from Figure 5.2. What does this come to?

The first probability at the top right of Figure 5.2 comes to 0.45%, as we have seen. The next two both come to 7.24%. Adding the three up gives 14.9%. About 15% of two card hands will include at least one ace. Many probability arguments can be illustrated with a tree diagram like this.

These tree diagrams also illustrate the way probabilities can be added and multiplied. We've just seen how you can work out the probability of 'Ace, Ace', 'Ace, Not Ace' or 'Not Ace, Ace' by *adding* the probabilities. If you deal a single card, the probability of getting a spade is 1/4, and the probability of

Figure 5.2 Tree diagram for hands of two cards

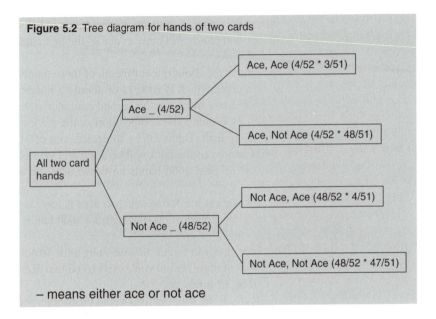

– means either ace or not ace

getting an ace is 1/13. Does this mean that the probability of getting an ace *or* a spade is 4/52 + 13/52 = 17/52?

No. The ace of spades will be counted twice: the right answer is 4/52 + 12/52 = 16/52. The probability 12/52 represents the probability of any of the spades *except* the ace. *When adding probabilities, you must check you aren't double counting anything.*

In Figure 5.2, the probability of two aces is 4/52 × 3/51, that is, we *multiply* the probabilities to get the probability of an ace first *and* an ace second. In Figure 5.1 the probability of H and H and H is obtained by *multiplying* 1/2 × 1/2 × 1/2.

The difference in Figure 5.1 is that the probability of H on the second or third toss is *independent* of what happens on the first, it is always 1/2. In Figure 5.2, on the other hand, an ace is less likely if the first card was an ace than if it was not an ace (3/51 instead of 4/51) because there are only three aces left. *Whenever you multiply probabilities, it is important to check if they are independent, and if they aren't, how they depend on each other.*

This is important in the next example too.

Jenny is applying for three jobs. She estimates her chance of getting the first job as one in two, her chance of getting the second job as one in three, and her chances of getting the third as one in four. What are her chances of ending up with at least one of the three jobs?

The first thing to ponder here is the meaning of these probabilities. For the first job, we can imagine a bucket' with two balls in it, one representing her getting the job and the other representing failing to get the job. We can think of these as possible futures for Jenny. Her assessment is that these are equally likely. This is inevitably more subjective than the judgement that heads and tails are equally likely.

Alternatively, if possible futures are difficult to imagine, we could let our balls represent similar people in a similar situation. We could call these clones 'jennys'. Then our bucket for the first probability contains two balls representing two jennys, one of whom gets the job while the other does not. Or we could combine the two images by thinking of jennys as possible futures for the real Jenny.

How can we build a bucket and ball model to deal with the whole problem? One tack is to imagine, say, 1000 jennys all applying for the three jobs. These jennys are the balls in the bucket. Each one of them represents a possible future for the real Jenny. We now need to think through the fate of these 1000 jennys. About 500 will get the first job, about 333 will get the second and about 250 will get the third. To work out how many get at least one of the jobs, we have to think about how many get the first but not the other two, the first two but not the third and so on. Then we add them up to find the number of jennys who end up with a job. In practice it is easier to work out the number of jennys who end up with *none* of the three jobs. This is a standard trick for working out probabilities. How many of the jennys will be left without a job?

Five hundred jennys will fail to get the first job. Two-thirds of these, or about 333, will also fail to get the second job. And three-quarters of these, or about 250 (0.75×333) out of the 1000, will fail to get the third job as well. So she has a 25% chance of ending up without a job. What is her chance of getting at least one of the jobs?

Obviously, this means she has a 75% chance (100% − 25%) of ending up with a job. This, of course, is on the assumption that the three probabilities are independent. There is actually a good argument for saying these probabilities are not independent, so the 75% answer is not quite realistic – see Exercise 5.8.8. *It is extremely important to check whether assumptions about independence are justified when calculating probabilities.*

I'll turn now to another example, where this was not checked, with disastrous consequences. In Section 1.2, we discussed the case of Sally Clark, who was accused of murdering two of her children. An 'expert' witness for the prosecution at her original trial claimed, wrongly, that the probability of having two SIDS (cot) deaths in a single family was 1 in 73 000 000. This figure is based on the following argument:

The probability of a child dying from SIDS is 1 in 8540 (0.000 117). There-fore, the probability of two children in the same family dying from SIDS is 0.000 117 times 0.000 117, which is 0.0 000 000 137 or about 1 in 73 000 000.

This is only valid if the probabilities are independent. To work out the true probability, we need to know the probability of a *second* baby dying from SIDS, given that the first child in the same family has already died. Do you think this is likely to be 0.000117, or higher or lower than this?

If there are risk factors which predispose some families to SIDS, these factors are likely to be much more prevalent among families which have already experienced SIDS, so the probability of a second SIDS case is likely to be higher than among the general population. There are undoubtedly such risk factors: estimates of this probability by experts range from 1% to 25%:[63] much higher than 0.000117. Suppose this probability (of the second child dying) were 25%. What does this make the probability of two children in the same family dying from SIDS?

One in 34 160, or 0.000029 (25% of 0.000 117). Much more than 1 in 73 000 000, which was the figure accepted in the original trial, and was part of the evidence which led to the conviction. Even the correct figure of 1 in 34 160 is liable to misinterpretation – see Sections 1.2 and 2.2. Be careful with arguments based on probabilities!

▶ 5.3 Working out probabilities by computer simulation

In Section 5.2, we saw how to work out the probability of Jenny getting at least one of three jobs. The method we used is reasonably straightforward, but only once you've seen the trick of working via the probability of her *not* getting any of the jobs. With many other problems, this method is far more difficult. Fortunately, there is an alternative which is often easier. This is simply to build a model of the balls in the bucket to allow us to make repeated random selections and so work out probabilities experimentally. In practice, the easiest way of building such a model is with a computer: this is known as 'Monte Carlo simulation' because we are using the computer to simulate chance events, like the roulette wheels in the casinos of Monte Carlo. It is the computer version of the 'lots of times' tactic.

Table 5.1 is a printout from a spreadsheet *jobs.xls* which is on the web. The 1s indicate that Jenny has been offered a job and the 0s that she has not. If you want to experiment with this spreadsheet (a good idea), you can either download it or key it in yourself (an even better idea and not too

Table 5.1 Computer simulation of 1000 jennys

Jenny number	Job A offer	Job B offer	Job C offer	Any offer
		Probabilities		
	0.5	0.333	0.25	
1	1	0	0	1
2	1	1	0	1
3	1	1	0	1
4	1	1	0	1
5	0	0	0	0
6	1	0	0	1
7	1	0	0	1
8	1	0	0	1
9	1	1	1	1
...	...	...	...	...
1000	0	1	0	1
		Estimated probability		0.74

1 represents a job offer; 0 represents no offer.

onerous).[64] It is important to get a feel for how computer simulation works, so if you aren't going to see it on a computer, I would suggest handcranking a bit of this simulation, as suggested in Exercise 5.8.4.

In the Job A offer column in Table 5.1, a formula is used which produces, at random, either 1 or 0, each with a probability of a half. In the Job B column, 1s have a probability of only a third, and in the Job C column the probability is a quarter. Each row of 1s and 0s represents a different 'run' of the simulation, corresponding to a different jenny clone. In the rows (jennys) shown, offers of Job A seem to be more probable than the probability would suggest (8 out of 10 instead of the expected 5 out 10), while the opposite is true of offers for Job C. Why do you think this is?

It's the luck of the draw. Remember that the formulae producing these numbers work at random. If you have the spreadsheet on a computer, your pattern of 1s and 0s will be different from Table 5.1. If you press F9, which recalculates the worksheet, you will see the pattern change.

The probability of 0.74 is worked out by counting the number of jennys with a job and dividing by the total number (1000). It is simply the proportion of jennys who have managed to get a job, which is our estimate of the probability. This answer is very close to the 75% we just worked out, but not quite the same. Why do you think the answer from the spreadsheet is not *exactly* 75%?

Again, it's the luck of the draw. The more jennys we take, the closer the simulation answer is likely to be to the answer worked out in the previous section. Even with 1000, the answer will not be exactly the same each time. On my computer, I got 74% the first time, next time (after pressing F9 to recalculate all the random numbers) I got 75%, then 76%, 74% again and so on.

What answer would you get from just the ten jennys shown in Table 5.1?

There are nine 1s and only a single 0 in the final column, so the probability is 9/10 or 90%. All the answers from the 1000 jennys above (74%, 75%, 76% and so on) were far closer to 75% than this. Simulating 1000 jenny clones provides a far more reliable estimate than simulating ten.

One of the advantages of spreadsheets is that you can change the contents of the cells and see what happens to the answer. What would Jenny's chance of getting a job be if the probability of getting each job was 0.5? What if the probability of getting the first job was 0.5, but the probability of getting the other two was zero? (Work these out in your head, or use the computer, or both.)

The first problem is effectively the same as tossing three coins – if, say, H represents getting the job and T represents failing to get it. You can now use Figure 5.1: the first seven boxes on the right-hand side all have at least one H, so she has at least one of the jobs. This means 875 (7 × 125) of the 1000 balls in the bucket represent her getting a job, so the probability is 875/1000 or 7/8 or 87.5%. Just like the earlier method, this assumes that jennys who get Job A have just the same chance of getting the other jobs as jennys who do not. We are assuming that the probabilities are *independent* (see Exercise 5.8.8). The second answer should be 0.5, which is simply the probability of getting the first job as this is the only achievable job on offer.

I'll use the UK national lottery as the next example of simulation. This also illustrates the idea of a probability distribution.

▶ 5.4 Simulating distributions of probabilities: the two bucket model

Sometimes we are interested not just in a single probability, but in the probability of each of a range of values. These are known as 'probability distributions' because they show how the probabilities are distributed between the possible values. The UK national lottery provides a good example to start with. Every few days, 49 balls, labelled from one to 49, are put into a specially designed machine, which then chooses six of them at random. To play, you pay £1 and try to guess the six numbers. The machine is carefully designed so that each of the 49 balls is equally likely to be chosen. Needless to say, your chance of winning the jackpot, getting all six balls correct, is very small indeed. But there are also prizes for getting five, four or three balls right. The question I want to look at is how we can work out the probability of winning these prizes. We could try listing all the (equally likely) possibilities, or using the lots of times tactic, but neither of these is particularly easy.

Instead, I'll use the much cruder method of Section 5.3, simulating the lottery on a computer. All we have to do is build a model of the lottery on the computer, run it lots of times and work out the probabilities of winning each of the prizes – just like we did for Jenny and her job. I have built this model in such a way that it will also be useful for lots of other problems. It will model the Poisson and normal distributions in the next two sections, and it also plays a part in most of the remaining chapters of the book. There are two versions of this model, `resample.xls` and `resample.exe`. The first is an Excel spreadsheet and the second is a stand-alone program you can use if you don't have Excel on your computer. The Excel spreadsheet is more flexible, but the stand-alone program is faster and can simulate many more 'times' than the spreadsheet. You may also find it easier if you are not familiar with spreadsheets. I'll start off with the spreadsheet.

Let's imagine you've entered the lottery and are choosing your six numbers. You might, for example, choose 21, 3, 49, 12, 7, 48. Or you might choose 1, 2, 3, 4, 5, 6. There are lots of possibilities. Then there are the numbers of the balls chosen by the machine. However, from the point of view of the probability of winning, it doesn't matter which numbers you choose because all 49 numbers are equally likely to be chosen by the machine. This means that we can simplify the lottery setup. Put 49 balls, labelled 1, 2, . . . 49, in a bucket and call this Bucket 1. Now stamp a second number on each ball – 1 on the six you have chosen, and 0 on the 43 you have not chosen. We can now focus on this second number and forget the original numbers.

The lottery machine draws six balls at random. Your score is then the number of these balls which have 1 stamped on them because these represent numbers you chose. For example, if you chose 21, 3, 49, 12, 7, 48, and the balls drawn by the machine were 6, 46, 3, 48, 49, 30, what would be stamped (0 or 1) on the balls drawn by the machine, and what would your score be?

The balls would be stamped 0, 0, 1, 1, 1, 0, and your score would be the sum (total) of these, 3. You've correctly identified three of the chosen numbers, which qualifies for the £10 prize.

The next step is to do this lots of times. Each time, draw six balls at random from Bucket 1 to represent another run of the lottery, stamp the score on another ball and put it in another bucket, Bucket 2. Then, when there are enough balls in Bucket 2, we can count up to estimate the probabilities. For obvious reasons, I'll call this the 'two bucket model'. The idea of the two bucket model is very simple. You draw samples from Bucket 1, and use each sample to work something out. Then you stamp this answer on another ball and put this in Bucket 2. The term 'resampling' comes from the idea that Bucket 1 is the original sample, and we are then drawing further samples, called 'resamples', from this. However, what we begin with here is not really a sample, so this term is not quite right. The phrase 'two bucket model' is more accurate, in that it avoids this problem and also fits the bucket and balls metaphor of this book. When I used *resample.xls* to simulate the lottery, the first resample gave me a score of zero and the second a score of one: the results of the first 200 are summarised in Table 5.2.

There are three linked worksheets in *resample.xls*. The first is for Bucket 1, the lottery machine containing 49 balls of which six are labelled 1 and the remaining 43 are labelled 0. The second is for a single simulated run of the lottery machine, that is, a single resample. The third collects together lots of such simulated runs and counts up the results; this is Bucket 2. If possible, do it yourself using *resample.xls*[65] or *resample.exe*.[66]

Table 5.2 is called a probability distribution because it shows the whole distribution of probabilities. It is based on 200 resamples: I ran the simulated lottery 200 times and put 200 balls in Bucket 2. If you are doing it on your own computer, your answers are almost certainly slightly different. If you press F9 to recalculate the spreadsheet, you should get another, slightly different set of answers. The probabilities in Table 5.2 are obviously not quite accurate. How could we make them more accurate?

We need more resamples (balls in Bucket 2, or simulated runs of the lottery). You could adjust the spreadsheet (click on the 'Read this' tab at the

Table 5.2 Lottery probability distribution based on 200 resamples

Number correct	No of simulated runs of lottery	Probability
0	88	44%
1	80	40%
2	30	15%
3	2	1%
4	0	0%
5	0	0%
6	0	0%
Totals	200	100%

Table 5.3 Lottery probability distribution based on 6 000 000 resamples

Number correct	No of simulated runs of lottery	Probability
0	2 614 916	43.58193%
1	2 478 326	41.30544%
2	795 036	13.2506%
3	105 752	1.762533%
4	5 860	0.09766667%
5	110	0.001833333%
6	0	0%
Totals	6 000 000	100%

bottom), but this becomes unwieldy if you want a very large number of resamples. It is better to use the program `resample.exe`. Table 5.3 shows the same simulation done on `resample.exe`. This time there are six million resamples (balls in Bucket 2). This took about two hours on my computer (not a particularly fast one). As you will see, the probabilities in Table 5.3 are similar, but not identical, to those in Table 5.2. The six million resamples in Table 5.3 give very reliable estimates of probabilities. If you try it on your computer, I can guarantee that the answers will be very similar to, but not of course exactly the same as, those in Table 5.3. If you don't believe me, try it!

According to the leaflet which you get when you enter the lottery, the probability of winning the £10 prize for getting three right is approximately 1 in 57. How does this compare with Table 5.3?

One in 57 is 1.75% which is very close to the 1.76% in Table 5.3. However, even Table 5.3 is not good enough for estimating the probability of winning the jackpot. This is obviously not zero: people have won. The difficulty here is that the probability is so low that we need an even larger number of resamples to get an idea of how big it is. According to the lottery leaflet, the probability of winning the jackpot comes to about 1 in 14 000 000. This means that we need about 100 000 000 resamples to get any sort of reasonable estimate. Unfortunately `resample.exe` will only do about 15 000 000 resamples, so we would need to run the program seven times and then combine the results, which would be quite easy to do but would take a long time.

The two bucket model will also simulate the two aces problem (Section 5.2). Can you see how?

An ace is the card of interest so use a 1 for each ace, and 0 for all other cards. Then the whole pack of cards comprises 4 1s and 48 0s. These go in

Bucket 1 (or in the 'sample'). Then each resample consists of just two cards and, as before, you are interested in the sum of these two cards because this will give the number of aces. Using `resample.xls` or `resample.exe`, you should be able to get answers very similar to those we got in Section 5.2.

The probability distributions for the lottery and number of aces in a hand of cards are examples of a type of distribution called the 'hypergeometric distribution' by probability theorists. If you look in the right textbook, you will find formulae (based on the mathematician's equivalent of the thought experiments in Section 5.2) for working out the probabilities in Table 5.2. (There is also an Excel function.) The reason this is worth the bother is that the formulae do not just apply to lotteries, but to other contexts as well, for example acceptance sampling in quality control (Exercise 5.8.5). Despite this, I wouldn't worry about the word 'hypergeometric'. It's not that commonly used. But there are two other probability distributions which are used much more frequently, and which are a little bit trickier to simulate. These are the 'Poisson' and the 'normal' distributions, which I'll look at in the next two sections with the help of the two bucket model.

It's also worth pointing out that the two bucket model – `resample.xls` or `resample.exe` – will simulate the three coins and the probability of heads (see Section 5.6), and `resample.xls` will deal with the birthday problem in Section 1.4.[67] The model is useful because it deals with such a wide range of problems.

▶ 5.5 The Poisson distribution: counts of random events

The Poisson distribution[68] gives us a way of working out the probabilities of a count of 'random' events. These are things that occur at random, but in such a way that they are equally likely anywhere or at any time. Incidences of rare diseases, defects in an industrial process, the decay of radioactive atoms, patients arriving at a hospital casualty department, people winning the jackpot on the national lottery are all examples of random events. The Poisson distribution can help us make some predictions about them, despite their randomness.

The goals scored by a football team are another good illustration. Manchester United, for example, scored 80 goals in 38 matches in the 1998–9 English Premier League season, an average of 2.1 goals per match. Sometimes they scored two, sometimes more, sometimes less, but the average was 2.1. There's no way of knowing in advance when goals will be scored; all we know is that their average rate of scoring was just over two goals per match.

As with the hypergeometric distribution, there is a mathematical formula (and an Excel function), but my approach here will be to simulate the distribution, so that you can see how and why it works. Fortunately, we can use exactly the same simulation model, the two bucket model, and `resample.xls` or `resample.exe`. Let's *assume* that

1. Goals are equally likely in each of the 90 minutes of all matches[69]
2. The average number of goals in a match is 2.1.
3. Goals are at least a minute apart. As you'll see later, this assumption is not essential, but it's helpful to start with.

The basic principle is to let Bucket 1 model the rate at which goals are scored and Bucket 2 contain balls representing simulated matches.

To start with Bucket 1, goals are scored at a rate of 2.1 per match. A tenth of a goal is not a real event, so we need to think of this as 21 goals in ten matches. We are going to build up the scores for each match, minute by minute. This means that we need to know the probability of scoring a goal in each minute. There were 21 goals in 10 matches, which lasted a total of 900 minutes. So we can put 900 balls representing these 900 minutes in Bucket 1, with 1 goal stamped on 21 of them, and 0 stamped on the rest. Can you see a simpler way of modelling this probability?

A total of 300 balls with 7 representing a goal would give the same probability since 7/300 is the same as 21/900. Or, even simpler, we could have 43 balls in the bucket with just one representing a goal. This reflects the fact that, on average, Manchester United scored a goal every 43 minutes. This is not quite accurate (the true figure is slightly less than 43), but it is good enough.

So each minute of each match can now be simulated by drawing one of these 43 balls out of Bucket 1. If it's got a 1 on it, a goal is scored. Then put the ball back, mix them up and draw again for the next minute. Repeat 90 times for the 90 minutes of one match. Notice that the ball is replaced after drawing it from Bucket 1. This is resampling *with replacement*. To model the lottery, the balls were not replaced: this is resampling *without replacement*. When I did this by computer, one goal was scored in the first 'match', in the 13th minute. In the next match, three goals were scored.

Now we have to put these scores on balls in Bucket 2: 1 on the first ball, 3 on the next and so on. The program `resample.xls`[70] simulates 200 matches, so we end up with 200 balls in Bucket 2, each with a number of goals stamped on it. Then it's easy to work out the proportion of the simulated matches with one goal, the proportion with two goals and so on. These are the estimates of the probabilities. The probabilities on my computer are 9.5% (0 goals), 23.5% (1 goal), 31.5% (2 goals), 27.5% (3 goals), 9.0% (4 goals), 3.5% (5 goals).

The highest score produced in the 200 simulated matches was 5 goals, and this occurred in 7 matches, giving the probability of 7/200 or 3.5%. If I press F9 to simulate another 200 matches, do you think I will get an identical set of probabilities?

No. The next time, the first probability was 14.5% instead of 9.5%. To get more reliable probabilities I need to simulate more matches, which is easily done.[71] If you did this, how could you decide if you had simulated enough matches?

Do it twice and see if the answers are similar.

However, we have made the rather dubious assumption that it's impossible to score more than one goal within a minute. This is obviously not quite true; it is just possible, but rather unlikely, to score two goals within a single minute. We can easily deal with this by dividing the match up into shorter intervals of time. Let's divide it into 15-second intervals. There are 360 intervals of this length in a match, so in 10 matches there are 3600 intervals. Twenty-one goals were scored in these 10 matches, which means that a goal is scored, on average, in one out of 171 15-second intervals. The question then is how many goals will be scored in a match of 360 of these intervals.

It's a little cumbersome to do this on the spreadsheet *resample.xls*,[72] so I have used *resample.exe* instead. In Bucket 1 (called the sample by the program) I put a single one and 170 zeros to represent the scoring rate of 1 goal in 171 15-second intervals. Each match is then represented by a resample comprising 360 15-second intervals, and I am, of course, interested in the sum of the goals scored. I have simulated 10 000 matches, which should give more accurate results than the 200 performed by *resample.xls*.

The results are in Table 5.4, together with 10 000 simulated matches based on one-minute intervals. I've also included probabilities worked out from the 38 matches that Manchester United actually played (these probabilities are simply the number of times they scored each number of goals divided by the number of matches). As you will see, both columns of simulated probabilities are very similar and both are very similar to the earlier results from the spreadsheet version. There is a very slight tendency for high-scoring matches (4, 5 or 6 goals) to be slightly more likely with the 15-second simulation than with the 60-second simulations. This is obviously because the shorter intervals give you the chance to score the occasional extra (simulated) goal. But the difference is tiny.

This means that the exact size of the interval into which the match is divided matters little. Obviously if you divided it into two intervals, first half and second half, this would not do because then the most goals that could be scored would be two, which is obviously unrealistic. But provided the intervals are small – so that the probability of scoring a goal in each is

Table 5.4 Probability distribution from 10 000 simulated and 38 real Manchester United matches

Goals scored	Simulated probability (15-sec intervals)	Simulated probability (60-sec intervals)	Probability from the 38 real matches
0	12.0%	12.4%	13%
1	25.6%	25.8%	29%
2	27.2%	27.3%	26%
3	18.6%	18.8%	16%
4	10.2%	9.9%	8%
5	4.2%	3.9%	3%
6	1.6%	1.3%	3%
7	0.4%	0.4%	0%
8	0.1%	0.1%	3%
9	0.05%	0.04%	0%
10	0.01%	0.01%	0%
Totals	100%	100%	100%

low – then it does not matter much. If you divided the match into five-second or even one-second intervals, the probabilities you would end up with would be very similar to those in Table 5.4. The *only* numerical information that is important is the average number of goals scored in a match (2.1). We then subdivide the match into short intervals, but the exact size of these doesn't matter.

What do you think of the comparison between the simulated probabilities in Table 5.4, and those worked out from the real matches?

They are very close. The most noticeable discrepancy is the eight goal figure. The simulated probability was very low, suggesting that such a score was almost impossible. However, it did happen – they beat Nottingham Forest 8–1. This suggests that the model may be a little wrong. Which of the three assumptions above (numbered 1, 2, 3) do you think may not be valid?

I would doubt the assumption that goals are equally likely in all matches. Nottingham Forest may have been a weak team against whom it was relatively easy to score. However, despite this, the overall fit of the simulation model is very good. You don't need the whole truth in statistics.

The other examples mentioned above can be analysed in a very similar way to the football scores. To take one example: if you're interested in the number of patients arriving at a hospital casualty department in an hour, you could divide the hour up into 10-second intervals, and then proceed just as before. And we'll come to another example in Section 8.1. Alternatively you can use the Poisson function in Excel,[73] which is based on the mathematical formulae for the Poisson distribution, which in turn are derived by imagining the process we have just been through. If you do this you will find the results are almost identical to the second column of Table 5.4.

But, you may wonder, why bother? If we know the goals scored in each match, why do we need to simulate them? There are a couple of reasons. The first is that if the model fits, there's a good chance the assumptions are right too: in other words, goals are scored at random. The second reason for the model's usefulness is for situations where there is no data, for example it could help us to predict the outcomes for matches next season. Or, if we know that arrivals to the casualty department are random and at a rate of six per hour, we could use the Poisson distribution to work out the most that we could reasonably expect in an hour, which could help us to decide sensible staffing levels (Exercise 5.8.6).

▶ 5.6 The normal distribution

This is another distribution which is useful in lots of different situations. It's so common that it's often assumed to apply everywhere but, as we'll see, there are many normal situations which are not statistically normal.

Imagine tossing a coin 100 times. How many times will it land head uppermost? Obviously around 50 times, but it might be 49 or 53. But what about 60? We want to work out how probable each of the possibilities are. Alternatively, imagine a maternity ward of 100 babies. How many of them are girls? Again about 50, but there may be a few more or a few less. This is essentially the same problem.[74] We will, of course, use the two bucket model. (This is even more normal than the normal distribution.) Can you see how to do this with the two bucket model. What do we put in the first bucket**?**

One ball to represent a boy and one to represent a girl. Or one to represent a head and one a tail. The easiest way to do this is to let 1 represent a girl (or a head) and 0 a boy (or a tail) or vice versa. Then if we add up the total we get the number of girls. (I'll talk about girls rather than heads from now on.)

We obviously want to take a resample of 100 *with replacement*, otherwise Bucket 1 will be empty after the first two babies. And we want to find the sum of this sample, since this will be the total number of girls.[75] My resample starts 1, 1, 0 . . . , or girl, girl, boy . . . , and the total number of girls is 56. When I recalculate the random numbers (function key F9), the total number of girls becomes 49, then 46. This corresponds to three different, randomly produced groups of 100 babies. The next stage is to produce lots of resamples so that we can fill Bucket 2 with enough balls to see the pattern. Figure 5.3 shows 200 000 simulated groups of 100 babies.[76]

Figure 5.3 Distribution of the number of girls among 100 babies based on 200 000 simulated groups of babies

```
73 to 77
68 to 72  -
63 to 67  -
58 to 62  XXXXXX-
53 to 57  XXXXXXXXXXXXXXXXXXXXXXXXXXXX-
48 to 52  XXXXXXXXXXXXXXXXXXXXXXXXXXXXXXXXXXXXXXXXXXXXXXXX-
43 to 47  XXXXXXXXXXXXXXXXXXXXXXXXXXXX-
38 to 42  XXXXXX-
33 to 37  -
28 to 32  -
23 to 27
```
X represents 1911 resamples; - represents fewer than this

This pattern is pretty stable. I can almost guarantee that if you do it, the results will be identical to mine. If you are in doubt about whether you have enough balls in Bucket 2 to see the stable pattern, try generating another set of the same size and see if you get the same pattern. If there's a substantial difference, you need more balls in the bucket.

The interesting thing about Figure 5.3 is that the pattern is one which occurs all over the place. There's a central hump and then the frequencies (probabilities) tail off symmetrically above and below. This is the so-called 'normal distribution'. If you browse the figures in this book, you will see that surprising number of them, but by no means all, have this characteristic bell shape: a hump in the middle and falling off symmetrically and gradually on both sides.

To take another example: the mean height of a 'nationally representative' sample of 18-year-old-males was 178 cm.[77] The median height was also 178 cm, and the 5th and 95th percentiles (Section 3.4.3) were 168 and 189 cm. Does this suggest that these heights are normally distributed?

Yes, at least roughly. The fact that the mean and median are the same suggests the pattern is symmetrical (Section 3.4.2), as does the fact that the lower percentile is roughly the same distance below the mean as the upper percentile is above it (10 cm versus 11 cm). Also, experience suggests that heights are likely to cluster round the mean, with very tall people and very short people being much rarer.

The pattern is likely to be a normal pattern as in Figure 5.4. This is produced using the Excel normal distribution function, which in turn is based on some complex mathematics which, in turn, is based on the assumption that the process works very like the two bucket model used to generate Figure 5.3. This function needs two inputs: the mean and standard

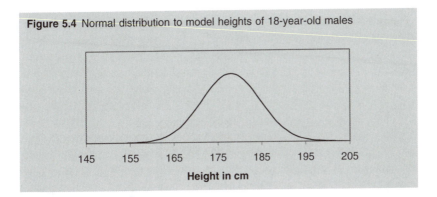

Figure 5.4 Normal distribution to model heights of 18-year-old males

deviation.[78] Figure 5.4 suggests that boys over 200 cm or under 155 cm are very rare!

Figures 5.3 and 5.4 are normal, statistically speaking. The scales are different, and Figure 5.4 looks more 'spread out'. How can we simulate something like Figure 5.4 using the two bucket model? There are actually many ways of doing it, but I'll start from Figure 5.3. To see how this is possible, let's change the story behind Bucket 1 slightly. Imagine that you are tossing a coin rather than having babies: if it lands on heads, you win £2.45, if it lands on tails, you win £1.11.[79] To model this we stamp 2.45 on one ball in Bucket 1 and 1.11 on the other. We now do exactly the same as before: make 100 random selections from Bucket 1 (representing 100 coin-tosses) and stamp the total on a ball in Bucket 2. Then repeat this many times. On my computer – using 200 resamples with `resample.xls` – the first total is £169.96 and the second £186.04. The mean of all 200 is £178.66 and the standard deviation is £6.79. The results are shown as a histogram (Section 3.4.1) in Figure 5.5, which looks roughly normal. Figure 5.5 is very similar to Figure 5.4 (except that one is a histogram and the other is smoothed to show the overall pattern). The point of doing this is just to show you how *any* normal distribution can be produced with the two bucket model, although it's not a terribly practical method.

The simulation approach does help to clarify the assumptions on which the normal distribution is based. You see the normal pattern whenever you have something which depends on adding up a large number of small, independent influences. All the balls in the bucket on which Figure 5.5 is based depend on 100 random events, each of which results in adding either 1.11 or 2.45 to the total. Do you think these numbers – 100, 1.11, 2.45 – have some deep meaning for the heights of 18-year-old boys?

No, obviously not. You could find many other ways of simulating a pattern

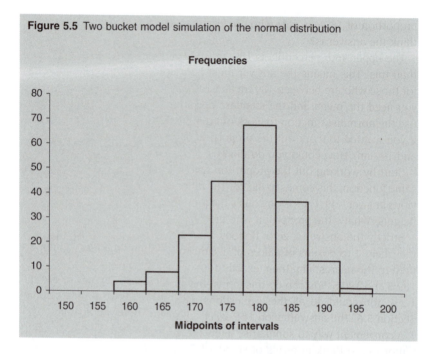

Figure 5.5 Two bucket model simulation of the normal distribution

like Figure 5.5. But you can be reasonably sure that the heights of 18-year-old males depend on a large number of factors and are not unduly dependent on any one of them. These factors will include various genes, the influence of nutrition and so on.

Of course, as I mentioned earlier, many distributions are *not* normal. Figures 3.1 and 3.2 are obviously not normal. Many distributions from real life are skewed like this. Despite this, the *average* alcohol consumption of groups of students will be much more normal than the figures for individual students in Figures 3.1 and 3.2. Each average depends on a number of different people and these different people are the independent factors which make the normal distribution work. Proportions of groups exhibiting some property behave in a similar fashion. This is the main reason why the normal distribution is important in statistics because typically we are working with averages of samples and similar quantities. However, when using computer simulation, you don't need to use this fact to work things out, you just run the simulation and see what happens.

5.6.1 Calculating normal probabilities
I'll use Figure 5.4 as an example. First, let's work out the probability of an 18-year-old male being less than 190 cm. Alternatively, think of it as the

proportion of 18-year-olds who are less than 190 cm. Roughly what do you think the answer is?

The upper 95th percentile is 189 cm (see Section 5.6) so 95% will be less than this. This means the answer must be a little more than 95% to allow for those who are between 189 cm and 190 cm. To work out an exact answer you need the mean and the standard deviation. If you have Excel, you can use the normdist function to work out a more exact answer – 96.3%.[80] What if you wanted to work out the proportion of boys who are between 185 cm and 190 cm? How could you do this?

Start by working out the proportion who are *less than* 185 cm. Using the same function, this comes to 85.2%. The difference between this and the previous answer – 11.1% – is obviously the proportion who are between the two heights. What's the proportion who are *exactly* 190 cm?

Strictly the answer is zero, nobody will be *exactly* 190 cm if you measure their height to dozens of places of decimals. However, if heights are measured to the nearest cm, then 'exactly 190' actually means anything between 189.5 and 190.5. You can do this in just the same way. The answer comes to 1.2%. You could do all these questions with the simulation we set up in Section 5.6. The answers won't be exact,[81] but they should be close.

A convenient way to summarise a few basic facts about the normal distributions is to think in terms of standard deviations from the mean. All the following could be verified either by simulation or from the Excel normdist function.

- About 68% of individuals lie within 1 sd of the mean
- About 95% of individuals lie within 2 sds of the mean
- About 99.7% of individuals lie within 3 sds of the mean.

Using the distribution in Figure 5.4, the mean is 178 and the standard deviation is 6.7, so, for example, 'within two sds of the mean' is the range between 164.6 ($178 - 2 \times 6.7$) and 191.4 cm. According to the normal distribution, 95% of 18-year-old boys have heights in this range. How many will be below 164.6 cm?

If 95% are in this range, 5% must be outside it. As the distribution is symmetrical, this means 2.5% must be in the bottom 'tail', and the other 2.5% in the top tail.

5.6.2 Simulating normal 'data'
It's also possible to generate normal 'data' with the norminv function in Excel.[82] It's possible to do this with the two bucket model (Figure 5.4), but this formula is far easier.

▶ 5.7 Similar concepts

'Bayes' theorem' is a an important part of probability theory, which is explained (in non-mathematical terms) in Chapter 6.

The distribution of the number of heads which you get when you toss a coin a given number of times or the number of girls you get if you have 100 babies (Section 5.6), are both examples of another standard probability distribution known as the 'binomial distribution' (binomdist in Excel).

Simulation techniques (Section 5.3) can be used for building models of specific situations. If, for example, you are thinking of marketing a new product, but are not sure how much it will cost to produce, how many you will sell, whether you will be sued by angry customers if it doesn't work and how much the damages are likely to be, what can you do? One answer is to set up a Monte Carlo simulation model to estimate the probabilities of the various possible outcomes. The Excel add-in @Risk[83] is very useful for building such models. It is also useful for getting a feel for the many probability distributions devised by probability theorists and probability modelling in general.

▶ 5.8 Exercises

5.8.1 What does one in three mean?

Three married brothers have heard that one in three marriages ends in divorce. Jim is divorced, so Joe and Jon were confident that their marriages would survive because Jim's marriage was the one in three. Then Joe's wife divorced him. He was surprised (and upset) because he thought the statistics showed he was safe. Any comments?

5.8.2 The Monty Hall problem

This is a well-known puzzle named after the host of a quiz show. You are a contestant on a quiz show who is shown three doors and told that there is a new car behind one door and nothing behind the other two. You are asked to choose one of the doors; if you choose the door with the car behind, you win the car, otherwise you win nothing. However, Monty, who can see what is behind the doors, gives you a clue. After you have made your choice, but before opening the door, he opens one of the two doors you haven't chosen to reveal there is nothing there (he avoids opening the door with the car behind it). He now offers you the option of changing your choice and choosing one of the other doors. There's obviously no point in choosing the door Monty has opened, so there are two reasonable options: stick to your original selection or choose the other door. What's the best thing to do and what are your chances of winning in each case? (You may be able to do this by listing equally likely possibilities. Alternatively you could imagine playing the game, say, 300 times.)

5.8.3 Lottery probabilities
What is the probability of winning the jackpot on the UK national lottery (see Section 5.4)? It may help to use a tree diagram like Figure 5.2. Is the lottery entirely a matter of chance? Are there any strategies for playing which would increase the amount you could expect to win?

5.8.4 Computer simulation without a computer
It is important to understand how computer simulation of probabilities works, so, particularly if you are not doing any of the computer exercises, it's worth running through one example without a computer. The easiest is Jenny's job – see Section 5.2 and Table 5.1. You will need a dice and two coins. Start by making a rough copy of Table 5.1, but without the 1s and 0s, and going down as far as Jenny number 20. Now toss the coin to see if Jenny 1 gets the first job – heads she does, tails she doesn't. Now use the dice for the second job; you can simulate a probability of 1/3 by saying that she gets the job if you throw one or two. Now toss both coins; the probability of two heads is 1/4 so this can represent her getting the third job. Repeat 20 times, and count up the number of jennys who get at least one job. Is it close to the expected 15? (Obviously you would get a more useful answer by simulating 1000 jennys, but you may not have the patience.)

5.8.5 Sampling to decide if a batch is acceptable
A firm decides whether to accept a batch of 100 components by taking a random sample of 20 of the components, testing them and accepting the whole batch if there is no more than one defective component in this sample. If there are two or more defectives, the batch is rejected. (This is known as an 'acceptance sampling plan'.) They are keen to reject any batches containing more than 5% defectives. Estimate the probability that their sampling scheme will reject a batch with just over 5% defective. Have you any suggestions for a better sampling scheme?

5.8.6 Using the Poisson distribution: hospital casualties and lottery winners
What is the maximum number of patients per hour a hospital casualty department should prepare for if the average rate of arrivals is six per hour? What assumptions is your answer based on, and are these assumptions realistic?

The probability of winning the jackpot on the UK national lottery is about

1 in 14 000 000. In the first 70 weeks the lottery ran, about 60 000 000 tickets were sold each week; nobody won on 13 occasions, and there were more than 50 winners on two occasions. Using the above probability, what is the average number of winners you would expect each week? Using the Poisson distribution, how often would you expect no winners and how often would you expect more than 50 winners? Have you any comments on the relation between these probabilities and what actually happened?

5.8.7 Using the normal distribution: heights and shares

According to a representative sample, the mean and standard deviation of the heights of 18-year-old girls in the UK in the 1990s were 163 cm and 5.8 cm. The 5th and 95th percentiles were 154 cm and 173 cm. The corresponding figures for boys were 178 cm and 6.7 cm, and 168 cm and 189 cm.[84] What proportion of girls were taller than the average boy? What proportion of boys were shorter than the average girl?

Exercise 3.11.5 involves producing a histogram of share returns. Much of the theory of stock markets assumes that share returns are normally distributed. Is this assumption justified for the three shares in *shares.xls* (and *sharesan.xls*)? You can check this by looking at the shape of the histogram, and also by comparing the percentiles of the distribution with the normal figures. For example, according to the normal distribution, the 2.5th percentile should be about two standard deviations below the mean, and the 97.5th percentile should be about two standard deviations above the mean. Work out the mean, sd and the two percentiles of the distribution of the share returns and see if these relationships are roughly right.

5.8.8 Independent or dependent probabilities?

The probability we calculated (in Section 5.2) for Jenny getting one of the three jobs was 75%. This depends on the assumption that the three probabilities are independent. Is this assumption justified and, if not, what can you say about the probability of her getting one of the three jobs? (The probabilities indicate that the first job is the easiest to get. If she fails to get this job, then isn't she very unlikely to get either of the other two?)

▶ 5.9 Summary of main points

- Equally likely arguments are the starting point for working out any probability.
- If this doesn't solve the problem, it may be possible to work out probabilities by imagining 'it' being repeated lots of times.
- If it is too difficult to list the equally likely possibilities or work out in

your head what will happen if 'it' is repeated lots of times, then you can use computer simulation.

- It's important to check the assumptions behind probability models, particularly the assumption that probabilities are *independent* of each other. They often aren't, which may make the answer very wrong.
- The two bucket model (or resampling) can be used to simulate many things, including the Poisson and normal distributions.
- The Poisson distribution enables you to estimate the probability of a given number of random events occurring. All you need to start with is the average (mean) number of events. You can then use simulation or an Excel function to work out the probabilities.
- The normal distribution enables you to work out the proportion of values of a 'normal' measurement which lie in a given interval. The inputs you need are the mean and the standard deviation. You can work out the probabilities either by simulation or by using Excel functions.

6 Possible Worlds and Actual Worlds: How can we Decide What's True?

This chapter looks at the process of 'statistical inference': using a limited sample of data to draw conclusions about a wider context. We start with the approach based on a famous theorem of probability, 'Bayes' theorem', and then move on to introduce two other approaches – 'confidence intervals' and 'null hypothesis tests' – which are explored in more depth in Chapters 7 and 8.

▶ 6.1 Introduction

In Chapters 2 and 5 we looked at probability. The basic idea here was to use our knowledge of how the world works to estimate probabilities of various events. We know the way the lottery works, how a game of football works and even how the weather works (roughly), and we can use this information to derive probabilities of winning the jackpot, scoring six goals or having fine weather at a particular time.

In this chapter I want to look at the opposite question. If we've got some observations from the world, some data, how can we decide how the world works? How can we go beyond the sample of data we have, and come up with the truth about a broader context? The short answer is that we usually can't decide, with certainty, what's true. But the statistical approach is to try to come up with some sort of probabilistic answer. For example, the data in Table 3.1 tells us that the mean alcohol consumption by the sample of 20 students on a Saturday night was 7.4 units. It also tells us that 12 of the 20, or 60%, drank too much, if we define 'too much' as more than three units, and that the males drank more than the females. But can we assume that these conclusions are accurate if we extend them to the broader context of students in general? Do they tell us the truth about whole world of student drinking?

Obviously they may give some hints, but a small, haphazard sample is not likely to be a very accurate or reliable guide to the general picture (see Section 3.2). The problem is to decide how accurate, how reliable, or what the error is likely to be.

The general problem of deriving general truths from particular observations (such as the 20 observations in the sample in Table 3.1) is called by philosophers the problem of 'induction'. If we are after complete certainty, there is no satisfactory solution. If observations of 100 swans show that all 100 are white, does it follow, with complete certainty, that all the swans in the world are white**?**

No, of course not. There are black swans, but our sample happens not to include any. However, particularly if we took care to ensure that the sample was a carefully chosen one (see Section 2.5), we might feel safe in coming up with a vaguer answer like 'there's a good chance that all swans are white'.[85] This process is known as 'statistical inference': trying to infer general truths from a limited sample of data. It is the statistical response to the problem of induction. This turns out to be more complicated, and more controversial, than you might expect. There are a number of approaches; the most commonly used is introduced in Section 6.6, with the main competition in Sections 6.4 and 6.5. I'll use the example in the next section to explain these approaches.

▶ 6.2 An experiment on telepathy

In January 2001, I did an experiment to try to demonstrate the existence of telepathic communication.[86] This is communication which does not rely on any of the known senses: by some unknown method one person becomes aware of what another person is thinking, despite the absence of any opportunity to communicate by means of sound, vision, touch or any of the other senses. I was in one room with a pack of playing cards which I shuffled thoroughly, then cut to display one of the cards to Peter, a volunteer, who concentrated hard on it. In another room, Annette, another volunteer, at the pre-arranged time tried to see if she could determine what card Peter was thinking about. She then wrote it down on a piece of paper. Annette got the card, the three of clubs, right! Afterwards she said that it felt as though she was guessing, but it was the three of clubs which floated into her mind when she was deciding what card to guess. We checked carefully, but there was definitely no way she could have known which card was chosen except by means of telepathy. She was as surprised by her success as Peter was. There were only two viable explanations: either Annette was guessing and was lucky, or she was communicating telepathically with Peter.

(In a series of experiments in the 1920s and 30s, the psychologist J. B. Rhine found a number of people who appeared to be telepathic (or to demonstrate extra-sensory perception – ESP).[87] In one series of experiments, Hubert Pearce Jr did a card-guessing experiment 8075 times, and got the card right on 3049 occasions. There were five cards in the pack, so guesswork would have produced about 1615 hits. Rhine argues that Pearce's performance is so much better than guesswork that ESP must be involved; others have taken the hypothesis that Pearce was cheating more seriously.[88])

▶ 6.3 Actual and possible worlds

We can think of these as two alternative 'hypotheses': the first hypothesis is that Annette was guessing and the second is that she was using telepathy. Or, we can think of these as two 'possible worlds'. Are we living in a world in which Annette could communicate telepathically with Peter or in a world in which she could only guess. Obviously we are just talking about one small aspect of the world, so the phrase 'possible world' may seem rather too flowery. However, it does draw attention to the fact that we need to imagine the possible ways the world might work. And the language of possible worlds is more natural in the next section when we start to put them on balls in buckets. So I'll stick with the language of possible worlds but remember it is equivalent to talking about a number of hypotheses concerning how the world works.

Let's think about these two worlds. It is important to imagine these worlds to see what they involve. You are probably familiar with guessing, but the world in which Annette was telepathic may not be so familiar. How telepathy works we do not, of course, understand. But we do need to be clear about how effective telepathy is. Perhaps it always works or perhaps it only works sometimes. If the latter, perhaps it works on, say, 50% of occasions. Perhaps it works when Annette is in a good mood or when the sun is shining. There are obviously lots of possible telepathic worlds. What we would obviously like is a way of saying how probable each of these worlds is. Perhaps the guessing world has a probability of 60%, the first telepathy world (in which telepathy always works) a probability of 10% and so on? This is obviously not easy; we haven't even got a complete list of the possible worlds.

If we know how the world works, it is reasonably easy to work out probabilities of events. The problem here is we want to do the opposite: use the events we have observed (Annette getting the card right) to work out how probable each possible world is. There is a way of approaching this problem, which is the subject of the next section.

▶ 6.4 Bayes' principle: the pruned ball method

The 'Bayesian' approach to statistics is based on a result of mathematical probability theory known as Bayes' theorem, named after its inventor the

Reverend Thomas Bayes, and published in 1763. Bayes' tomb, in Bunhill Fields in London, has become a shrine for Bayesian statisticians.[89]

As the approach in this book is non-mathematical, I will describe this theorem in terms of bucket and ball models. I'll call the resulting idea 'Bayes' principle' or, more graphically, the 'pruned ball' method. It is the exact equivalent of Bayes' theorem: the answers we get from this method are identical to those obtained with the mathematical version.[90] Let's see how it works and why the balls get to be pruned.

The concepts involved here are a little bit odd, so I will start by changing the situation slightly in order to reduce this oddness. Let's imagine that telepathy is a gift enjoyed by, say, 10% of the population. In the world I would like you to imagine, 10% of the population is telepathic and the other 90% are not. In effect, I am asking you to imagine different people instead of different possible worlds. Furthermore, let's imagine that telepathy is always accurate. If Annette is telepathic, she will always get the card right.

Now let's use the lots of times tactic (Section 5.2). Imagine, say, 1000 people doing this experiment. One hundred of them will be telepathic and the remaining 900 won't be telepathic. Remember that we are interested in what happens 'on average' to work out probabilities, so we can assume it'll be exactly 100 telepathic people. So get 1000 balls, write 'telepathic' on 100 of them and 'non-telepathic' on the other 900. Annette is one of these, but we don't know which one. The point of the model is to find out if she is more likely to be one of the telepathic ones or one of the others.

The next step is to imagine what will happen when these 1000 people do the telepathy experiment. How many of the telepathic people will guess the card correctly?

All 100 of them will guess right, as we are assuming that telepathy is always completely accurate. Put a tick on these 100 balls. How many of the other 900 will guess the card correctly?

These are all guessing and have a one in 52 chance, so we'd expect 900/52 or about 17 of them to guess correctly. Put a tick on these 17 balls. The model is summarised in Table 6.1.

Now remember that Annette *has* guessed the card correctly. This means she must be represented by one of the balls with a tick on it. How many balls have a tick on them?

There are 117 balls with a tick: 100 representing telepathic people and 17 representing lucky guessers. These are the only possible balls which are consistent with the evidence. Annette must be one of these. We can *prune* (discard) the rest, leaving just the first column in Table 6.1. So what is our estimate of Annette being telepathic?

The probability of her being telepathic is 100/117 or about 85%. Of the 117 who guessed correctly, almost six times as many achieved this by telepathy as by guesswork.

Table 6.1 Telepathy experiment: number of balls in different categories

	✓ (Card right)	Card wrong	Total
Telepathic	100	0	100
Non-telepathic	17	883	900
Total	117	883	1000

But, of course, the idea of telepathy being a gift enjoyed by 10% of the population doesn't really ring true. What we really want to know is whether we are living in a world in which Annette is telepathic or one in which she is not. Let's try and see how we can make sense of the bucket and ball model in terms of possible worlds. Instead of 1000 people, imagine the balls representing 1000 possible worlds. One hundred of these are worlds in which Annette is telepathic, the rest are non-telepathic worlds in which Annette can only guess. As they are all represented by a ball in the bucket, they must be equally likely. So the probability of a telepathic world is 100 out of 1000 or 10%. This is our initial assumption, equivalent to the assumption that 10% of the population enjoyed the gift of telepathy. This 10% is known as a 'prior probability'. It is our assessment of the probability of Annette being telepathic *before* we do the experiment. (We'll return to this prior probability in more detail – why it's necessary and what happens if we change it – in Section 6.4.1.)

The argument is now similar to before. Annette will guess correctly in all 100 telepathic worlds and 17 of the others. Put a tick on these and prune (remove) the balls without a tick. As before, we are left with 117 balls with a tick, of which 100 represent worlds in which Annette is telepathic, so the probability of such a world being the actual world, and of Annette being telepathic, is 85%. This is different from the prior probability of 10%. What has changed?

The point is that the prior probability was assessed *before* we had the result of the experiment. Now we know the result of the experiment, we can prune the balls which are not consistent with this evidence and work out the new probability. This (85%) is called a 'posterior probability' because it is derived *after* getting the evidence.

Bayes' principle shows how the evidence changes our assessment of the probability from 15% to 85%. We start by envisaging a collection of equally likely possibilities. Evidence gathered then rules some of these out, and we can work out probabilities based on the ones that are left.

Of course, in practice, we'd want to take this experiment further and try again to see if Annette can get a second card right. Imagine that Annette does succeed the second time too: another card is drawn at random from the pack of 52 cards, Peter concentrates on it and it is correctly identified by Annette. In the telepathy worlds, the probability of this is still 100%, so if we start off with the same bucket of 1000 balls as before, she will get the card right in all the 100 telepathic worlds. So put a tick and 'telepathy' on 100 balls. What about the 900 non-telepathic worlds in which she can only guess? In how many of these will she get both right?

She'll get the first one right in 900/52 or about 17 worlds as before. She'll get the second right too in about one in 52 of these, or about a third of a world. So put a tick and 'non-telepathic' on a third of a ball. (If you don't like the idea of a third of a world, you could start off with more balls in the bucket, say, 10 000. You should end up with just the same answer.) Now prune the balls in the bucket which are not consistent with the fact that Annette has got both cards right. How many balls are left, and what's the probability of telepathy being involved this time?

There are 100 telepathy balls, and a third of a ball representing her succeeding by guesswork. This means that telepathy is now 300 times as likely as guessing, and the probability of telepathy is 100/100.33 = 99.7%. The evidence is now much stronger, which is reflected in the new posterior probability.

6.4.1 Strengths and difficulties of Bayesian statistics

This is the basis of a Bayesian approach to the problem. Bayesian statistics is something that some statisticians feel passionate about. To them it is obviously the only right approach, to others it is equally obviously misguided and to many others it is too complicated to bother with in practice. The main thing to be said in favour of the Bayesian approach to statistical inference is that you get what you probably want: probabilities of the various competing hypotheses. You end up with a clear statement that there's a 99.7% chance that Annette is telepathic.

The main competing approach is null hypothesis testing (introduced in Section 6.6), where you do *not* end up with this probability. In Section 1.2, we looked at a newspaper report on a cancer cluster at Aldermaston which stated that the 'probability of chance occurrence' was 1 in 10 000 000. However, this does *not* mean the probability that the cancer is a chance occurrence is 1 in 10 000 000, from which we could deduce that there are 999 999 chances in 10 000 000 that there is something sinister causing it (see Section 1.2). On the other hand, the Bayesian answer *would* (if we had it) tell us the probability that there is a sinister cause to the cluster.

There are, however, problems with the Bayesian approach. The first is whether the probabilities attached to possible worlds are *meaningful*. Does it make sense to envisage 1000 possible worlds – initially equally likely – and argue that the probability of the actual world being a telepathic one is 100/117 because 100 of the 117 worlds which are consistent with the evidence are telepathic worlds?

Some would say yes. Others would say no; Annette is either telepathic or she isn't and there is no sense in attaching a probability to it. The doubters would claim that probability makes sense when applied to events which may or may not happen, but not to possible worlds or hypotheses.

The next problem is the *origin* of the prior probability. Where did the 10% initial probability come from? This is an important part of the argument: if you took, say, 1% or 50% instead, the answer would be different (see Exercise 6.7.1). In this case the likely source of the prior probability would be subjective opinion (Section 2.3): my feeling was that telepathy is possible but not that likely, say, 10%. But if the prior probabilities are subjective, this means the answer is, to some extent, subjective too.

A little thought should convince you that this is inevitable. Suppose you believe telepathy is impossible. Your prior probability is 0%. Then, whatever happens in the experiment, you will interpret it in terms of guesswork. You will put *no* balls representing telepathic worlds in the bucket and the answer will be that Annette is not telepathic. Your prior beliefs have influenced the conclusion in this case, so it's surely reasonable to expect they will in other cases too. So, if you want a posterior probability out at the end, you must put a prior probability in at the beginning. However, the more evidence there is, the less important this prior probability will be to the final result: compare the conclusion from Annette getting one card right (85% posterior probability) with the conclusion from getting two right (99.7%) in Section 6.4.

The final difficulty is that of *complexity*. In this example we have just two possible worlds: in practice we are likely to want to put far more possible worlds into the bucket. For example, we might want to consider a telepathy world where telepathy works on 90% of occasions, and another where it works on 80% and so on. In the Aldermaston example, the underlying interest is in the effect of the nuclear installation on cancer rates: to model this sensibly we would want to consider different strengths for this effect. This complexity hurts at three points. First, we need to work out a prior probability for *each* of the possible worlds. Then we've got to go through the mental gymnastics involved in working out how likely the experimental evidence is from the perspective of each possible world. And finally, the answer is not a simple probability like 85%, but a whole distribution of probabilities (Section 5.4). The exercise in Section 6.7.1 should give you some idea of all this.

So Bayesian statistics as an approach to statistical inference – inferring general truths from samples of data – has its problems. You will find comparatively few research reports use Bayesian methods. But the

Bayesian perspective is a helpful ideal to have at the back of your mind.

On the other hand, Bayes' principle, or the pruned ball method, has many uses where it is less controversial, for example in medical diagnosis (Exercise 6.7.2), or in establishing guilt in criminal investigations (Exercise 6.7.3). It is an important aspect of probability theory.

▶ 6.5 Confidence intervals

The mean number of units drunk on Saturday night by the students in Table 3.1 is 7.4. If we want to generalise this to the broader context of students in general, some error is inevitable because the sample is only a small one. A convenient way of expressing the likely size of this error is by means of a 'confidence interval'. This is the subject of Chapter 7, so I will just give a very quick introduction here.

Using the method to be explained in Chapter 7, the 95% confidence interval for the mean number of units drunk on Saturday night *by the wider group of students* is 4 to 11 units. We don't know what the true mean for all the students is, but the data we have allows us to say, with about 95% confidence, that it will be somewhere between 4 and 11 units. But we can't say exactly where.

This might seem a very different type of problem to the problem of assessing how likely a hypothesis, or a possible world, is. But the differences are superficial. In the present example, we are choosing between the hypothesis that the mean is about 7, about 6 or about 8 and so on. The confidence interval is just a convenient way of attaching a level of 'confidence' (roughly the same as a probability) to a group of these possible worlds. Could we apply the confidence interval idea to the telepathy example**?**

Yes, but it would get complicated. Exercise 6.7.1(b) distinguishes three telepathy worlds: one where telepathy works 100% of the time, one where it works 50% of the time and one where it doesn't work. Going further, you could distinguish between a 100% telepathy world, a 90% world, an 80% world and so on. Then Bayes' principle would allow you to work out a posterior probability for each. This could then be the basis for your confidence intervals.[91]

Confidence intervals have lots of advantages. They're relatively easy to interpret, and tell you something useful. We'll return to them in Chapter 7, and again in Chapters 8 and 9.

▶ 6.6 Null hypothesis testing

This is the approach which has cornered the market in many fields of application. With the telepathy example, I think it is a reasonable approach, but in many situations there are real difficulties in the use and interpretation of these tests. I'll introduce the idea briefly here, but I'll return to it in much more detail, and look at some of the problems, in Chapter 8.

The starting point in any null hypothesis test is the 'null hypothesis'. This is usually an assumption along lines like there is *nothing* going on, or *no* difference or *no* relationship between two variables. In this case the null hypothesis is that there is no telepathy involved, so Annette is guessing. Then we work out the probability of getting results like the ones we've got, or more extreme, *on the assumption that this null hypothesis is true*. What is this probability in the experiment in which Annette gets one card right?

The probability is one in 52, or 1/52 or 1.9%. Notice that the null hypothesis needs to be clear-cut so that we can work out these probabilities. This probability is often called a *p* value.

Now, suppose she gets two cards right. Again, assuming the null hypothesis is right – she's guessing – what's the probability of her doing this well?

This comes to 1/52 × 1/52 or 0.04% (if you want, you can imagine her guessing lots of times as in Section 6.4). This suggests that Annette is very unlikely to get two cards right by guessing, which is surely pretty convincing evidence for her being telepathic. Would you accept this evidence that Annette is telepathic?

If you said no, it is probably because you think telepathy is more or less impossible, so the chance explanation, although a long shot, must be the correct explanation because it is the only possibility. If you said yes, then you must have accepted that telepathy is possible. But there is no right answer here. It depends on how strong you would need the evidence to be in order to accept the telepathy hypothesis.

It would be nice to know the probability that the guessing world is the actual world. Can we assume that this is also 0.04%?

No, we can't! This is a quite different probability. It is different for just the same reason that the probability that a rich man is a successful bank robber is different from the probability that a successful bank robber is a rich man (the first probability is likely to be low, the second almost 100% – see Section 2.2). The only way of working out the probability that Annette is guessing is to use Bayes' principle (Section 6.4). On the other hand, the probability of 0.04% does give us some idea of how *plausible* the guessing hypothesis is. It does suggest that if she is guessing, she's very lucky indeed! Obviously the lower this probability, the less *plausible* the guessing world is. But it is *not* the probability of the guessing world.

The advantage of null hypothesis testing as a way of analysing the telepathy experiment is that it's relatively simple. We don't need to worry about prior probabilities, or about imagining how the telepathy worlds might work. I'll return to this in more detail in Chapter 8.

▶ 6.7 Exercises

6.7.1 Telepathy

It is worth playing with the example in Sections 6.2–6.4 to get a feel for how Bayes' principle and p values work.

(a) What difference does it make to the posterior probabilities if the prior probability of Annette being telepathic were 0%, 1%, 50% or 100%? Work out the posterior probabilities in each case. Are they what you would have expected?

(b) Instead of the two possible worlds, now imagine three. In the first, telepathy is impossible, this is the guessing world. In the second world, Annette can do telepathy, but not reliably; she guesses the right card on 50% of attempts, but gets the other 50% wrong. The third world is a world in which telepathy always works. In the first world the probability of telepathy working is 0%, in the second it is 50%, and in the third it is 100%. Suppose that the prior probability for the 0% world is 90%, for the 50% world it is 5%, and for the 100% world it is also 5%. What are the posterior probabilities after she's done the experiment once and guessed correctly?

(c) Imagine that Annette had been through the process of guessing 20 cards, and had got three correct. This is not terribly good, but is certainly better than you would expect from chance. What would you expect from chance? Using the null hypothesis that she is guessing, what is the p value for this result? Use `resample.xls` or `resample.exe` (see Chapter 5) to work out the probability of getting three or more right. Would you be convinced by this evidence?

6.7.2 An unreliable test for a disease

One person in a thousand is known to suffer from a serious disease. A test is available to detect whether patients have the disease before symptoms become apparent, but unfortunately this test occasionally gives the wrong answer. The data available shows that 5% of healthy patients produce a positive test result, and 1% of patients with the disease produce a negative result. Both of these are, of course, errors. A patient comes for the test. The result is positive. The patient, of course, goes away very worried. As the test is positive, either the patient has the disease or the test is wrong. Which is the more likely, and how much more likely?

6.7.3 Forensic evidence in a court of law

Dan is being tried for a murder on a remote island. The *only* evidence against him is the forensic evidence – blood samples taken from the scene of the crime match Dan's. The chance of such a match happening if Dan were in fact innocent, and the match were just a coincidence, is calculated (by the prosecution's expert witness) as 1 in 10 000 (0.0001). The defence's expert witness, however, points out that the crime could have been committed by any one of the 40 000 people on the island. There is no evidence – except the blood sample – to link Dan, or any other individual, with the crime. If you were on the jury, would you find him guilty? What do you think is the probability of his guilt? (If you think the answer is 0.9999, you are very, very wrong: this is known as the 'prosecutor's fallacy', which was one of the problems in the trial of Sally Clark – see Section 1.2.)

6.7.4 Rhine's ESP experiments

What is the p value for the series of ESP trials by Hubert Pearce (see the end of Section 6.2)? Does this prove the existence of ESP? (To simulate the null hypothesis, use `resample.exe` – see Chapter 5. You will need to press c after the opening screen to set the program to allow you enter a resample size of 8075.)

▶ 6.8 Summary of main points

Statistical inference – using a sample of data to infer more general truths – is the statistical response to the problem of induction. Three approaches are introduced:

- The Bayesian approach leads to the posterior probabilities of the competing hypotheses, which is generally what you want. However, in practice, the approach is often too complicated as an approach to statistical inference.
- Null hypothesis tests involve estimating the probability of obtaining results 'like' those obtained *if* the null hypothesis is true. These probabilities, often known as 'p values', give us a measure of the plausibility of the null hypothesis we are testing. Low p values indicate that the null hypothesis is not very plausible, so the alternatives are more likely. We return to this in Chapter 8.
- The third possibility is to set up confidence intervals. This is the subject of Chapter 7.

7 How Big is the Error?
Confidence Intervals

In Chapter 6, we looked at methods of statistical inference: approaches to drawing inferences from samples of data about more general truths. One of these approaches is to use the data to produce an interval (or range), within which we can be confident the truth lies. These are called 'confidence intervals', and are the subject of this chapter. They can also be used to estimate how large a sample you need for a given purpose.

▶ 7.1 Introduction

Political opinion surveys in the UK are typically based on a sample of 1000 electors, which is a tiny fraction of the British electorate. This is the magic of statistics: at first sight it ought to be impossible to predict how 40 000 000 people will vote by asking a mere 1000 of them, and yet the predictions, while not perfect, are generally not far off. The question tackled in this chapter is how accurate such samples are likely to be.

The obvious starting point is to ask why opinion polls might not give accurate results. Why do you think that asking a sample of 1000 electors about their voting intentions might not provide the whole truth about what will happen in an election?

There are two categories of reason, each corresponding to a difference between the opinion poll and the election. The first is simply that the opinion poll is not the election. People are asked how they *would* vote, some time before the actual election. Their expressed voting intention may not correspond with the way they actually vote. Even if the pollsters asked the whole electorate, this problem would still remain, and we could not be sure that the results were accurate. These are 'measurement errors': the errors due to the fact that the method of 'measuring' voting intentions – asking hypothetical questions before the actual election – may not be accurate.

The second problem is that we have only asked 1000 of the 40 000 000 electors. Conclusions based on such a sample may not be reliable because the sample may not be typical in some way. If the survey were to be repeated with a new sample, drawn in the same way, the conclusions may be different. The errors due to the fact that conclusions are drawn from a limited sample are called 'sampling errors'.

Confidence intervals are designed to indicate the extent of sampling error only. We assume there is no measurement error. For example, the conclusion that 45% of voters will vote for the Labour Party may be qualified by the statement that the sampling error is 3% with 95% 'confidence',[92] implying that there is a 95% chance that the true proportion of Labour voters is somewhere between 42% (45% *minus* 3%) and 48% (45% *plus* 3%) – this is the 'confidence interval'. Instead of coming up with a single, precise, point estimate, the idea is to derive a less precise but more realistic estimate, an interval within which we can be reasonably (95% or whatever) sure that the truth will lie. As we'll see, not only can we draw reliable conclusions from a tiny sample, it is also possible to use this sample to estimate the accuracy of the conclusions, without access to any further information.

The other side of the coin is assessing how small a sample we can get away with. If a sample of 20 will do, why bother with a larger one? How this is all achieved is the subject of this chapter.

The starting point is the assumption that samples are taken at random, or can reasonably be considered random (see Section 2.5). The approach I am taking here is known as 'bootstrapping'.[93] The basic idea is to use a computer simulation of randomness to see the effects of the randomness on the sampling process. It does this by taking repeated 'resamples' from a sample of data. The software we will use is the same as the software introduced in Section 5.4 – `resample.xls` and `resample.exe`. In Section 5.4 we referred to the underlying model as the two bucket model; in this chapter, as the first bucket is always a sample, I'll use the term resampling. But it's essentially the same idea.

▶ 7.2 Bootstrap confidence intervals

I'll start with another example to emphasise the point that confidence intervals can be used in many different contexts. It has the additional advantage that it is a typical questionnaire survey, a very common potential application for this sort of analysis. The example uses some data[94] from a questionnaire sent to 650 of the 4500 members on the mailing list of a society of accountants: 105 of them (16%) responded. One of the questions required respondents to indicate their agreement on a six-point scale, ranging from 'not at all' to 'strongly', with the statement: 'I'd welcome the opportunity to socialise more with other accountants.' The responses were coded using 0 to represent 'not at all' and 5 to represent 'strongly'.[95] Seven of the 105 respondents to the questionnaire failed to answer this question, leaving 98 responses.

Table 7.1 Data from question about socialising with accountants

Response	Frequency (no. of people responding)
0	42
1	21
2	16
3	6
4	9
5	4
All responses	98

These responses ranged from 0 to 5, with a mean (average) of 1.3. Remember that we are assuming there are no measurement errors: when someone says they would 'strongly' welcome the opportunity to socialise with accountants, they really do mean it (Table 7.1).

These responses, however, are from only 98 members, about 1 in 46 on the membership list. Obviously the responses from another group of 98 members would almost certainly be different. The idea of a confidence interval is to express this uncertainty as a statement of confidence of the true mean (or median or any other measure) lying in a specified range. The conventional confidence level is 95%[96] and the confidence interval derived by bootstrapping is 1.0 to 1.6 (the method used is explained below). This means that we can be 95% confident that the mean *of the whole population of members* on this question would lie within this range. The converse, of course, is that, on average 5% of 95% confidence intervals will be wrong in the sense that the truth will lie outside the interval. Notice that the confidence interval refers to the whole population (all 4500 members), not just the sample. This is the reason for the uncertainty: we have only looked at a sample, so we cannot be sure about the average of the whole population.

If we had the answer to the question from all 4500 members, we could assess the size of the error due to using samples of 98 simply by taking a few hundred such samples from this population. In fact, of course, the whole problem is that we only have one sample of 98, so the next best thing is to use this sample to guess what the population would look like. The sample of 98 comprises about 1 in 46 of the whole population of 4500 members, so the obvious way to do this would be to make 46 copies of the sample. For example, four respondents answered 5 to the question, so the 'guessed population' would contain 46 times as many members answering 5, that is, there would be 184 5s in the guessed population (Table 7.2).

Table 7.2 Guessed population for question about socialising with accountants

Response	Frequency
0	1932
1	966
2	736
3	276
4	414
5	184
All responses	4508

We can now draw lots of random samples of 98 scores from this guessed population and see how much they vary. These samples are called 'resamples' because they are drawn from the original sample (or, more precisely, from 46 copies of the original sample). In terms of buckets and balls, the procedure is to put 4508 balls labelled 0, 1, 2, 3, 4 or 5 in Bucket 1. Now mix them up thoroughly, put on a blindfold, draw out 98 to represent the first resample, and work out the mean score of these 98. Now put this mean on another ball and put this in Bucket 2. Repeat this a few thousand times, and you'll be in a good position to see how accurate samples of 98 are.

This is, of course, exactly the same two bucket model as we met in Sections 5.4, 5.5 and 5.6. The process is shown in Figures 7.1 and 7.2, which are two screens from the output from the program *resample.exe*.[97]

Figure 7.1 shows the first resample, and is designed to show you what is going on. The first randomly chosen response from the guessed population is 3, the second is also 3, the third is 4 and so on. These are selected at random, by the computer, from the 4508 'people' in the guessed population. The computer selects a complete resample of 98 responses in this way, works out the mean (the average) which comes to 1.5, and plots it on a simple tally chart. You can run off as many resamples as you want to ensure you understand what the program is doing. Each resample mean will be represented by a new X on the tally chart.

Figure 7.2 shows a similar tally chart with 10 000 similar resamples. This shows you the contents of Bucket 2. The 2.5 and 97.5 percentiles of this distribution, as worked out by the program, are 1.02 and 1.59, which we'll round off to 1.0 and 1.6. This means that 2.5% of the resample means are below 1.0, and a further 2.5% are above 1.6. The majority, 95%, are between these two limits. *The conclusion is that there is 95% chance that the mean of a*

Figure 7.1 First resample (question on socialising)

Mean of a resample of 98 (no replacement, N = 4508)
1st resample: 3 3 4 1 4 1 4 1 0 4 1 0 1 1 3 5 2 4 1 1 1 1 0 1 1 2 0 0 4 2 3
1 0 0 1 1 2 1 1 0 0 4 4 1 2 4 1 1 0 1 4 0 2 3 3 1 1 1 5 0 5 1 1 0 2 0 1 0
2 0 2 1 1 2 0 1 5 1 5 0 0 0 0 1 1 1 0 2 1 4 0 0 0 0 0 1 1 1
Mean of 1st resample is 1.5
1.7
1.6
1.5   X
1.4

Figure 7.2 Resample distribution (question on socialising)

Mean of a resample of 98 (no replacement, N = 4508) 10 000 resamples
2.0
1.9   -
1.8   -
1.7   X-
1.6   XXXXXX-   *97.5 p'tile*
1.5   XXXXXXXXXXXXXXXXXX-
1.4   XXXXXXXXXXXXXXXXXXXXXXXXXXXXXXXXXXXXX-
1.3   XXXXXXXXXXXXXXXXXXXXXXXXXXXXXXXXXXXXXXXXXX-
1.2   XXXXXXXXXXXXXXXXXXXXXXXXXXXXXXXXXXXXXXX-
1.1   XXXXXXXXXXXXXXXXXXXXXX-
1.0   XXXXXX-   *2.5 p'tile*
0.9   -
0.8   -
0.7   -
0.6

X represents 60 resamples; - represents fewer than this.

sample of 98 drawn from this guessed population will lie between 1.0 and 1.6. Few were outside this range, and none, for example, were as high as 2.

The corresponding figures from a run of another 10 000 random resamples were identical. If you don't believe this, try it yourself. Although individual resamples are to some extent unpredictable, if we take enough of them we can predict the pattern surprisingly accurately. If in doubt about the number of resamples to simulate, the best thing to do is to try more and see if the answers change.

However, the difficulty with this, of course, is that it is derived from a guessed population, not the real population. The trick now is to think in terms of the errors we would make in using individual resamples to find out about the guessed population. Then we can use this to guess about the errors we are making in using real samples.

The mean (average) of this guessed population (Table 7.2) is obviously the same as the mean of the original sample (Table 7.1): 1.3. This is the centre of the distribution in Figure 7.2. The first resample shown in Figure 7.1 has a mean of 1.5. If we were to use this to estimate the mean of the whole guessed population, what would the error be?

The error would be 0.2: the estimate would be 0.2 too high. Now think about each of the resamples with a mean of 1.0 in Figure 7.2. What would be the error in using these to estimate the mean of the whole guessed population?

The error would be −0.3, that is, the estimate is 0.3 less than the true mean of the guessed population, 1.3. This means that we can look at the mean on each of the balls in Bucket 2, and stamp the error, +0.2, −0.3 or whatever, on it as well. These errors are shown in Figure 7.3, which is identical to Figure 7.2 except that the numbers have been rescaled to represent the errors rather than the means themselves.

Figure 7.3 shows that 95% of the errors are in the range −0.3 to +0.3: we can be 95% sure that the error in the mean of a resample of 98 responses will be no more than 0.3: we will refer to this maximum likely error as the 'error limit'. Errors of 0.5 or 0.6 were very rare, errors of 0.7 and above did not happen in any of the 10 000 resamples. This is all based on 10 000 resam-

---

Figure 7.3 Error distribution (question on socialising)

```
Error (based on Figure 7.2)
+0.7 |
+0.6 |-
+0.5 |-
+0.4 |X-
+0.3 |XXXXXX-                                               97.5 p'tile
+0.2 |XXXXXXXXXXXXXXXXXX-
+0.1 |XXXXXXXXXXXXXXXXXXXXXXXXXXXXXXXXXXXXXXX-
 0.0 |XXXXXXXXXXXXXXXXXXXXXXXXXXXXXXXXXXXXXXXXXXX-
-0.1 |XXXXXXXXXXXXXXXXXXXXXXXXXXXXXXXXXXXXXXX-
-0.2 |XXXXXXXXXXXXXXXXXXXX-
-0.3 |XXXXXX-                                                2.5 p'tile
-0.4 |-
-0.5 |-
-0.6 |-
-0.7 |
```

X represents 60 resamples; - represents fewer than this.

ples from the guessed population, which are, in effect, some experiments on an imaginary population. We don't know what the real population is like, but by experimenting on an imaginary one, it is possible to infer the size of error we may make when using a single, real sample. In this case the 95% error limit is 0.3 units. The assumption is that the guessed population is sufficiently like the real population for this estimate to be realistic. Common sense suggests, and experience shows, that with reasonably large samples, this assumption is justified.

The actual sample mean (which is the basis of all the resamples) is, of course, 1.3, and if the error range is +/–0.3, this means the confidence interval extends from 1.0 to 1.6. We can be reasonably (95%) certain that the truth about the average response to this question from all 4500 members would lie within this range. We can be confident of this, despite the fact that most members have not answered the question. This range, 1.0 to 1.6, is just the same as the percentiles in the resample distribution (Figure 7.2), so *we can use the resample distribution directly as a confidence distribution and use it to read off confidence intervals*. (There are a few assumptions here which we'll consider later.)

In rough terms, the argument is that the resample tally chart (Figure 7.2) gives a picture of the likely size of sampling error. Providing this is roughly symmetrical (so that we don't need to distinguish between positive and negative errors), this can also be interpreted as a confidence distribution for the population value, since the best guess is the centre of the distribution, and errors are reflected by discrepancies from this central value. A standard 95% confidence interval goes from the 2.5th to the 97.5th percentile of this resample distribution. We can also use the distribution to read off probabilities directly.

For example, what would your estimate be for the probability of the mean of the whole population being 1 or less?

The 2.5 percentile mark in Figure 7.2 tells us that this is about 2.5%. What about an 80% confidence interval. What percentiles do you need for this?

The 10th and 90th percentiles. This, of course, all depends on the assumption that the random resampling process mirrors the real sampling process reasonably closely. In fact, the actual sample comprised those members who bothered to respond to the questionnaire. Is such a selection close enough to a random selection?

Your guess is as good as mine, but the confidence interval is largely meaningless if this assumption does not hold.

In the next section we'll look at large populations, which may be too large to make a guessed population. This leads to a useful shortcut, 'resampling with replacement'.

▶ 7.3 Large populations: does size matter?

The argument above takes account of the size of population (that is, the number of members of the society) in a very direct manner: by constructing a guessed population of the appropriate size. Let's see what difference the size of the population makes. Imagine, first, a smaller society: say 196 accountants. We can produce a guessed population by taking just two copies of the sample of 98. Using the method described above, this leads to a confidence interval of 1.1 to 1.5. This is a bit narrower than the previous one. Why do you think the interval is a bit narrower?

Imagine the process of selecting one of the resamples of 98. We start with two copies of the sample (Table 7.1), so there will be eight balls labelled with a 5 in Bucket 1 at the start. Now suppose that, say, six of these have been drawn out by the time we've drawn out 50 of the 98 balls in the resample. There are now only two 5s left, so the chances of drawing another 5 is now much reduced. If, on the other hand, no 5s had been drawn in the first 50 balls, the chances of drawing a 5 will be slightly increased (because there are fewer balls left but the same number of 5s). Either way, the composition of the bucket changes as you draw the resample in such a way that unusually high or unusually low averages are less likely than they would be with a larger guessed population. This means that the confidence interval is likely to be slightly (but, as we saw, only slightly) narrower than it would be with a larger guessed population in Bucket 1. The extreme case would be to put just one copy of the sample in Bucket 1. Then every resample will be the same, because there are only 98 balls there.

At the other extreme, say we have a society of 98 million accountants. This population can be guessed by taking a million copies of the sample. In this case, however, the removal effect – the way that the contents of the bucket and the probabilities change as balls are removed from the bucket – is negligible because removing 98 balls from a bucket containing 98 million doesn't make any practical difference to the pattern of those remaining. For *every* ball in the resample, the probability of selecting a 5 is effectively 4/98, because the proportion of 5s in the bucket does not change appreciably.

7.3.1 Bootstrapping by resampling with replacement

This suggests a rather easier approach called 'resampling with replacement'. This means that we resample from the sample itself (without making extra copies), but each member of the resample is *replaced* in the sample before drawing the next member of the resample. This means every member of the resample is drawn from the same sample, which is used to represent the guessed population. *Resampling with replacement is a useful device for mimicking a large or infinite population.*

In this case, we want to take a resample of 98 from the original sample of 98. Put 98 balls in Bucket 1 to represent the responses in the sample (Table 7.1). Now select one ball at random and write down the response it represents. Put the ball back and mix Bucket 1 thoroughly. Repeat 98 times for a resample of 98. Work out the mean of these 98 responses, and put this on a ball in Bucket 2. Repeat a few thousand times.

There are likely to be more of some values in the resample than there are in the original sample, and fewer of others. (Otherwise, each resample would be identical to the original sample, which would be pretty pointless.) One resample with replacement, for example, was: 0 0 0 0 2 5 0 2 0 0 1 2 1 2 2 2 1 0 4 2 3 5 1 2 3 2 2 1 5 1 0 0 5 2 4 4 3 0 0 1 0 0 2 4 0 0 1 4 0 1 2 0 1 4 0 0 0 0 0 0 1 0 0 2 1 0 1 1 0 4 1 5 4 4 3 0 0 1 4 0 0 4 1 0 2 5 3 0 0 0 1 0 1 1 0 0 3. This contains six 5s, whereas another resample contained only three. Doing this leads to almost the same confidence interval as for the population of 4508: 1.01 to 1.59.

These results illustrate one of the important but counterintuitive results of statistics: namely that the size of the population has remarkably little impact on the magnitude of sampling error. The width of the confidence intervals shows that a random sample of 98 provides very nearly as accurate a guide to a population of 98 million, as it does to a population of 4500. Even with a population of 196, the confidence interval was only slightly narrower (1.1 to 1.5, instead of 1.0 to 1.6) than it was for the larger populations. So you need a similar size sample to find out about students in a typical college, as you do to find out about the entire population of Germany, provided the samples are random ones and the underlying patterns in both populations are similar. If you doubt this, just imagine the populations represented by buckets, and run through the process of taking samples from each. The size of the population just does not matter much. On the other hand, as you will see in the next section, the size of the *sample* is crucial.

In the reminder of this chapter, I will stick to sampling with replacement, because it gives almost identical results and is simpler to do.

▶ 7.4 What is the smallest sample we can get away with?

The error limit from our sample of 98 at the 95% confidence level is a mere 0.3 on a scale from 0 to 5. Bearing in mind the vagueness of the question, this seems unnecessarily accurate. Could we have made do with a smaller sample, which would probably give a less accurate result? To answer this, we need to backtrack to the stage at which the survey is set up. When doing a questionnaire survey like this, it is always a good idea to do a pilot study before the main survey, to check that the questions are understood in the intended way and that there are no unforeseen problems (see Section 10.2.2). Let's imagine that the first 10 questionnaires correspond to such a pilot study. This pilot sample also had responses ranging from 0 to 5, but the mean was more, 2.3 instead of 1.3 for the whole sample of 98. We can now explore the effect of different sample sizes using this pilot data: 5 4 0 4 4 1 2 1 2 0. This works just the same as before, except that our sample now comprises just 10 numbers.

Is it possible to find out about samples of 20 from this sample of 10?

Yes. If we resample *with replacement*, each ball is put back in the bucket after being chosen so there are always 10 balls in the bucket. (Alternatively, we would make 450 copies of the sample to get a guessed population but this is more trouble and will produce much the same answer.) We can choose a resample as large as we like, and so find out about samples of any size. In this way we can experiment with big samples, even though the pilot sample itself is only 10 strong. Table 7.3 shows the results with sample sizes of 20, 98 and 500. Each line in the table is produced by `resample.exe`, but you could also do it with `resample.xls`.

If you've got time, and a computer handy, I'd suggest that you try this yourself. It shouldn't take more than a few minutes, and running the simulation yourself is the best way of bringing it to life and checking that you really understand what's going on. If you haven't got a computer, have a go at Exercise 7.8.1 which uses a dice instead.

The important figures in Table 7.3 are the error limits (the difference between the centre and the extremes of the confidence interval). The error limit for a sample of 98 is estimated at 0.34, slightly more than the figure estimated from the sample itself (0.3 as described above), but close enough to be helpful. The error is smaller with the larger sample of 500. Is this what you would have expected?

The whole point in taking a large sample is to get a more accurate, or reliable, estimate. So the errors should be less. The simulation is confirming

Table 7.3 Estimated 95% confidence intervals and error limits based on pilot sample of 10

Sample size	Mean	Estimated confidence interval	Estimated error limit
20	2.30	1.55 to 3.05	0.75
98	2.30	1.96 to 2.64	0.34
500	2.30	2.15 to 2.45	0.15

what should be common sense, but it is also telling you *how much* less the error is with larger samples.

What is an acceptable error here? We might say that 0.75 would be satisfactory: getting within 0.75 of the true mean would be close enough. This can be achieved with a random sample of 20, far smaller than the actual sample used. A sample of 98 is much larger than necessary. By experimenting with different sample sizes, it is easy to see how large a sample we need to get results of an acceptable degree of accuracy.

▶ 7.5 Other statistics: proportions, quartiles, correlations and so on

As well as asking about the mean response to the question, we might also be interested in how varied the responses to the question were. The sample responses ranged from 0 to 5 (the full range of the scale), so this must be true of the population as well (since the sample is part of the population), but this does not tell us in much detail how varied the responses were. To assess this, we could look at the quartiles. The upper quartile of the sample, for example, is 2. We can use resampling in just the same way to see how influenced by sampling error this is likely to be. Instead of getting the computer to work out the mean of each resample, we get it to work out the upper quartile. The intervals I got (from 10000 resamples again) are: 95% confidence interval for upper quartile: 2 to 3.

Another question in the questionnaire asked if respondents had been to the annual dinner in the last three years.[98] Of the 105 respondents, 70 said no, 12 said yes and the remaining 23 did not respond. At first sight, questions to which the response is yes or no appear very different because the answer is not a number. However, if we use the coding scheme of 0 for no and 1 for yes, the mean (average) corresponds to the proportion answering yes. What does this come to in this case?

The mean is 12/82 or 0.15 or 15%. In other words, 15% of respondents had been to the annual dinner. We can now resample from this data set, using the mean in just the same way as in the original example. Figure 7.4 shows the results from `resample.xls`. The column headed 'proportion' contains some of the 200 resample results calculated. The percentiles are set to 2.5 and 97.5, which tells us that the 95% confidence interval for the proportion of the whole membership attending the dinner extends from 7% to 23%.

The 3% error in the percentage voting for a particular party in political opinion polls based on a sample of 1000 electors can be worked out in just the same way (Exercise 7.8.2). We can do the same with anything calculated from a random sample: means, medians, interquartile ranges, correlations

Figure 7.4 Top of Lots of resamples sheet of `resample.xls`

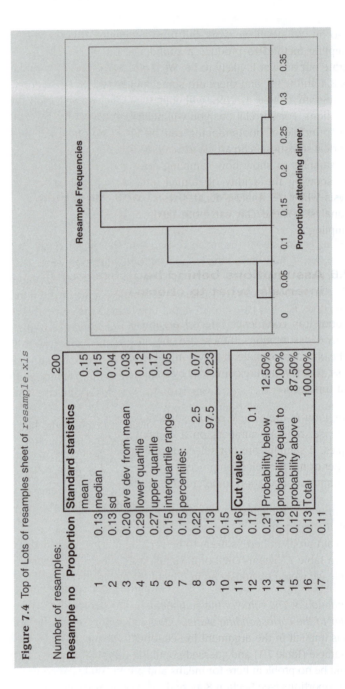

Number of resamples: 200

Resample no	Proportion	Standard statistics	
1	0.13	mean	0.15
2	0.13	median	0.15
3	0.20	sd	0.04
4	0.29	ave dev from mean	0.03
5	0.27	lower quartile	0.12
6	0.15	upper quartile	0.17
7	0.15	interquartile range	0.05
8	0.22	percentiles:	
9	0.13	2.5	0.07
10	0.15	97.5	0.23
11	0.16	**Cut value:**	
12	0.17	0.1	
13	0.21	Probability below	12.50%
14	0.18	probability equal to	0.00%
15	0.12	probability above	87.50%
16	0.13	Total	100.00%
17	0.11		

Resample Frequencies

Proportion attending dinner

and so on. Whatever we work out from a sample of data, we can use the resampling method to produce a confidence interval, which tells us how accurate our answer is likely to be. We'll meet some more examples in Sections 8.4 and 9.3.2, and there are some suggested exercises in Section 7.8. The program *resample.exe* will cope with all the above statistics except correlations. For correlations you will need to use *resample.xls*.[99]

The principle of bootstrapping can be taken beyond the estimation of numerical statistics: in an article in *Scientific American*, Diaconis and Efron[100] give examples to show how sampling error may impact the generation of maps showing the acidity of rainfall, and the preliminary stage of data analysis when the analyst decides which variables are worth including in the analysis. These can can both be investigated using the principle of resampling.

▶ 7.6 Assumptions behind bootstrap confidence intervals: what to check for

The bootstrap confidence interval argument in Section 7.2 depends on a number of assumptions. If these are only approximately true, the results may also be only approximate. If they don't hold at all, the answers may be meaningless. (But if you were convinced by Section 7.2, I wouldn't worry too much about this section.)

Assumption 1: The sample can reasonably be considered random
Otherwise, random numbers on a computer cannot be used to simulate samples. If samples are not selected randomly, the question then becomes whether or not the selection process is sufficiently close to being random for the computer simulation to be credible. Use your judgement.

Assumption 2: The guessed population is reasonably 'similar' to the real population
The main problem here is likely to be very small samples. The sample of 10 used in Table 7.3 seems OK, but if we just used the first two members of this sample we would obviously be in difficulties. Again, use your judgement!

Assumption 3: The value of the statistic derived from the data is reasonably similar to the corresponding statistic derived from the guessed population
This is implicit in the argument in Section 7.2. In the example, the mean of the sample (Table 7.1) and guessed population (Table 7.2) are both 1.3. There should be no problem here for means and proportions, differences of means and proportions (see Section 8.4), and most other statistics you are likely to use.

*Assumption 4: Assumption 3 holds, and the distribution of resample
statistics is reasonably symmetrical about the value of the statistic
derived from the data*

If the distribution were not symmetrical about the value derived from the
data, it would not be reasonable to ignore the distinction between positive
and negative errors as we did in Section 7.2. This is easily checked. Figures
7.2 looks symmetrical (about 1.3), and Figure 7.4 looks *roughly* symmetrical
(about 0.15), but see the discussion of the next assumption. Exercise 7.8.4
illustrates the problem when the distribution is not symmetrical.

*Assumption 5: It is reasonable to talk of the error distribution
independently of the true value of the population parameter*

The argument in Section 7.2 assumes that the error distribution (Figure 7.3)
applies whatever the true population value is. To see the difficulty here, let's
have a closer look at Figure 7.4. One of the resample proportions (not shown
in the figure) was 30.5%. Running through the argument in Section 7.2, this
resample has an error, compared with the true proportion in the guessed
population (15%), of +15.5%: it is 15.5% too high. This suggests that the
actual sample value, 15%, may suffer from a similar error, in which case the
true population proportion would be *minus* 0.5%. This is obviously impossible. Similarly, a resample proportion of 30% would imply a true proportion
of 0%, which is also impossible, because there would be no 1s in the population so the observed 15% could not have happened. Another of the resample proportions was 29% (no. 4 in Figure 7.4): by a similar argument this
corresponds to a true population proportion of 1%. But if the population
proportion were 1%, the resample distribution would be far more skewed
than Figure 7.4; most of the resamples would be 0%, 1% or 2% and then it
would gradually tail off.[101] The bootstrap idea is to assume the same error
distribution applies to all possible values; this may be roughly OK between
the 2.5 and 97.5 percentiles, but it is not at all accurate at the extremes.

Problems are likely to arise with Assumption 5 if the resample distribution
suggests that the boundary value – zero in the case of Figure 7.4 – is a possibility, but in these cases the resample distribution is likely to be skewed by
this boundary (30.5% is possible but –0.5% is not), so Assumption 4 will fail.
In practice, I would suggest checking the first four assumptions, which are
easy to check. If these are OK, in particular, if the resample distribution is
symmetrical, Assumption 5 should be OK too.

▶ **7.7 Similar concepts**

In most books on statistics you will find formulae for confidence intervals
for the mean and for proportions. These are based on mathematical proba-

bility theory, and usually give very similar, but not identical, results to the bootstrap method. You will also find that these formulae for the confidence interval for the mean are built into SPSS[102] and into Excel.[103] On the other hand, you will find very little on confidence intervals for other statistics, like the quartiles, correlation coefficients and standard deviations. There are *no* well-known formulae for confidence intervals for these. Sometimes, the bootstrap approach is the only option. We will return to confidence intervals in Chapters 8 and 9.

▶ **7.8 Exercises**

7.8.1 Bootstrapping with a dice

You will need two mugs, a dice and some scrap paper for this exercise. The idea is to give you a feel for how bootstrapping works without using a computer (although you could use a computer as well). Suppose you have the weights (in grams) of random samples of six apples from two batches (this is similar to Table 3.3):

Batch 1: 130, 124, 124, 120, 121, 124
Batch 2: 173, 192, 36, 166, 119, 31

The task is to use bootstrapping to derive a 50% confidence interval for the mean weight of apples from each batch.

Put the dice in one mug. This is Bucket 1. Let 1 on the dice represent the first weight in the sample (130 for Batch 1), 2 represent the second (124) and so on. Throw the dice six times: write down the weights the answers represent, work out the mean and write it on a piece of paper, screw it up, and put it in the other mug, Bucket 2. (Notice that the dice is like sampling with replacement because there are always six possible results.) Repeat 20 times. Now tip the 20 'balls' out of Bucket 2, and arrange them in order of size. You want the 25th and 75th percentiles. Repeat for Batch 2. Which batch has the wider confidence interval? Ninety-five per cent confidence intervals really need more balls in Bucket 2, but can you make a rough guess from your results? How do they compare with the 50% intervals?

7.8.2 Opinion polls

A poll asks 1000 people if they will vote Labour; 350 of them say yes, which suggests the percentage voting Labour will be 35% in the whole electorate. To see how accurate this is, use a code of 1 for a Labour voter and 0 for others. The sample then comprises 350 ones and 650 zeros. The mean of the sample is 0.35, which is simply the proportion voting Labour. Key this data in,[104] and run off some resamples. The normally quoted error for this sort of poll is 3%. Do your results agree with this? What would the confidence interval be for a sample of 100 people, of whom 35 say they will vote Labour?

7.8.3 Experimenting with the drink data

The data file *drink20.xls* is a random sample of 20 of the 92 cases in *drink.xls* (see Section 3.1). This gives you the chance to see how confidence intervals derived from a sample compare with the whole 'population', in this case the 92 in the bigger file. There is a lot you can do here, for example:

- Paste the Satunits and Age data into the two variables in the Sample worksheet of *resample.xls*. Now paste four copies underneath the original data so that you have a total guessed population of 100.
- Use the spreadsheet to work out 95% and 50% confidence intervals for the mean and median of the units drunk on Saturday. Use the columns in the worksheet for resampling *without* replacement. How do the 95% and 50% intervals compare?
- Compare the intervals you get with the actual values from *drink.xls*. Remember, a 50% confidence should have 50% probability of including the true value. Any comments?
- Do the same for the 80th percentile (Section 3.4.3), and the correlation (see Section 3.7.3) between the two variables.
- Repeat the exercise resampling *with* replacement using just the 20 rows in *drink20.xls*. Are the results similar?
- Work out the confidence intervals using all the data in *drink.xls*. These intervals should tell you about a wider population of students, of course. How do these intervals compare with those you worked out from *drink20.xls*?

7.8.4 Estimating world records from a small sample of club runners

This is a deliberately silly example to illustrate the problems when Assumptions 1–5 in Section 7.6 do not hold. The mile times of six runners from an athletics club are: 250, 300, 290, 360, 310 and 340 seconds. The problem is to use this data to estimate a confidence interval for the world record, that is, the fastest mile time – the minimum – for the whole population of the world.

The obvious approach is to use bootstrapping, taking the *minimum* of resamples of six (with replacement) as the resample statistic. When I did this (and you should get similar results from *resample.xls* or *resample.exe*[105]) the results were that the 95% interval for the minimum of resamples of six extended from 250 to 310 seconds. Using the method of

Section 7.2, this would be the confidence interval for the population minimum, that is, the world record. Does this make sense? How does this example fit the five assumptions? Can you think of any ways of improving the method?

▶ 7.9 Summary of main points

- Confidence intervals are a very useful approach to statistical inference. They give you an idea of the size of the sampling error you can expect when using data from a sample to come to conclusions about a wider population.
- Bootstrapping provides a very flexible method of working out confidence intervals for many different statistics. The basic idea is to use a sample of data to produce a *guessed population*, and then draw lots of *resamples* from this guessed population to see how much they vary, and so how accurate the real sample is likely to be.

8 Checking if Anything is Going on: Tests of Null Hypotheses

This chapter looks at how you can 'test a null hypothesis', an assumption that there is nothing going on, or no relationship between two variables. This is a very common approach to assessing the strength of evidence for statistical conclusions. However, you need to be careful about interpreting the answer, a probability known as a 'p value' or a 'significance level'. It is often possible to use a confidence interval (Chapter 7) instead, which may be more informative and less liable to misinterpretation.

▶ 8.1 An example: testing the hypothesis that a doctor is not a murderer

In January 2000 the doctor Harold Shipman was convicted on 15 counts of murdering his patients. A subsequent inquiry came to the conclusion that there was good evidence that he had killed at least 215 patients over a 23-year period. There was clear evidence of 16 murders in 1993, 11 in 1994, 30 in 1995, 30 in 1996 and 37 in 1997. Many lives could have been saved if Shipman's crimes had been detected earlier. The obvious way of doing this would be to monitor deaths rates of general practitioners' patients in order to check that they are within the 'normal' range and not suspiciously high.[106]

Shipman had 3600 patients and the crude death rate in Britain is 1.1% per year; this means we would expect, under 'normal' circumstances, that 1.1% of these 3600 patients would die every year. In other words, we would expect about 40 deaths among Shipman's patients each year. But not, of course, exactly 40. It may, in practice, be a few less or a few more. In 1994 Shipman killed 11 patients. If his practice was otherwise 'normal', this would mean that 51 patients died, instead of the expected 40. If you were responsible for monitoring these figures, would this be sufficient to make you suspicious?

If you said yes, your suspicions would be very frequently aroused. Let me explain.

Figure 8.1 shows the probabilities of different numbers of deaths in a particular year if the long-term average death rate is 40 deaths per year. This is

Figure 8.1 Probability of different numbers of deaths (mean = 40)

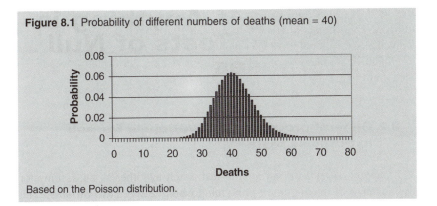

Based on the Poisson distribution.

based on the Poisson distribution (see Section 5.5).[107] What do you think is the probability of 51 or more deaths in a particular year?

Using the spreadsheet to work out the exact answer gives 5%.[108] It should be obvious from the diagram that this is roughly right.

Figure 8.1 is based on the assumption that the deaths are 'normal', in the sense that there is nothing unusual involved.[109] If Shipman's practice followed this pattern, without any excess deaths due to murder, this is what we should expect. This pattern will obviously be different for practices with different numbers and types of patients, for example practices with a larger number of patients or predominantly old patients would expect higher death rates. However, to keep the argument simple, let's suppose there are 10 000 practices in the country, each with 3600 patients. Let's also imagine that you decide to check any practice with 51 or more deaths during a year. If *all* practices were following the normal pattern (Figure 8.1), without any unusual circumstances, random fluctuations, as shown in Figure 8.1, will still mean that some practices will reach this threshold of 51 deaths. How many practices would you expect to reach 51 or more deaths in a typical year?

Five per cent of 10 000 is 500 practices. You would have 500 practices to check. Shipman's death rate would be similar to that in 500 practices with no unusual circumstances whatsoever.

So, to make Shipman stand out from the crowd, you would need to put the threshold higher. If the threshold was 60 (20 above the expected 40), Figure 8.1 shows a very low probability of this number of deaths under normal circumstances, using the spreadsheet formula the probability comes to 0.2%, or 2 in 1000. How many of the 10 000 practices would reach this level (under normal circumstances)?

Twenty. This would probably be a viable number to monitor, but even at this level, it's important to remember that some practices could simply be unlucky. This threshold level would mean that Shipman would have been flagged as exceptional in 1995, 1996 and 1997, but *not* in 1993 or 1994. This argument is an example of null hypothesis testing. I'll explain the general idea and then relate it to the Shipman problem.

▶ 8.2 General procedure and rationale for null hypothesis tests

Null hypothesis tests are an approach to statistical inference (Section 6.1), the business of making inferences that go beyond the data you've actually got. The data may tell you, for example, that death rates are higher than average, but what can you infer from this? Is it chance, or is there some systematic factor at work? The general procedure for *any* null hypothesis test is very simple:

- *Step 1: Formulate the null hypothesis.* This is an imaginary world, in which the thing which really interests you does *not* happen. In the Shipman analysis, the null hypothesis is that there is no difference (on average, in the long term) between the normal death rate and the death rate among Shipman's patients.
- *Step 2: Estimate the p value.* This stands for 'probability', of results like those actually observed, or more extreme than those observed, *if the null hypothesis is true*. In the Shipman example, as explained in Section 8.1, the *p* value for 51 deaths is 5%, while the *p* value for 60 deaths is 0.2%. It tells you how likely the results are to have occurred, *if* the null hypothesis is true. (An alternative term for a *p* value is 'significance level'.)
- *Step 3: Draw your conclusions.* The *lower* the *p* value, the *less* plausible the null hypothesis is, and so the *more* plausible it is that something unusual is occurring. For example, a value of 5% indicates that the results would occur, by chance, in 5% of practices. A value of 0.2% corresponds to only 20 out of 10 000 practices by chance. The latter is obviously far stronger evidence against the null hypothesis that it's all chance.

There are a large number of recipes for hypothesis tests (see Section 8.8) in statistics books. They all follow this logical structure; the differences between them lie in the nature of the null hypothesis and the method by which the *p* value is estimated. These tests are very widely used and it is important to understand the underlying rationale. Unfortunately, this is more difficult than it may seem. The idea is counterintuitive to many people, and it is very easy to misinterpret the results of these tests (see Section 8.6).

The important thing to remember is the null hypothesis. Whenever you see a p value, there must be a null hypothesis on which it is based. The null hypothesis represents a possible world. *It is important to imagine this possible world and see how it works.* Then you will be in a position to see how the p value is estimated, because it is always estimated on the assumption that the null hypothesis is true. The null hypothesis is a *baseline assumption* against which reality is tested. If you have a suspicion that a doctor may be murdering his patients, you set up a baseline to represent normal performance and compare the actual figures with this. Then, if the p value is low, the data you have observed is unlikely to have arisen from this baseline, so the baseline is likely to be wrong.

We have looked briefly at null hypothesis tests in earlier chapters. In Section 1.2, the figure of 1 in 10 000 000 for a probability of chance occurrence of a cancer cluster at Aldermaston is a p value based on the baseline assumption that there was no unusual cause of cancer in Aldermaston. Does this strike you as being strong evidence against this baseline assumption?

Yes. It's very powerful evidence that Aldermaston did not follow the usual pattern. There must have been some special cause of the excess cancer cases.

In Section 6.6, we tested Annette's telepathic powers against the null hypothesis, or baseline assumption, that she was guessing. We considered two experiments: one gave a p value of 1.9%, and the other gave a p value of 0.04%. Which gives the more convincing evidence against the baseline assumption that she is guessing, and so for the hypothesis that she is telepathic?

Obviously the second probability, because it is *lower*. (This corresponds to the experiment in which she got two cards right.)

I'll move on now to some further examples of null hypothesis testing but remember that they all follow the same basic pattern.

▶ 8.3 Testing a hypothesis that there is no relationship

In practice, most useful null hypotheses are to the effect that there is no relationship between two variables. This is the baseline with which we can compare the actual data. In the case of monitoring doctors to spot future Harold Shipmans, the null hypothesis is that there is no relationship between the identity of a doctor and the death rate among patients; there are no systematic causes of differences between death rates in different practices. Any differences observed are just random fluctuations. Figure 8.1 shows the pattern which we would expect from these random fluctuations. It represents this null hypothesis.

In that example, we were comparing a sample of data with a baseline about which we have fairly definite information. The method we look at next is useful when the comparison is between two or more samples of data. It's called an 'approximate randomisation test':[110] randomisation because the null hypothesis is simulated by randomisation, and approximate because the answer from a simulation is never exact. An alterative name would be 'shuffle test', for reasons that will soon become apparent. The next three subsections show how it can be applied in different situations.

8.3.1 Comparing two means

Table 3.5 shows that, among the sample of 20 in Table 3.1 (see Section 3.1), females drank an average of 3 units of alcohol on Saturday nights, whereas males drank 13 units. This suggests that males drink more than females. How big is this difference? (A trivial question but it's important you see how differences are measured.)

The difference between the female and male averages is 10 units. I worked it out as female mean – male mean which came to minus 10, but you may have done the opposite. (Remember that the mean is just the ordinary average.) The plus or minus sign tells us which sex drinks more.

If we are just interested in this sample on the one Saturday night, this is all there is to it. The males did drink more. But what if we want to make some inferences which go beyond the sample and refer to students in general? What null hypothesis would you suggest?

The obvious null hypothesis is that there is no difference, on average, between the amounts that male and female students drink on a Saturday night. This hypothesis refers to the wider context, or the population, which the sample represents. (It's obviously not true of the sample.) The next step is to estimate the p value. This, remember, is based on the assumption that the null hypothesis is true. So, imagine a world where there are no differences, on average, between the amounts drunk by males and females. The difficulty, of course, is that our information about this world is rather limited. We're trying to draw some inferences from our sample of 20 students, so we must assume that this data is all we have. Among these 20 students, males do drink more, so how on earth can we model a world in which this is not true? Have you any ideas about what we could do? (Don't worry if you haven't.)

In the imaginary world of our null hypothesis, the amount drunk has no relation to the sex of the student. The 12 females (Table 3.5) will drink much the same as the 8 males. So imagine the amount drunk by each student is stamped on a ball and put in a bucket. Now draw 12 balls out at random for the 12 females. The 8 balls left represent the males. Each ball in the bucket is equally likely to end up in the female or the male pile, reflecting the fact that we are assuming there is no difference between males and females.

I'll call this a *resample* because it involves taking a sample from a sample. Finally, work out the difference between the two means for the resample. When I did this, the balls representing the females were: 1, 0, 1, 4, 0, 12, 2, 26, 24, 6, 5, 10; and those representing the males were: 5, 15, 3, 3, 7, 19, 0, 4. Notice that these are just the figures in the Satunits column in Table 3.1, shuffled[111] and dealt into two piles. What is the difference between the means?

The mean for the females is 7.6, and for the males 7.0, giving a difference of 0.6. In this resample, the females drink more, but not as much more as the males did in the real sample. The next resample I drew gave a difference of −6.7: the males drank more this time. What do you think we do next?

Take lots of resamples so that we can estimate a probability distribution (Section 5.4) for the difference between the (simulated) female and male means. Remember, this is all based on the null hypothesis assumption that there is, on average, no difference between the male and female figures. This is where we need a computer. The spreadsheet program `resamplenrh.xls` (resample no relationship hypothesis) is designed to test a null hypothesis of no relation between two variables. If you have a computer it would be a good idea to download the file and follow the example through;[112] if not you should be able to see what's going on from my account.

We have worked through through the first resample above. The second gave a difference between the two simulated means of −6.7, the third 2.7 and so on. The program does this 200 times. The result is shown in Figure 8.2. The horizontal scale here represents the *difference* between the two means. The bars are a histogram (Section 3.4.1) representing the resampling distribution: this shows that the commonest value of the difference between the means from the resamples was around zero, and they were all between −10 and 10.

The actual value from the sample in Table 3.1 (−10 units) is shown as a vertical line. Remember this represents what really happened; the histogram is based on the null hypothesis assumption that there's no difference between males and females. Do you think the actual value is consistent with the null hypothesis? What do you think the *p* value is? What would your conclusion be?

It isn't really consistent with the null hypothesis because the value of −10 does *not* fall within the range that occurred in the 200 random simulations. The *p* value, according to the program, was 0%, none of the 200 resamples had a mean of −10 or less. This difference of −10 is unlikely to be the result of chance, as represented by the histogram in Figure 8.2. The conclusion is that we can be fairly confident that male students do drink more than females

Figure 8.2 Resample distribution of difference of means

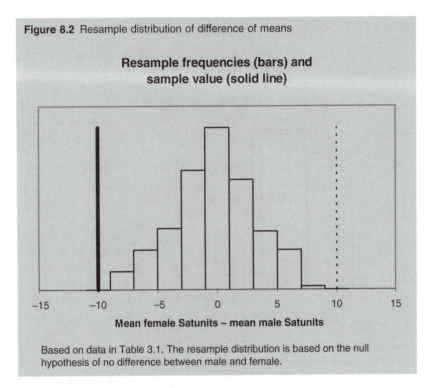

Resample frequencies (bars) and sample value (solid line)

Mean female Satunits – mean male Satunits

Based on data in Table 3.1. The resample distribution is based on the null hypothesis of no difference between male and female.

in a broader context than this sample. (The dotted line in Figure 8.2 represents the scenario in which females drink 10 units more than males. This is the mirror image of the actual result of −10. We'll see what it's for in Section 8.5.1.) Pressing the key F9 on the computer reruns the simulation. Next time, the pattern of the graph was slightly different, and the *p* value was 0.5%. But it is still a small probability.

8.3.2 Comparing more than two means

What if we wanted to compare the amounts drunk on the Saturday by students on the three courses in Table 3.1? With two groups we can work out the difference by subtracting the mean of one group from the mean of the other, but this won't work with three groups. Here we have to use the 'range', the difference between the largest and smallest mean. The answer is always positive. If you split the data in Table 3.1 into three subgroups – one for each course – what are the mean amounts drunk on Saturday and what is the range of these means?

The three means are 10.6 (FB), 2.2 (FP), 5.7 (PP), so the range is 10.6 – 2.2 or about 8.4. Now we can do just the same as before and simulate 200 resam-

Figure 8.3 Resample distribution of range of means (sample of 20)

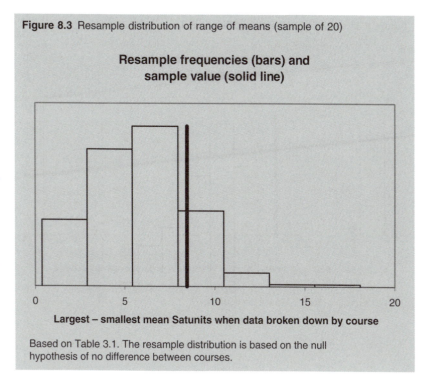

Resample frequencies (bars) and
sample value (solid line)

Largest – smallest mean Satunits when data broken down by course

Based on Table 3.1. The resample distribution is based on the null
hypothesis of no difference between courses.

ples on the assumption that there is no relation between the course and the
amount drunk.[113] The result is in Figure 8.3.

Using Figure 8.3, what do you think the *p* value is?

According to the spreadsheet the probability is 12.5%, that is, 25 of the
200 simulated resamples produced a range of means greater than or equal
to 8.4. It should be obvious from the diagram that this is a reasonable answer.
What would you conclude from this?

Compare the actual value from the sample with the histogram, which
represents the null hypothesis that it's all chance. The conclusion is that
this discrepancy between the courses could well have arisen by chance.
Can you conclude that there is definitely *not* a difference between the
courses?

No! There is quite a big difference in the sample of 20. This pattern may
or may not be repeated if we took a larger group of students. We can't tell
from this sample of data.

We have, of course, a larger sample of 92 from which Table 3.1 is drawn
(`drink.xls`). In fact the pattern in this sample is similar. The range of
means comes to 6.7. Let's now use this data to test the null hypothesis that

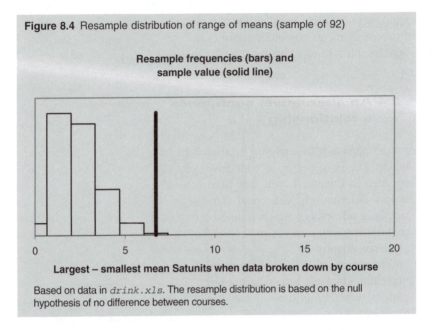

Figure 8.4 Resample distribution of range of means (sample of 92)

Resample frequencies (bars) and
sample value (solid line)

Largest – smallest mean Satunits when data broken down by course

Based on data in `drink.xls`. The resample distribution is based on the null
hypothesis of no difference between courses.

there's no difference between the courses. The result is in Figure 8.4. What
do you think the p value is this time? Why is it different from before?

The p value is 0%. This pattern is very unlikely to have arisen by chance.
The graph in Figure 8.3 is more spread out than Figure 8.4. This is because
Figure 8.3 is based on a much smaller sample (there are only three PP students in Table 3.1), which is likely to be much more variable in the random
resampling process. The larger the sample, the less spread out the graph is
likely to be.

8.3.3 The difference of two proportions and other possibilities

Is the proportion of male students who smoke the same as the proportion
of female smokers? We can test this null hypothesis in just the same way as
we tested the null hypothesis about drinking. A smoker is coded as 1 and a
non-smoker as 0, and then the average (mean) represents the proportion (see
Section 7.5). The process is then exactly the same as before.

We might also be interested in the correlation between the number of cigarettes smoked each day and the amount drunk on Saturday night. Are the
big drinkers also the big smokers? Kendall's correlation coefficient, for all 92
students, comes to 0.10 (Section 3.7.3). But would this pattern be repeated,
or is it a fluke? We can test the null hypothesis that there is no correlation
by a very similar method.[114]

And there are other possibilities. You might be interested in the difference of two medians, or any other statistic describing the relation between two variables. I'll turn to a slightly different approach to these problems now.

▶ 8.4 An alternative: confidence intervals for a relationship

Another approach to analysing relationships, such as those considered in Section 8.3, is to set up a confidence interval. Confidence intervals are explained in Chapter 7: you may need to read this chapter to follow this section. (Alternatively, you could skip this section.) This approach has a number of advantages which should become clearer when we've looked at the problems with p values in Section 8.6. I'll be brief here: for more detail please see Chapter 7.

In the sample of 92 students from which Table 3.1 is drawn, there were 46 female non-smokers, 12 female smokers, 20 male non-smokers and 14 male smokers. What proportion of males and females smoked? What is the difference?

The proportion of female smokers is 12/58 (21%), and the proportion of males is 14/34 (41%). The difference is −20% if we use the female – male difference as in Section 8.3.1. The proportion of male smokers is 20% more than the proportion of female smokers. But this is based on a sample of 92, and so won't be completely accurate.

Figure 8.5 shows the bootstrap confidence distribution for this difference.[115] This is based on resampling from the data to obtain an indication of how much samples are likely to vary, as explained in Chapter 7. The 95% interval extends from −40% to 0%. This indicates that we can be 95% confident that the true difference, among the wider population from which the sample is drawn, will be somewhere in this interval.

What can we say about the null hypothesis that there is no difference?

The null hypothesis that the difference is zero is right on the edge of this confidence distribution. This suggests it's possible but unlikely.

More precisely, the bootstrap resampling tells us that there is a 95% probability that the difference between a sample result and the truth about the whole population is 20% or less. (This is the error limit as explained in Section 7.2.) This means that there's a 5% probability that the difference between the sample and population answers is more than 20%. Now remember that the null hypothesis is that the difference is zero, and the difference we have observed is 20%. This means that if we can assume the pattern in Figure 8.5 applies to the null hypothesis, the probability of observing a difference of 20% or more if the null hypothesis is true is 5%. This is the p value. Are you confused?

Figure 8.5 Confidence distribution for difference between proportion of female smokers and proportion of male smokers

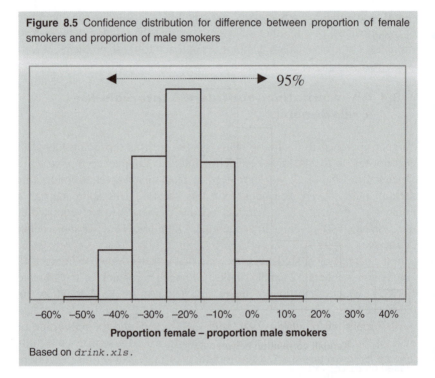

Based on `drink.xls`.

I got confused writing it, so a little confusion is understandable! Fortunately, the point is simply that if the null hypothesis value – zero – is on the edge of a 95% confidence interval, the p value is 5%. If it's outside the interval, the p value is less than 5%. If it's inside, the p value is more. As I hope common sense would suggest.

You can plot a confidence interval for a correlation coefficient (Section 3.7.3) in just the same way.[116] The result is Figure 8.6. The 95% confidence interval extends from −0.04 to +0.22. According to the simulation, there is a 9.5% probability that the real correlation is zero or negative.[117] This puts the figure of 0.10 in Table 3.8 in context, and shows us what the likely extent of sampling error is. If you wanted to analyse this by means of a null hypothesis test, what would the null hypothesis and the p value be?

The null hypothesis is that the true, population, correlation is zero. Zero is firmly inside the 95% confidence interval, so the p value must be more than 5%. A more exact answer would be 9.5% or 19%; the distinction between these is explained in Section 8.5.1. Either way, the evidence against the null hypothesis is not very strong.

Figure 8.6 Confidence distribution for Kendall correlation between drinking and smoking

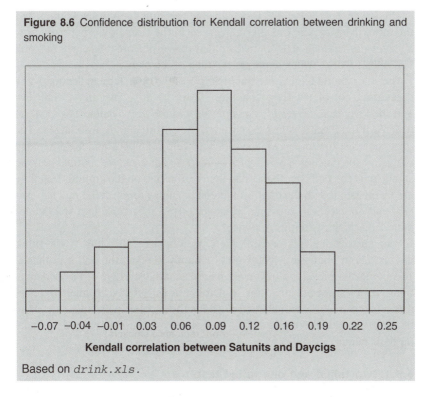

Kendall correlation between Satunits and Daycigs

Based on `drink.xls`.

▶ 8.5 The interpretation of *p* values

You may have come across a research report which quotes *p* values (or significance levels). Or you may have analysed your own data and worked out your own *p* values. In either case, you need to be clear about their interpretation. As we saw in Section 8.2, a *p* value is simply a probability worked out on the basis of a null hypothesis. However, sharp-eyed readers will have noticed that Step 3 of the procedure in Section 8.2 is rather vague. You are told to draw your conclusions, but not told how to do so. This is deliberate, because I think any firm rule may be misleading: some of the reasons for this should be clear from Section 8.6.

To understand what a *p* value means, you must imagine the null hypothesis: an imaginary, possible world, set up to provide a baseline against which to compare what has actually happened. Imagine that you are living in this fictional world, and visualise what the probability means. *You cannot understand a* p *value without being clear about the null hypothesis on which it is based.*

The lower the p value, the less plausible this null hypothesis world is and the more plausible are the alternatives. So in the telepathy experiment, low p values (for example 0.04%) indicate that the results are unlikely in this null hypothesis world, which supports the idea of telepathy.

The rule which I might have put in Step 3 of the procedure in Section 8.2 is to choose a cut-off level of probability – 5% or 1% are conventional choices – and then say that *the result is significant and the null hypothesis should be rejected* if the p value is *less* than this. If the cut-off significance level is 1%, the telepathy experiment, which yielded a p value of 0.04%, and the difference of two means (Section 8.3.1), which yielded a p value of 0%,[118] would both be significant. The null hypotheses can then be rejected on the grounds that they are inconsistent with the data. Would you be happy to reject the null hypothesis that Annette was guessing, in favour of the alternative that she is telepathic, on the basis of this evidence?

Your answer depends on how likely you consider telepathy. If you think it's just about impossible, you won't be happy to reject the null hypothesis. The significance level is a (reversed) measure of the strength of the evidence: 1% may not seem adequate for something as far-fetched as telepathy. The rule may not seem reasonable here. That's the problem with rules: they may be too rigid. The alternative is just to give the p value and let readers make up their minds.

8.5.1 Two-tailed and one-tailed tests

At the end of Section 8.4, I gave two different p values for the null hypothesis that a correlation was zero: 9.5% or 19%. The distinction is between a 'one-tailed' and 'two-tailed' test. If you are prepared to count a correlation in either direction as 'extreme' in Step 2 of the procedure in Section 8.2, then the p value should include both tails. If you would count a negative correlation between smoking and drinking as evidence against the null hypothesis of no correlation, as well as a positive correlation, then you want a two-tailed test. This may be a rather arbitrary decision. If in doubt, standard practice is to go for two tails.

What about the general practitioner test in Section 8.1? If we monitor practices with 60 or more deaths in a year, is this a one-tailed or two-tailed test?

This is clearly one-tailed. Death rates below normal would have quite different implications. On the other hand, if the aim was to find practices with unusual death rates in either direction, we would want a two-tailed test – the p value would be the probability of 60 or more *or* 40 or less. Two-tailed p values are, of course, usually twice as big as one-tailed ones.

▶ 8.6 Why *p* values can be misleading: things to watch for

Null hypothesis tests and their resulting *p* values are very widely cited in research reports. There are, however, major problems in their use and interpretation. I've divided the problems into three categories explained in Sections 8.6.1, 8.6.2 and 8.6.3. If your interest is in interpreting research results, then these sections should alert you to points to check for in assessing the credibility of the conclusions. If you are doing the research, these difficulties have implications for how you should be analysing your data.

8.6.1 Is the *p* value interpreted correctly?

Surprisingly often, the answer is no. There are two common fallacies. I'll return to the telepathy experiment (Section 6.2) to illustrate them. Let's imagine, again, that Annette has got one card right, and we decide to test the null hypothesis that she's guessing and is not telepathic, with a significance level of 1%. Then, as we saw before (Section 6.6), the *p* value comes to 1.9% (1/52), so the evidence is not strong enough to reject the null hypothesis at this level of significance. Does that mean we should *accept* the null hypothesis that she's guessing?

No, of course not. She's got one right so it's hardly evidence against telepathy. She couldn't have done any better! If a result is not significant, this means the evidence is not strong enough to reject the null hypothesis. This may be because the null hypothesis is true, or it may simply be because there is not enough evidence. It does not provide positive evidence for the null hypothesis.

The second fallacy is that as the *p* value is 1.9%, the figure of 98.1% (100% – 1.9%) appears to suggest that the *probability* of Annette being telepathic is 98.1%. What do you think of this argument?

It's rubbish! The probability of 1.9% is the probability of getting the observed result, *assuming* that it's due to chance. It is *not* the probability that it's due to chance. What does the probability of 98.1% actually represent?

The chance of her getting the card wrong, *assuming* she's guessing. This is not very interesting.

The general fallacy is the idea that 100% minus a *p* value tells you anything useful about the null hypothesis.[119] It doesn't. If you want to know the probability of the telepathy hypothesis being true, you need to use the Bayesian approach (Section 6.4).

Both problems stem from the difficulties in understanding the definition of *p* values. Any short definition is liable to be misleading, for example the *British Medical Journal's* 'the probability that an observed difference occurred by chance'[120] is ambiguous about whether the probability is that of the chance hypothesis, or that of the observed difference happening. Remember that you must imagine the world of the null hypothesis, and then the p value is the probability of certain events in this imaginary world.

8.6.2 Is the null hypothesis worth testing?

I came across an academic article recently where the researchers had given out a questionnaire with a question (on accountancy, as it happens) to which people had to respond Yes, No or Don't know. They then tested the null hypothesis that respondents were equally likely to give each of these three answers. The results showed that there were very few Don't know answers. The p value was very low, so the results were deemed very significant.

The problem here is that this null hypothesis is a very silly one, which is almost certainly false. If the question had been 'Are you female?', there wouldn't have been many Don't know responses, and the same applies to many other questions. The hypothesis is very silly, so getting evidence that it's false is not very interesting.

On another occasion, a student came to me who was interested in demonstrating that manufacturing firms with an 'export orientation', that is, they researched the potential for exporting and took the idea seriously, were likely to export more than those which had no such orientation. He proceeded by setting up a null hypothesis that there was no relation between exports and export orientation. And, when his results came in, it turned out that the p value was low: there was evidence against the null hypothesis, and so for the idea that export orientation and exports are linked. Firms with high export orientation *did* export more than those without this orientation. Have you any comment?

Imagine the world of the null hypothesis. Some firms will be export oriented: they will find out about potential customers abroad and about how to supply them. Other firms are not export oriented. They won't do this research. They won't get to know about customers abroad. The null hypothesis is that the group that knows all about exporting will export about the same amount as the group that knows nothing. This hypothesis is not really credible. How can firms export if they don't know anything about it? The evidence against this null hypothesis is not really interesting because the hypothesis is too silly to take seriously.

8.6.3 How big is the observed effect?

In ordinary English the word 'significant' means big or important. In statistics it refers only to the strength of the evidence: a significant effect is one which signifies a real effect that cannot reasonably be attributed to chance, as represented by the null hypothesis. Sometimes a result may be significant

Table 8.1 Differences between shop X and shop Y: *p* values

Aspect of service	Shop X: mean customer rating	Shop Y: mean customer rating	Difference X – Y	Level of significance (p)
Queuing time	1.46	6.38	−4.92	0.000
Helpful/friendly staff	7.49	7.19	0.30	0.003
Range of produce	6.39	6.45	−0.06	0.201

in the statistical sense but not in the ordinary English sense. Problems may then arise if people think that statistics is written in English. In this respect at least, it isn't.

Table 8.1 shows the results of a survey to compare the customer service offered by two supermarkets, Shop X and Shop Y.[121] The shops are organised in very different ways, and the survey was set up to investigate customer reactions. The data was obtained from a sample of customers who rated each shop on a scale ranging from 1 (very bad) to 9 (very good). What would be your main conclusion from these results?

The shops are very similar in terms of the last two aspects of service: differences of 0.30 and −0.06 on a nine-point scale do not seem very important. However, Shop Y is far better in terms of queuing time: a difference of −4.92 is obviously important. Using a significance level of 1%, which of these three results are significant?

The first two *p* values (0.000 and 0.003) are less than 1%, so these two are significant. There is strong evidence for a real difference which will extend to customers not yet surveyed. The third result is not significant.

The problem arises with the second of these three results. This is statistically significant, despite the fact that the size of the difference is very small, so it is not significant in the ordinary sense of the word. How do you think the researchers managed to get such an impressive (that is, low) significance level despite this small difference?

The sample must have been very large, probably thousands of customers. The larger the sample, the smaller chance fluctuations in the mean are likely to be, and so the lower the *p* value (other things being equal) – see Section 8.3.2.

Some researchers have a regrettable tendency to forget the size of the effect (difference, correlation or whatever) and focus only on the significance level. This is the sort of unhelpful, black and white thinking deplored by advocates of fuzzy logic (Section 4.6). The remedy is to make a point of always noting the size of any effect. Then, if it's not big enough to be interesting, forget it. Only bother to check the *p* value if the size of the effect is big enough to be interesting.

▶ 8.7 Choosing a method of inference: *p* values and other approaches

We've now looked at three broad approaches to statistical inference: Bayes' principle (Section 6.4), null hypothesis tests and confidence intervals (Chapter 7 and Section 8.4). How should you choose which is best for a particular purpose? Bayes' principle has the advantage of giving you useful answers in a way which many regard as logically rigorous. If you have two simple hypotheses you are comparing, as in the telepathy experiment (Section 6.1), then there is a case for using the Bayesian approach. But in more complicated situations, the Bayesian approach may be far too complicated (Section 6.4.1).

The next contender is null hypothesis testing. This is by far the commonest approach, but there are difficulties as we saw in Section 8.6. Take care to avoid these traps. If you do decide on a null hypothesis test, the problem is then how to estimate the *p* values. There's a brief guide to some of the conventional approaches in Section 8.8. In terms of the methods covered in this book, there are two alternatives. Firstly, you may be able to see how to use some of the probability theory to simulate the null hypothesis. Figure 8.1 is one example; see also Exercise 10.5.1. Secondly, you may be able to use the approximate randomisation (shuffle) method, described in Section 8.3, and implemented on `resamplenrh.xls`. This is surprisingly flexible, as you'll see in the next section when we look at its relation to some of the standard approaches.

The third method of inference is to derive confidence intervals (Chapter 7). If you have measured a mean, a median or a correlation from a sample and want to know how reliable a guide your result is likely to be if extended to a wider context, then this is the obvious method. If you have a null hypothesis of no overall relationship between two variables, and you can measure the size of the relationship in a sample, then a confidence interval for this relationship (see Section 8.4) answers all the questions that a null hypothesis test does and more. For example, Table 8.2 analyses the same results as Table 8.1, but in confidence interval format.

Can you tell from Table 8.2 which *p* values would be significant at the 1% level?

You should be able to. The confidence level in the table is 99%, which meshes with the significance level of 1% (see Section 8.4). Zero – the null

Table 8.2 Differences between shop X and shop Y: confidence intervals

Aspect of service	Shop X: Mean customer rating	Shop Y: mean customer rating	Difference X – Y	99% confidence interval for difference
Queuing time	1.46	6.38	–4.92	–4.81 to –5.01
Helpful/friendly staff	7.49	7.19	0.30	0.15 to 0.45
Range of produce	6.39	6.45	–0.06	–0.20 to 0.10

hypothesis value of no difference – is within the third interval, but outside the first two. This means that the third result is *not* significant, but the first two *are* significant at 1%. In addition, of course, the confidence interval gives you an indication of how big the difference is. The second one, for example, is clearly different from zero, but not by much.

In general, if measuring the relationship in this way is possible and convenient, confidence intervals are more useful than null hypothesis tests.[122] They avoid the problems discussed in Section 8.6.1 (their interpretation is far more obvious), Section 8.6.2 (there is no hypothesis so it can't be a silly one) and Section 8.6.3 (they tell you the size of the relationship).

▶ 8.8 Similar concepts

If you work with a definite cut-off significance level (for example 5%), there are two kinds of 'error' you can make when testing a null hypothesis. A 'Type I error' occurs when you conclude that the null hypothesis is false when it is actually true, and a 'Type II error' occurs when you fail to conclude that the null hypothesis is false when it is false. However, Type II errors are not really errors: failing to find significant evidence against the null hypothesis does not mean it's true. It may simply indicate you haven't tried hard enough.

There are a large number of methods of testing null hypotheses, referred to as 'tests'. Each test is appropriate to a particular type of situation. The aim, in all cases, is to derive a *p* value or significance level. The randomisation test, explained in Section 8.3, is one of these tests, but one which is not very commonly used. It will, however, do the job of the following tests, which are commonly used:

• 'Analysis of variance (one way)' also known as ANOVA, is for testing a null hypothesis of no difference between the mean measurements of subgroups (Sections 8.3.1 and 8.3.2). In SPSS use Analyze – Compare means – One-way ANOVA. The dependent variable is the number variable (Satunits in the example in Section 8.3.1) and Factor is the variable which defines the subgroups (Sex in Section 8.3.1, Course in Section 8.3.2).

- In the particular case of two subgroups (Section 8.3.1), a 't test' (unmatched data) will do the same job. In SPSS, use Analyze – Compare means – Independent samples t test.

- The 'chi square' test can be used for comparing proportions (Section 8.3.3) and, more generally, for looking at relations between category variables (see Section 3.5). In SPSS use Analyze – Descriptive statistics – Crosstabs. Then paste one of the variables (for example Sex) in as a Row variable, and another as a Column variable (for example Course). Then click on Statistics and put a tick in the Chi square box.

- Alternatively, there are methods in textbooks for working out p values and confidence intervals for the 'difference of two proportions'.

- SPSS will provide p values as part of the results for most of its procedures. The randomisation test is an alternative to some of these, for example – Analyze – Correlate – Bivariate will give you p values (Section 8.3.3) as well as correlation coefficients.

The randomisation test will not give identical answers to these tests because of differences in the exact definition of the null hypothesis.[123] The answers should, however, be similar. The randomisation test should give you a good idea of the underlying rationale of all these tests.

If you want to compare a pair of variables, each relating to the same cases, you can use the 'paired samples t test', or the 'sign test' – see Exercise 8.9.2 for an example.

Analysis of variance can also be used to analyse far more complex hypotheses, incorporating more variables and the 'interactions' between them (see Chapter 9). In SPSS, use Analyze – General linear model. We will return to this in Chapter 9, although a detailed treatment is beyond the scope of this book.

The analysis of death rates in Section 8.1 illustrates the principle behind a 'Shewhart control chart',[124] a well-established quality control method.

It is also helpful to be aware of hypothesis testing as a general idea. In some fields of enquiry, there is a tendency to assume that if you want to be scientific, you have to test hypotheses, which means statistical hypothesis testing. Neither of these assumptions is reasonable. Much of science does not involve testing hypotheses.[125] And where it does, the format is usually rather different from statistical null hypothesis testing. One influential philosopher, who has popularised the idea that science works by subjecting hypotheses to rigorous testing, is Karl Popper.[126] But he is not talking about the statistical testing of null hypotheses; instead he is advocating the testing of hypotheses which say something interesting, not by statistical methods, but by searching for situations in which the hypotheses don't work. The hypothesis in the title of Section 8.1 is that a doctor is *not* a murderer. For Popper, the only interesting hypothesis would be that he *is* a murderer. The phrase 'hypothesis testing' has different meanings in different contexts.

▶ 8.9 Exercises

8.9.1 Working out *p* values by shuffling cards

Do the simulation example in Section 8.3.1 (or 8.3.2) by shuffling cards instead of using a computer. You will need 20 cards; business cards would do. Write the Satunits figure for each student in Table 3.1 on one of the cards. Now, to simulate the null hypothesis, you shuffle the cards and then deal one pile of 12 to represent the females and another of 8 to represent the males. Work out the mean of each and the difference and start to plot a diagram like Figure 8.2. Twenty shuffles should be enough to see the rough pattern. Alternatively use some data of your own.

8.9.2 Do students drink more on Saturday night than Sunday night?

The data in Table 3.1 seems to suggest they do. The best way to analyse this is to put the difference (Satunits – Sununits) in another column, and then work out a confidence interval for this difference using `resample.xls` or `resample.exe` and the bootstrap method of Chapter 7. What does this suggest about the null hypothesis of no difference? An alternative method of analysis is suggested in Exercise 10.5.1. This is called the 'sign test' (in SPSS use Analyze – Non-parametric tests – 2 related samples). Yet a third possibility is the 'paired sample t test' (in SPSS use Analyze – Compare means – Paired samples t test). The pairing refers to the fact that you have a pair of figures for each person. This differs from comparing males and females, which is unpaired because you are comparing separate groups of people. How do the three methods compare?

8.9.3 Big and small samples

The example in Section 8.3.1 uses a sample of only 20. You should be able to get a better result with the whole sample of 92 in `drink.xls`. Try the analysis with the larger sample. Is the result 'better'? In what sense?

8.9.4 Agreement between reviewers of academic papers

Academic papers are normally reviewed by other academics to see if they are acceptable. At a recent conference, each of the 58 papers submitted was reviewed by two other academics. Ideally, these two reviews should agree, because they are supposed to be reviewing the same paper by the same criteria. An analysis of this process[127] found that there were a total of 116 reviews (two for each paper), of which 69 were 'good', and the rest were 'bad'. However, looking at the reviews for each individual paper, there was agreement between the two reviewers for only 50% (29) of the papers. For the other 50%, one review was good and other bad. Any comments? Is this statistically significant? Is it significant in any other way?

8.9.5 A test of a new treatment for cancer

A small clinical trial of a new treatment for a type of cancer found that the new treatment did work better than the old treatment, but the difference was not statistically significant. Does this mean that the new treatment is ineffective and should be abandoned?

8.9.6 Are old accountants more sociable than young accountants?

Use the data in `accquest.xls` to find out.

▶ 8.10 Summary of main points

- A null hypothesis is typically a 'nothing interesting happening' hypothesis. Its purpose is to be used as a baseline with which reality can be compared. The null hypothesis *always* refers to a wider context than the sample, for example the whole population from which the sample is drawn.
- The *p* value, or significance level, gives you a measure of how plausible this null hypothesis is. The *lower* the *p* value, the *less* plausible the null hypothesis is. So low *p* values suggest that the null hypothesis is wrong.
- In practice, null hypothesis tests are very easy to misinterpret. They should be treated with care.

9 Predicting the Unpredictable or Explaining the Inexplicable: Regression Models

This chapter shows how you can use some data on one or more variables (for example people's diet and exercise habits) to try to predict the value of a further variable (for example on their general health). Models to do this are called 'regression models'. We start with the single variable case and then move on to 'multiple regression models' which use several variables to make the prediction. We also look at how we can assess the accuracy of regression models, the circumstances under which they may be misleading and how they can be used; often the aim is to try to *explain* something rather than to predict it.

▶ 9.1 Introduction: predicting earnings on the Isle of Fastmoney

The data in Table 3.1 shows that the male students drank an average of 13.4 units of alcohol on the Saturday, whereas the females only drank 3.3 units. This means that if we wanted to predict how much a randomly chosen student would drink next Saturday, a reasonable guess might be 13.4 units if the student was male and 3.3 if female. However, we would not expect this guess to be at all accurate. If we had more information, like the student's age and other variables, we should be able to make a much more accurate prediction. But we still wouldn't expect to be 100% accurate.

This is the subject of this chapter: making predictions like this as accurately as possible. I'll illustrate the methods we can use drawing examples from an imaginary island known as the Isle of Fastmoney. This island used to have another name, but ever since a couple of students at the college on the island did a small survey and found that high earners on the island could run substantially faster than those earning less, the older name has been forgotten in favour of the name coined by the local paper, the Isle of Fastmoney. Every year on the island there is a 10 km race. Most of the population enter, and all finishers are given a medal with their name and time engraved on it.

It's taken very seriously and the times are generally pretty fast. The survey found, much to everyone's surprise, that there was a negative correlation (Section 3.7.3) between the time individuals recorded in the race and their annual earnings, especially if allowances were made for age and sex. There was a definite tendency for the higher earners to record faster times in the race. Other surveys since have found a similar pattern.

In the last couple of years, pressure from a cycle manufacturer on the island has resulted in a cycle race being added to the island's calendar. The results show a very similar relationship with earnings: the high earners seem to be able to cycle faster. The most recent survey was based on a sample of 50 male islanders and 50 female islanders. These were drawn at random from the population of the island aged between 20 and 60 who entered both the running and the cycle race (about 10 000 people). This is a 'stratified' sample because we draw the males and the females separately and ensure that we have the right proportion of each (50%) in the final sample.[128]

The data in Table 9.1 shows eight males and eight females drawn, randomly again, from this sample. (Table 9.1 is on the web as `iofm16.xls`, and the whole sample as `iofm.xls`.) How can we predict earnings from the race times and the other variables in Table 9.1? And can these predictions help us

Table 9.1 Subsample of data from the Isle of Fastmoney

Refno	Sex	Sexn	Age	Height in cm	Run 10 km	Cycle 10 km	Earn000e
1	F	1	42	170	61	24	106
2	F	1	53	165	87	35	17
3	F	1	27	161	71	28	18
4	F	1	53	170	83	34	11
5	F	1	23	161	56	20	15
6	F	1	53	168	69	29	40
7	F	1	32	162	67	28	25
8	F	1	51	167	66	29	156
9	M	0	46	174	70	27	37
10	M	0	49	187	53	23	143
11	M	0	33	180	64	28	12
12	M	0	48	182	77	33	20
13	M	0	49	177	58	21	79
14	M	0	24	189	48	17	6
15	M	0	31	176	50	20	59
16	M	0	35	190	52	21	66

Sexn is a numerical coding of sex: 1 for female and 0 for male. The Run 10 km and Cycle 10 km columns are the race times to the nearest minute. Earn000E is earnings in thousands of euros. Data is in `iofm16.xls`.

understand the factors which determine earnings on the island? These questions are the subject of this chapter.

▶ 9.2 Straight line prediction models: linear regression

The simplest form of model is based on a single category variable. Does Table 9.1 suggest that we can predict anything about islanders' earnings from their sex (M or F in Table 9.1)?

Not much. The average earnings of the females in Table 9.1 are 48.5 thousand euros, and the corresponding figure for males is 52.75. But this is a slight difference, which would provide a very unreliable prediction.

The next simplest possibility is to base a prediction of earnings on a single number variable, such as the time in the 10 km run. Figure 9.1 shows the relationship between these two variables as a scatter diagram (Section 3.7.1). This figure seems to show the expected correlation between the two variables: most of the high earners seem to have fairly fast (low) race times. But this relationship does not look strong enough to make a useful prediction.

This is not the case with relationship between the run time and the cycle time in Figure 9.2. This figure suggests that it would be possible to get a reasonable estimate of the time an individual took for the cycle race from their time in the run. For example, what would your predictions be for two runners: one with a run time of 60 minutes, and the other with a time of 80 minutes?

Figure 9.1 Relationship between 10 km run time and earnings (based on sample of 16)

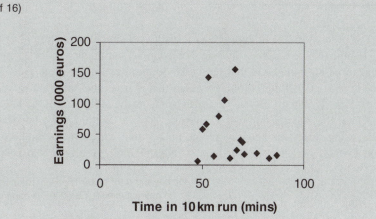

Figure 9.2 Relationship between 10 km run time and 10 km cycle time (based on sample of 16)

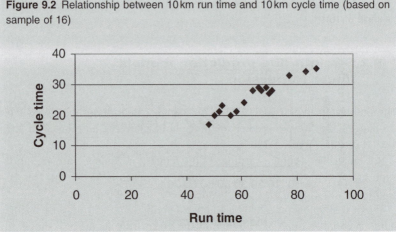

Runners who finished in about 60 minutes took about 20–25 minutes in the cycle race. Similarly, the graph suggests that a time of 80 minutes for the run is likely to imply a time of 30–40 minutes for the cycle ride. The slightly scattered pattern emphasises the obvious point that we should not expect these predictions to be exact.

A prediction can be represented on the graph as a line. Figure 9.3 shows a prediction line superimposed on Figure 9.2. It's obviously *not* a good prediction line, but it will do to explain how prediction lines work, and how we can decide how good they are. The vertical axis (cycle time) is the variable we are trying to predict, so we have to assume it is *dependent* (in some sense) on the other variable, the run time. This is known as the 'independent variable' because we assume we have a way of measuring this independently of the other variable.

The prediction line in Figure 9.3 makes a very simple prediction: that the cycle time will be half the run time. For example, the prediction for a runner who takes 60 minutes is that they take 30 minutes for the cycle race. The line consists of all the points for which this is true. The half (0.5) is called the 'slope' (gradient) because it corresponds to the steepness of the line. In this case the line goes up half a unit for every one unit along the horizontal axis. If the slope was 2.5, it would go up 2.5 units for every one unit along, and it would look steeper. (The important terminology is summarised in Table 9.7 below.) What is the prediction from the line in Figure 9.3 for a runner who takes 80 minutes?

Using this line, a run time of 80 minutes corresponds to a cycle time of 40 minutes. Alternatively, using the rule on which the line is based, cycle time

Figure 9.3 One line for predicting 10 km cycle time from 10 km run time (based on sample of 16)

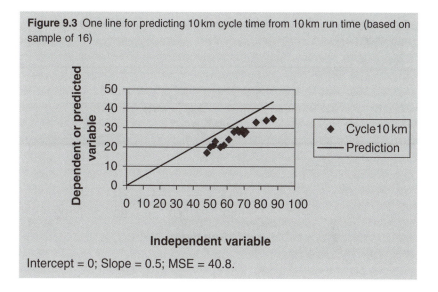

Intercept = 0; Slope = 0.5; MSE = 40.8.

is half the run time. How good are the predictions made by the line in Figure 9.3?

They all look too high. The line is consistently above the points representing the actual race times. To compensate for this, we need to lower the line. We can do this by changing the starting point.

The prediction line in Figure 9.3 starts from zero: it crosses the vertical axis at the point where the dependent variable is zero. The line in Figure 9.4 starts lower, at the point where the dependent variable is −5. This is known as the 'intercept' because it intersects the vertical axis at this point. It is the value of the dependent variable where the independent variable is zero. What is the intercept of the prediction line in Figure 9.3?

The intercept is 0. The line in Figure 9.4 looks a better predictor than the one in Figure 9.3. What we need is a way of measuring how accurate a prediction line is likely to be. Then we should be in a position to find the most accurate possible line.

I'll explain the way this is done in relation to Figure 9.3. The basic idea is to work out the error we would make in using the prediction line to predict each of the cycle times, and then work out a sort of average error. Some of the results are in Table 9.2. The Excel workbook `pred1var.xls` uses this method to work out prediction lines.[129] The last row in Table 9.2 (no. 14) corresponds to the point on the left of the cluster of points in Figure 9.3. The run time is 48 minutes, so the predicted cycle time is half this, 24 minutes. The actual cycle time is 17 minutes, so the error in the prediction is 24 minus

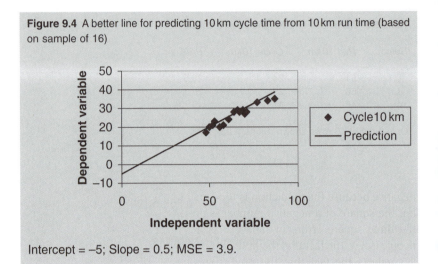

Figure 9.4 A better line for predicting 10 km cycle time from 10 km run time (based on sample of 16)

Intercept = −5; Slope = 0.5; MSE = 3.9.

Table 9.2 Calculation of error and square error for Figure 9.3

Refno	Run 10 km	Cycle 10 km	Prediction	Error	Square error
1	61	24	30.5	6.5	42.25
8	66	29	33	4	16
14	48	17	24	7	49

Only three of 16 rows shown. Slope = 0.5; intercept = 0.

17 or 7 minutes. This 7 minutes corresponds to the vertical gap between the point and line in Figure 9.3. The smaller these errors are, the closer the line will fit the points and the more accurate any prediction is likely to be.

To assess the overall performance of the line, we need some measure of average error. The obvious way to do this is perhaps to use an ordinary mean. However, this leads to a few problems (see Exercise 9.9.4); the preferred measure is the 'mean square error' (MSE). To work this out you square the errors and then take the mean of these squares. For the last row in Table 9.2, the square error is 49, and the mean of the three square errors in the table is 35.75. If we include all 16 people in Table 9.1, the MSE comes to 40.8.

Figure 9.4 is based on an intercept of −5 (instead of 0). What would the three errors and square errors in Table 9.2 be with this intercept?

The intercept is now −5, so to work out the predictions you need to add this on. The answers are in Table 9.3. Note here that the middle error is

Table 9.3 Calculation of error and square error for Figure 9.4

Refno	Run 10 km	Cycle 10 km	Prediction	Error	Square error
1	61	24	25.5	1.5	2.25
8	66	29	28	−1	1
14	48	17	19	2	4

Only three of 16 rows shown. Slope = 0.5; intercept = −5.

negative because the prediction is too small (the point lies beneath the line), but the square of a negative number is positive (see Note 18). The mean of the three square errors in Table 9.3 is 2.42. The overall MSE from all 16 people is 3.9. The fact that the MSE for Figure 9.4 is much less than for Figure 9.3 reflects the fact that the prediction line in Figure 9.4 is much more accurate.

Can we do better? Can we find a line with an even lower MSE? To see if this is possible, we can use the Excel Solver,[130] which will find the values of the slope and the intercept which lead to the lowest possible MSE. In this case, Solver tells us that the lowest possible MSE is 2.2, which is achieved by setting the slope to 0.45 and the intercept to −3.0. A value of 2.2 for the MSE is better than 3.9, although the graph (Figure 9.5) does look very similar.

The prediction line in Figure 9.5 is called a 'least squares' prediction line, or a 'best fit' line. It's also known as a 'regression line' for reasons that are less obvious.[131] What prediction does this regression line give for the cycle time for someone who takes 50 minutes in the 10 km run?

It's clear from Figure 9.5 that the answer is about 20 minutes. To get the exact prediction from the line, we need to add the intercept (−3.0) to the slope (0.45) multiplied by the run time:

Prediction = −3.0 + 0.45 × 50 = 19.5 minutes.

The intercept in Figure 9.5 is the cycle time for a person who can do the run in zero time. This comes to minus 3 minutes. Does this make sense?

This intercept does not much make sense as a prediction. The regression line only makes sensible predictions towards the right of Figure 9.5 as this is where the data is.

The slope determines the amount of extra time we need to add on to take account of the run time. The slope of 0.45 means that if you have two people whose run times differ by one minute, their cycle times are likely to differ by 0.45 minutes.

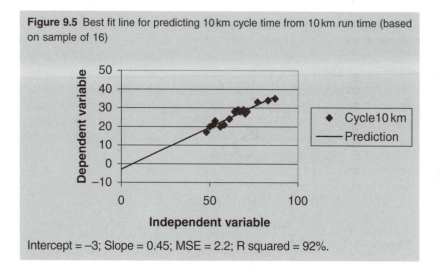

Figure 9.5 Best fit line for predicting 10 km cycle time from 10 km run time (based on sample of 16)

Intercept = −3; Slope = 0.45; MSE = 2.2; R squared = 92%.

We'll now turn to the original prediction problem: predicting earnings from the 10 km run time (Figure 9.1). Exactly the same method (using the spreadsheet `pred1var.xls`) leads to the prediction line in Figure 9.6. The slope here is negative (−1.4): the line goes downhill, indicating that people with bigger (slower) race times earn less. The value of the MSE for Figure 9.6 is a lot more, 1893. How useful do you think this prediction line is? What problems can you see?

There are lots of difficulties: this is a good illustration of many of the problems with regression, which we will look at later. Compared with Figure 9.5, the scatter in the diagram suggests that the prediction is likely to be very inaccurate. The ends of the line seem particularly unrealistic: it is unlikely that people with run times longer than 100 minutes will earn negative amounts, for example. Earnings are likely to depend on the other variables too (for example age), so a prediction which ignores these is unlikely to be very accurate. And the sample of 16 is unlikely to be sufficient to come up with reliable conclusions. We'll see how we can do better in Section 9.4.

We've seen how to use the Excel Solver to work out regression lines. It is also possible to work out the slope and intercept by means of mathematical formulae which are built into Excel and SPSS. They are the basis of the Excel functions forecast (which gives the predictions), slope and intercept.[132] There is also a Regression tool (see Section 9.5). You should find these functions give identical answers to the Solver method, and they are certainly easier to use. The main advantage of the Solver method is that it makes it clear what is going on. It is also more flexible: you can adjust the method to try rather different types of model (for example Exercise 9.9.4).

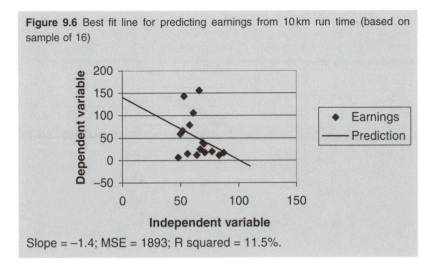

Figure 9.6 Best fit line for predicting earnings from 10 km run time (based on sample of 16)

Slope = −1.4; MSE = 1893; R squared = 11.5%.

▶ 9.3 Assessing the accuracy of prediction models

9.3.1 A measure of error reduction: R squared

The errors – the difference between the prediction line and the actual values – look a lot smaller in Figure 9.5 than in Figure 9.6. This suggests that a prediction based on Figure 9.5 is likely to be much more accurate than one based on Figure 9.6. The measure we used – MSE – seems to confirm this: the MSE is 2.2 for Figure 9.5 and 1893 for Figure 9.6. However, this comparison is not entirely fair. The values of the dependent variable in Figure 9.6 (earnings) are larger and more spread out than those in Figure 9.5 (10 km cycle time), so any errors are likely to be larger for this reason. There is a simple way round this. This is to think in terms of the *proportional reduction in mean square error* which the prediction produces. To do this, we need to start with the error before we have the prediction line. If you were faced with the task of predicting an individual's 10 km cycle time from the data in the cycle 10 km column of Table 9.1, *without* using any of the other variables to help you, what would your best guess be?

The obvious answer is the mean. (The median would be another possibility – see Section 3.4.2 – but I'll use the mean as this is the conventional approach.) The mean time for the cycle race comes to 26 minutes. What would the square error be if we were using this 26 minutes as our prediction for person 14 (Table 9.1)?

The actual time was 17 minutes, so the error is 9 minutes, and the square error is 81 minutes. This is a lot more than the 2 in Table 9.3, and the square error from the best fit line in Figure 9.5, which comes to 2.7. (Overall, of course, the best fit line is better than the model in Table 9.3, but it is not better for this particular point.) The mean square error from taking this prediction of 26 for all points is 27.6. This quantity is called the 'variance' of the cycle times and is one of the standard statistics built into software.[133] It is a measure of how spread out the cycle times are. The method of working it out is the same as for the standard deviation (Section 3.4.4) except that you don't take the square root in the last step. The variance is the square of the standard deviation.

So the MSE without the prediction line (the variance) is 27.6, but with the prediction line in Figure 9.5 this is reduced to 2.2. What is the proportional reduction in error?

The reduction in error is 25.4 (27.6 − 2.2) which is 25.4/27.6 or 92% of the original error. This prediction line reduces the MSE by 92%. It is likely to be a good prediction. How would expect Figure 9.6 to compare?

The variance of the earnings is 2139, and the MSE from the prediction line is 1893. The prediction obviously hasn't made much difference: the proportional reduction (R squared) is 0.115 or 11.5% {(2139 − 1893)/2139}.

The proportional reduction in mean square error from a regression line is also known as 'R squared'. This is because it turns out to be the square of the Pearson correlation coefficient (Section 3.10), and a standard symbol for this is r. This should seem reasonable because the closer the correlation coefficient is to zero, the lower R squared will be, the more scattered the scatter diagram (Section 3.7), and the less accurate any prediction line is likely to be.

Go back to the three scatter diagrams in Figure 3.7. For each of the three diagrams, what would the regression line look like, and what would R squared be?

For the first two diagrams (with a correlation of +1 and −1), the prediction line would follow the points exactly, and R squared would be +1 or 100%, indicating that the error has been reduced by 100%. The predictions are completely accurate. (Remember that the square of −1 is +1.) In the third case, the variable on the horizontal axis is obviously of no help in predicting the other variable. This means that the prediction line would be a horizontal line at the level of the mean of the dependent variable. As the correlation is zero, R squared will also be zero, which confirms that the prediction does not reduce the error at all. R squared gives a good indication of the likely value of a regression line. There are, however, snags; we'll come to some of the problems in later sections.

9.3.2 Confidence intervals
In the last section we saw how R squared can be used to measure how useful a regression line is. A slightly more direct question is to ask how big the

error is likely to be. The first approach to this is to use the MSE. We saw that this is a bit like the variance, and its square root is a bit like the standard deviation. The MSE for the prediction of earnings in Figure 9.6 is 1893, so the 'standard deviation' is 44 (thousand euros, of course). This is the standard deviation of the errors, often called the 'standard error' of the prediction. If the error distribution is normal (Section 5.6), we can use this to estimate a confidence interval for the error:[134] the 95% interval will extend from −2 sds to +2 sds, or −88 000 euros to +88 000 euros. For example, the prediction from Figure 9.6 for someone who can do the run in 90 minutes is that they will earn about 15 000 euros. The confidence interval derived from this is that we can be 95% sure that this runner will earn something between 103 000 euros and losing 73 000 euros (since 15 − 88 is negative). This is not an impressive prediction, but the pattern in Figure 9.6 should not encourage you to expect a good prediction.

What is the equivalent confidence interval for the error from Figure 9.5 (with an MSE of 2.2)?

The standard error comes to 1.5 so the 95% confidence interval extends from 3 minutes below the prediction line to 3 minutes above it. This is a much more acceptable error for a useful prediction.

There are a few difficulties with this method. It fails to take account of the fact that the regression line itself may be inaccurate because the sample is small. It depends on the errors being normally distributed (see Section 5.6). And it's based on an average error; it ignores the fact that the predictions are likely to be more accurate for some values than for others.

The next approach, bootstrapping, gives us a way of largely avoiding the first two problems (but not the third). I'll start with a slightly different question: how accurate is the estimate of the slope? The slope is an important piece of information in its own right. The slope of −1.4 means that running a minute quicker corresponds to, on average, an extra income of 1.4 thousand euros. But how accurate is the estimate of the slope based on such a small sample?

To find out, we can use the bootstrap method (Chapter 7). The method is just like the method we used to estimate the confidence interval for a correlation (Section 8.4), except that here we are analysing the slope. The principle is to resample from the sample of 16 with a view to seeing how much the slope estimated from samples of 16 will vary between samples. (You will probably need to read Chapter 7, and Section 8.4 to follow this fully.)

When I used `resample.xls` to work out the 95% confidence interval for the slope of Figure 9.6,[135] it came to −3.1 to +0.4. This indicates that the slope is very uncertain: there is a reasonable chance it may even be positive. This confidence interval is based on simulation with only 200 resamples; if you do it on your computer the answer may be slightly different. It is also possible to get confidence intervals for the slope from the regression procedures in Excel and SPSS (Section 9.5).

Making a prediction from the regression line in Figure 9.6 is a bit of a waste of time, so I'll return to Figure 9.5 to illustrate how we can find a confidence interval for the prediction error. (Again, this builds on Chapter 7.) We need to draw resamples of 17 from the data in Table 9.1. The first 16 are used to set up the regression model, and the 17th is used to make a prediction and then find the error, that is, the difference between the actual value and the prediction. When I used *resample.xls*,[136] the first resample of 17 led to an error of −1.5, the next to an error of +1.3 and so on. The 95% confidence interval extended from −2.8 to +2.5 (based on results from 200 resamples.) As expected, this is similar to the −3 to +3 minutes we got above. The resampled answer should be more realistic because it avoids making assumptions about the errors being normally distributed and it takes account of sampling error, the likelihood of differences between one sample and another.

▶ 9.4 Prediction models with several independent variables: multiple regression

The prediction line for earnings in Figure 9.6 is based on only one variable, the 10 km run time. We are likely to be able to get a better prediction using more than one variable. Earnings, for example, seem to increase with age, so age should help to improve the prediction. The regression model can easily be extended to include any number of independent variables. We could include all five independent variables in Table 9.1. There are, however, good reasons for not doing this, which I will explain in due course. The variables I'll use for the first model, to try to get a better prediction of earnings, are Sexn, Age and Run 10 km.

It's easy to draw a line on a graph to represent the prediction from one variable (for example Figures 9.5 and 9.6). This is not possible with more than one variable, so the prediction can't be represented by a line on a graph. The phrase 'prediction line' no longer makes sense. Instead, we can refer to a prediction, or regression, 'model': this is simply the rule for making the prediction. (The prediction lines in Figures 9.5 and 9.6 are also models.)

The first column in Table 9.1 gives sex coded as F or M. For the regression model, we obviously need to code this numerically: the convenient coding scheme is to use 0 for one sex and 1 for the other. This gives the variable Sexn, which is known as a 'dummy' variable (because it's not a genuine numerical variable). This trick can always be used for category variables which can take one of two values. (The situation where there are three or more values, for example the three courses in Table 3.1, is a little more complicated.[137])

The procedure is now, more or less, identical to before. The interpretation of the answer is, however, a little more complicated, so I'll adjust the variables to make the conclusions more user-friendly. (This adjustment is not essential: you will get the same answers without it, but they may be harder to visualise.)

The intercept in Figure 9.5 is the predicted 10 km cycle time for someone who takes zero time in the 10 km run. This makes little sense! We could have improved matters by giving the independent variable, the run time, another base, say 50 minutes. The new variable would then have been *time above 50 minutes*. The first person in Table 9.1 with a time of 61 minutes would score 11 minutes on this new variable, and the 14th, with a time of 48 minutes, would score −2 minutes. If we had done this, the predicted times, and the slope, would have been unchanged. (If you don't believe this, try it.) The intercept would obviously have been different (19.5 minutes), but the value now has a reasonable interpretation: the 10 km cycle time corresponding to a 50 minute run time.

I'll take 50 minutes as the 'base value' for the new run time variable. A similar difficulty will occur with the age: I'll take 20 years as the base here. (It doesn't matter what base you take from the point of view of the final predictions: they will always be the same.)

The 'base case' is now someone who scores zero on all three independent variables, that is, a male (Sexn = 0) aged 20 with a 10 km run time of 50 minutes. There may or may not be such a person in the sample, but such a person could exist. You should be able to imagine him. The equivalent of the intercept for a multiple regression is the predicted value for this base case: the 'base prediction'.

Table 9.4 shows how a three variable prediction model works. Each of the three independent variables has its own slope: I have (arbitrarily) chosen 3 for the three slopes and the base prediction. Table 9.4 is based on `predmvar.xls`. I'll take the first row as an example. There are four components to the model. The first is the base prediction, that is, the prediction for our base case. We've arbitrarily set this to 3. The next component is due to sex. The first person is female, which means she is predicted an extra 3 units of income. We get this by multiplying the slope (3) by the value in the Sexn column (1). For a male, this component would be zero because males are coded as 0. Next we come to the age component. She is 42, so her age over 20 is 22 years, and the component due to age is 3×22 or 66, because we have assumed a slope of 3: income rises by 3 for each extra year of age. Similarly, the final component from her 10 km run time comes to 33 (3×11). And adding up all four components gives a final prediction of 105. This is very close to her actual earnings of 106, but this is just luck!

Notice that the underlying assumption is that we can start off from a prediction for the base case, and then add on separate components for each

Table 9.4 Calculation of three variable prediction model (three slopes and base prediction equal to 3)

						Prediction model			
		Data					*Additional component for:*		
Ref	*Sexn*	*Age 20+*	*Run 50+*	*Earnings*	*Base prediction*	*Sexn*	*Age 20+*	*Run 50+*	*Prediction*
1	1	22	11	106	3	3	66	33	105
8	1	31	16	156	3	3	93	48	147
14	0	4	-2	6	3	0	12	-6	9

Only three of 16 rows shown. Age 20+ means age over 20; Run 50+ means run time over 50 minutes. Overall MSE is 8981.

independent variable. Furthermore, we're assuming that each component can be derived by multiplying some number, the slope, by the value of the variable. Do you think this is realistic?

Probably not, but the question is whether it's good enough to be useful. We'll return to this question in Section 9.6. What is the mean square error of this model for the three cases in Table 9.4?

The square errors are 1, 81 and 9 with a mean of 30.3. However, these three cases fit the model much better than the rest: the overall MSE is 8981. The variance of the earnings is only 2139, so this model has managed to *increase* the error. Not surprisingly – in view of the fact that we set everything to 3 quite arbitrarily – this is a very bad model. To get it to fit better, we must use the Solver to find the three slopes and the base prediction which lead to the lowest possible MSE. The result of doing this is in Table 9.5. Whatever values of the three slopes and the base prediction you try, you will not manage to make the MSE lower than the value in Table 9.5 (677).

Note that the MSE (677) is now a lot less than it was for the model we started with (8981). It's also less than it was for the best fit model for predicting earnings from the run only (1893). The prediction fits better, as we expected. This is reflected in a bigger R squared (0.68 compared with 0.115 for the earlier model), which can be calculated in exactly the same way. We can use this model to make some predictions. What earnings would you predict for a 60-year-old female who can do the run in 52 minutes?

The prediction from the model is $13.9 + 33.2 + 4.0 \times 40 + (-4.3) \times 2 = 198$. What difference would it make if her run time was 48 minutes?

The only difference is that her time is now below the base of 50 minutes,

Table 9.5 Three variable regression model for earnings based on subsample of 16

Base prediction (all independents = 0)	13.9
Slope – sexn	33.2
Slope – age over 20	4.0
Slope – run time over 50 minutes	–4.3
MSE (mean square error)	677
RMSE (square root of MSE)	26
R squared	0.68
Number of cases (people)	16

so she scores –2 minutes, the component from the run becomes positive,[138] and the prediction becomes 215.

Which of the three independent variables – sex, age and run time – do you think has the biggest influence on earnings?

You might have said sex, on the grounds that this has the biggest slope in Table 9.5. Or you might think age because this has the biggest component (4.0 × 40 = 160) in the prediction above. Or you might think run time on the grounds that if she was a more typical 60-year-old who took, say, 90 minutes for the run, her run component would be –4.3 × 40, or –172. This would make the run component the biggest of the three. The point here is that the question is difficult to answer, because it depends on what you mean. Be careful and don't jump to unwarranted conclusions.

As well as using the model to make predictions, you can also use the slopes as an indicator of the way things work. Are the slopes in Table 9.5 what you would expect?

The age slope (4.0) indicates that, on average, the older inhabitants of the island earn more, at a rate of 4000 euros per year older. The negative slope for the run time indicates that the larger (slower) the race time, the less people earn, with one minute slower corresponding to a decrease of earnings of 4300 euros. This is in line with the original survey (see Section 9.1). The slope for sexn indicates females are likely to earn 33 200 euros more than similar males. Notice that this gives a slightly different picture from the single variable analyses in Section 9.2. The males in Table 9.1 earn slightly more, on average, than the females, so the slope we would expect for sexn is negative. Similarly, the negative slope for the run time is not so pronounced (–1.4 instead of –4.3). Why the differences?

The multiple regression slope for the run time (–4.3) takes account of the other variables. For example, there is a tendency for the fast runners to be younger and male. Being faster seems (on this island) to be associated with

Table 9.6 Five variable regression model for earnings based on subsample of 16

Slope – sexn	14.2
Slope – age	3.8
Slope – height	−1.4
Slope – run time	−8.3
Slope – cycle time	8.9
MSE	518
R square	0.76

Note that the slope for age is the same as the slope for age over 20; similarly for run time and run time over 50.

higher earnings, but being younger and being male are associated with lower earnings. The multiple regression tries to separate these influences. The single variable regression obviously can't do this.

So why not put all five variables in? If we do this, the results are Table 9.6. I have used the unadjusted variables for this regression: this make no difference to the slopes. The main oddity here is the slope for the cycle time (+8.9). This seems to indicate a strong tendency for the slower cyclists to earn more. As the fast cyclists tend to be the same people as the fast runners (Figure 9.2), this seems very odd indeed.

It is this strong correlation that is responsible for the problem. The run time and the cycle time both provide very similar information, so the regression can pick up this information from one, the other or some combination of both, depending on small quirks of the data. The model is unstable; the slopes may be quite different with another, very similar, sample. This is an important principle: it is important not to include strongly correlated independent variables in a multiple regression.

The other point to watch is that adding another variable is *always* likely to reduce the error (MSE) and increase the R squared (which has improved from 0.68 for the three variable model to 0.76). R squared can never go down if you add another variable, because Solver could always find the previous solution by setting the new slope to zero. This means that any variable, even one with no relation at all with the dependent variable, may appear to help. It is important to remember the context, and only add variables if it is reasonable to expect them to add some useful information.

It is a good idea to look at the confidence intervals for the slopes to see what the likely error is (see Section 9.3.2). The bootstrap method for deriving confidence intervals for multiple regression requires more sophisticated software than `resample.xls`,[139] so you need to use the Regression tool in

Excel or SPSS, as explained in the next section. The confidence intervals for the slopes in the models we have just set up (using the Excel Regression tool) are very instructive. For the three variable model, the 95% confidence interval for the sexn slope is −5 to 72. In other words, it could well be negative. On the other hand, the interval for the run time is −6.3 to −2.3. This is quite a wide interval, but it's all negative. We can be reasonably sure that the 'true' relationship is a negative one. This is not the case with the single variable regression: the confidence interval here was from −3.1 to 0.4. Turning to the five variable model, the confidence interval for the run slope is now much wider (−14.0 to −2.7) and that for the cycle time is even wider (−2.9 to 20.5). This confirms what we said above about the five variable model being unreliable.

▶ 9.5 Using the regression procedures in Excel and SPSS

You will find that SPSS uses a lot of jargon, and some of it does not correspond to the terms used in Excel. Table 9.7 summarises the important concepts, and gives some of the alternative names used for them. In Excel, use Tools – Data analysis – Regression for a full set of statistics and various scatter plots; these are useful for checking for any patterns that may indicate problems with the model (see Section 9.6). In SPSS use Analyze – Regression – Linear. You will need to click on Statistics then Confidence intervals if you want confidence intervals and Plots if you want plots.

As well as slopes, intercepts and confidence intervals, Excel and SPSS will give you p values (otherwise known as 'significance' or 'sig' levels); one for each of the slopes, one for the intercept and an overall one for the whole model. These are explained, in general terms, in Chapter 8.[140] The p value for the whole model is based on the null hypothesis that there is no relationship between the independent variables and the dependent. The p values for the slopes and the intercept give you some, but not all, of the information provided by the confidence intervals (Section 9.3.2). I would suggest focusing on the confidence intervals.

For a single independent variable, you can also use the Excel functions, forecast, slope and intercept (see Section 9.2), and if you right click on the points of a scatter diagram, you will be invited to add a trendline to the graph. The linear one is the regression line explained in Section 9.2; there are also some other options.

Table 9.7 Regression terminology

Concept	Alternative names
Regression model	Prediction model Least squares model Best fit model
Independent variable A variable used to help predict values of the dependent variable	Xs or X values Predictor variable Explanatory variable
Dependent variable The variable whose values are predicted or explained	Ys or Y values Predicted variable Explained variable Response variable
Error The difference between the actual value of the dependent variable and the value predicted by the model	Residual
Mean square error (MSE) The mean (average) of the squares of the errors for the predictions for the data on which the model is based	

R squared
The proportional reduction in MSE provided by the model.
    For a single independent variable, R squared is equal to
    the square of the (Pearson) correlation coefficient. R
    squared = 1 suggests a perfect prediction; R squared =
    0 suggests a useless one
	Proportion of
	    variance explained
	    by the model

Slope
Each independent variable has a slope indicating its
    impact on the prediction of the dependent variable. The
    predictions from two values of the independent variable
    separated by one unit will differ by the value of the slope
	X coefficient
	Regression
	    coefficient
	β (beta)*
	b

Intercept The predicted value if all independent variables are zero	Constant Base prediction

* Although some books reserve this term for the 'standardised' coefficients, see, for example, Lewis-Beck (1993: 56).

▶ 9.6 Things to check for with regression

If you've got some data comprising a few cases, and at least two variables, you will have no difficulty in building a regression model. But it may not make much sense. Always ask yourself the following questions.

Is the underlying model reasonable?
There are three checks you can do here. First you can have a look at the graphs. Figure 9.5 suggests that a straight line prediction is reasonable. Figure 9.6 suggests that it isn't. It's more difficult to do this with multiple regression, but both Excel and SPSS will produce graphs (plots) which give you some idea of any major discrepancies.

The second check is R squared. This, remember, tells you the extent to which the model has managed to reduce the error in making a prediction (MSE), so low values indicate that the model is not very useful. The value of 11.5% for Figure 9.6 indicates this model is much less useful than Figure 9.5, with its R squared of 92%. R squared depends on the number of variables and the number of cases, so be careful about using it to compare models with different numbers of variables or cases.

The third check is to see if the model makes sense in terms of your under-standing of the situation. Look back at the model in Table 9.5. This implies that being female is worth an extra 33.2 thousand euros. The figure is the same regardless of age and run time. Similarly, the run time slope of −4.3 seems to imply that cutting one minute off your run time leads to an extra 4.3 thousand euros (on average). This is assumed to be the same for fast runners and slow runners, for males and females and for the young and the old. This can really only be a guess. You can use R squared as a crude measure of how good a guess it is.

What about sampling error? Is the sample large enough for the model to be reliable?
Check the confidence intervals for the slopes and the standard error of the prediction (Section 9.3.2). These should reveal how accurate estimates are likely to be. If you are using the Excel Regression tool or SPSS, strictly, the method for estimating these depends on the assumption that the errors should not show any strong relationship with any of the variables. You can check this using the plots provided by the package. If everything looks random, you should be OK. Any obvious pattern and the answers may be misleading.

Should you leave any variables out? Or include any extra ones?
The main thing to check is that there are no very high correlations (that is, approaching +1 or −1) among the independent variables (see Section 9.4). If there are, you should leave out one of the correlated variables. This is the reason for excluding the cycle time (strongly correlated with run time) and height (strongly correlated with sex) from the first model for earnings (Table 9.5).

You then need to come to a judgement about whether extra variables contribute enough to be worth putting into the model. Remember that the model will always squeeze something out, even if there's nothing useful there. SPSS has some built-in procedures for making this decision, search for Help on Stepwise.

▶ **9.7 Cause, effect, prediction and explanation**

Let's return to the story of the Isle of Fastmoney. Over the years, the knowledge of the relationship between earnings and 10 km run time has had an impact on the life of the island. Ambitious people, keen to earn a lot, typically take their running seriously and train extensively. And employers have taken to using the relationship as a guide to recruitment: they are keen to employ fast runners and are willing to pay them more. In fact, they have largely ceased to take any notice of academic qualifications. Potential students have responded to this by staying away from the college and enroling at the gym. The economic performance of the island does not seem to have suffered, but the college is nearly bankrupt!

In Section 3.9 we saw the difficulties of using data from surveys to come to conclusions about causal relationships. The Isle of Fastmoney illustrates these difficulties well. There are many plausible hypothesis about causal relationships here:

- *Hypothesis 1*: People who can run faster can move around faster, work faster and get more done, so are likely to earn more.
- *Hypothesis 2*: A high salary means people have more money to spend and can afford a better diet or the right drugs, and employ the best training methods, so are likely to do better in the race.
- *Hypothesis 3*: There is a psychological quality of single-mindedness which can be applied both to work and running. Some people have it; others don't. Those who have it both run faster and earn more.
- *Hypothesis 4*: Employers *believe* that fast runners are more productive and so are prepared to pay them more.

All these hypotheses are consistent with the data. We've no way of knowing how much truth there is in each of them, which is a pity, because the four hypotheses have very different implications. For example, suppose Hypothesis 4 is true and the other three hypotheses are false. What would you do if you were an employer on the island?

It would be tempting to seek employees with poor run times in order to avoid paying exorbitant salaries for fast runners who are not likely to be any more productive.

If, on the other hand, there is some truth in Hypothesis 1, this would not be a good idea because slow runners are likely to work more slowly. But if Hypothesis 1 is false and Hypothesis 3 is true, it might still be worth employing fast runners because running fast is an indicator of determination. This is despite the fact that running fast is of no direct benefit.

The situation is even more confusing than this discussion suggests if we think there may be *some* truth in *all* the hypotheses: a fuzzy approach to truth (Section 4.6) seems more helpful than the crude assumption that each hypothesis must be true or false.

What regression allows us to do here is to *control*, or make allowances or adjust, for any variables we know about. The model in Table 9.5 tells us the relationship between earnings and 10 km run time if we make allowances for age and sex. Whatever age and sex we consider, the model predicts that a difference in run time of 1 minute will correspond to a difference in earnings of 4.3 thousand euros, with the negative sign indicating that the two differences go in opposite directions. This is just a model. We haven't got the data to make the comparison for real, so the regression enables us to compare hypothetical scenarios. Don't forget that regression models are based on assumptions which are seldom fully realistic (Section 9.6). They are guesses. Treat them with caution.

Could we use regression to test the truth of the four hypotheses above**?**

If we had data on some of the variables mentioned – diet, single-mindedness and so on – we may be able to derive some regression coefficients (slopes) to come to some tentative conclusions about the truth of each hypothesis, in a fuzzy sort of way. However, we would need to be careful. Observing a relationship between two variables can *never* prove conclusively that one causes the other (Section 3.9). To demonstrate this possibility, we would need to do an *experiment* (Section 10.1.3 and Exercise 10.5.2).

In this chapter I've described regression models as methods for making predictions. This is convenient for explaining how they work. In practice, however, we are often more interested in the understanding that the models give us, than in making predictions. On the Isle of Fastmoney, the predictions of earnings are useful because of the insights they give into how to make money. Similarly, a model of the relationship between smoking and lung cancer is more likely to be used to understand what causes lung cancer, than to predict who is going to die and when. This is recognised in some of the alternative regression terminology (Table 9.7). The independent variables are also called 'explanatory' variables because they help to explain the variations in the dependent variable. The errors are called 'residuals' because they are the bit left over which you can't explain. And R squared can be described as the proportion of the variation in the dependent variable which is *explained* by the regression model.

▶ 9.8 Similar concepts

Models like Table 9.5 are normally written in symbols:

$$y = 13.9 + 33.2x_1 + 4.0x_2 - 4.3x_3$$

where x_1 is sexn, x_2 is age over 20, x_3 is run time over 50 minutes and y is predicted earnings. The general form is:

$$y = a + b_1x_1 + b_2x_2 + b_3x_3$$

The SPSS procedure General linear model (Analyze – General linear model – Univariate) combines the idea of regression with that of 'analysis of variance' (see Section 8.8). Independent category variables are called 'factors', and number variables are referred to as 'covariates'. Sex would be a factor in explaining income on the Isle of Fastmoney and age would be a covariate. The 'effect' of the factor sex is 33 (Table 9.5): this is another way of describing the slope of a dummy variable. If you click on Options – Display means, SPSS will produce means of female and male earnings 'adjusted' to particular values of the covariates. This provides essentially the same information as the slope for sexn in Table 9.5.

This procedure also allows you to analyse 'interactions' between the effects of the independent variables. For example, the effect of sex (on earnings) may be different for different age groups. If this is so, the model in Table 9.5, which assumes that you can measure the slope for each independent variable irrespective of the values of the other variables, may be unrealistically simple. You will need to refer to the SPSS manuals to see how SPSS deals with interactions.

The single variable regression model in Section 9.2 is called a 'linear' model, because the prediction line is straight (not because it's a line, as you might expect). The multiple regression model in Section 9.4 is of a similar form and is also described as linear. It is possible to use exactly the same least squares argument to build other, non-linear models. If you right click on the points of an Excel scatter diagram, you will be invited to add a trendline: there are several non-linear possibilities on offer.

A recent alternative to multiple regression is an 'artificial neural network' (ANN). These are designed to mimic the way natural neurons in the brain recognise patterns. They provide a way of making predictions without assuming any sort of linear model.

▶ **9.9 Exercises**

9.9.1 Predicting earnings with the full sample of 100

In Section 9.2 we saw how to predict 10 km cycle times and earnings from the 10 km run time, and in Section 9.4 we saw how to set up a model to predict earnings from three of the variables (Table 9.5). These are all based on a subsample of 16. Obviously more accurate results would be possible if we used the whole sample of 100 in *iofm.xls*.

(a) Use *pred1var.xls* and *iofm.xls* to set up a model for predicting cycle time from run time. Check you understand how the spreadsheet works. How closely do the results agree with those in Section 9.2? How fast do you think you could run 10 km? Use your estimate to work out a predicted cycle time.

(b) Do the same thing for the prediction of the earnings from run time. Use the model to predict your earnings if you lived on the island. How much extra would your predicted earnings be if you could run 5 minutes faster? You should find R squared is less than in (a). What does this indicate?

(c) Use *predmvar.xls* to do the same for the prediction of earnings from sexn, age, and run time. Use the model to predict your earnings if you lived on the island. How much extra would your predicted earnings be if you could run 5 minutes faster?

(d) Finally, use the Excel Regression tool, or *resample.xls*, to work out confidence intervals for the slopes you found in (a), (b) and (c). Any comments?

9.9.2 Understanding drinking habits

Suppose you wanted to explain the amount students drink in terms of the other data in *drink.xls*. What's the best model for doing this and how good is it? Which are the most useful predictor variables?

9.9.3 Predicting returns on the stock market from what's happened in the past

A considerable amount of research has been done to see if it is possible to predict returns on the stock market from past data (see Exercise 3.11.5 for an explanation of what is meant by 'returns'). One such study[141] produced a regression model to predict the return which investors would receive from investing in a particular company's shares for a period of four years, from the return they would have received if they had invested in the same shares over the previous four years. The data on which the model was based were the returns for a sample of large companies over consecutive periods of four years. The regression coefficient cited was −0.112, and the value of R squared was 0.0413. What do these results mean? What implications do they have for investors? What else would you like to know?

9.9.4 Why square the errors?

You may have wondered why we square the errors and work out the mean square error in Section 9.2. Wouldn't it be easier to ignore any negative signs and just take the mean of the errors? This would be the mean absolute error (MAE). The snag with doing this is that you may end up with lots of different 'best fit' models, some of which may be intuitively unreasonable. To see the problem, try using both methods with this data:

Values of independent variable: 0, 0, 1, 1
Values of dependent variable: 1, 5, 3, 7

It is quite easy to do this without a computer: just draw a scatter diagram, sketch some possible best fit lines, and work out MSE and MAE (try a line with intercept 3 and slope 2, and another with intercept 1 and slope 6). Alternatively use *pred1var.xls*.[142]

9.9.5 What's the relationship between the model for predicting B from A, and the model for predicting A from B?

You should be able to see the answer by experimenting with different patterns of data. I would start with the data in Section 9.9.4 above, then try the patterns in Figure 3.7. The worksheet *reg2way.xls* may help.

▶ 9.10 Summary of main points

Suppose you have some data consisting of at least two number variables, for each of a number of cases. You can use this data to build a regression model for predicting values of one of the variables (the dependent variable) from values of one or more of the others (the independent variables). You can then use your model to make predictions (often very rough ones) for new cases and help you understand how the dependent variable depends on the independent variables(s). Take care of regression models: many of them are less sensible, accurate or reliable than they may look.

10 How to do it and What Does it Mean? The Design and Interpretation of Investigations

To use statistics you need to get some data. This final chapter looks at some of the different ways of acquiring data about the world – surveys, experiments and so on – and at a few of the practicalities of designing investigations and analysing data. We finish with some tentative suggestions for the situation in which, despite this book, you're stuck: you aren't sure which method to use, or you don't understand the results of an unfamiliar technique.

▶ 10.1 The logic of empirical research: surveys, experiments and so on

Your underlying motive for studying statistics is likely to be that you want to find out about, or make better sense of, the world. You might want a better understanding of how the world works, or you might want a prediction about a specific situation, perhaps to back up a decision to do one thing rather than another. To do any of this, you will need some empirical data. Then you can analyse this in the various ways we've met in earlier chapters: by means of graphical or numerical summaries (Chapter 3), by means of probability models (Chapter 5) or regression models (Chapter 9), or by using the information to derive confidence intervals (Chapter 7), test hypotheses (Chapter 8) or assess the probability of these hypotheses being valid (Section 6.4). But you need to start by getting the data.

How can we get information about the world? There are lots of possibilities and lots of different ways of categorising these possibilities. For my purposes here, I'll distinguish the following three categories.

10.1.1 Common sense and subjective judgements

This is rarely mentioned in lists like this, but it is important. How do you know that the probability of heads is 50%, that all 49 balls are equally likely to be drawn in the lottery, that telepathy is not possible or that a clock on an aeroplane keeps the same time as a clock on the ground? In most cases your answer would probably be along the lines of 'it's obvious that . . .'. We all have a vast store of things we take for granted. We don't bother to research these things; we just take them for granted – life is too short to check every-thing. However, it is sensible to be cautious. Some of these assumptions occasionally turn out to be wrong. The coin may be biased or the lottery may be fixed. Telepathy may be possible. And Einstein's theory of special relativ-ity avoids the common-sense assumption that clocks on aeroplanes keep the same time as clocks on the ground. Sometimes, it is worth questioning and checking these common-sense assumptions. But in general we just accept them.

As the above examples show, some probability estimates depend on this sort of assumption. The business of statistics, however, is more concerned with situations where we have no obvious answer: we need to collect some data and find out. We need to undertake some empirical research.

10.1.2 Non-interventionist research: surveys and case studies

A survey is simply the process of collecting data about a group of people, organisations, countries, events or whatever the units of analysis are. The data is normally collected from a sample, but the purpose would typically be to find out about a target population, or some other context which goes beyond the sample from which the data was obtained (Sections 2.5 and 3.2). The aim is to collect information without intervening in any way, which may be more difficult than it sounds. You need to bear in mind that the very act of asking people may put ideas their head and alter what they do or what they think. The results may not be as pure as you think.

With any empirical study, there is a trade-off between the size of the sample and the depth in which each case is studied. One issue is how large the sample needs to be for statistical purposes (Section 7.4). You may, however, have decided to research a particular case, or a small number of cases, for the reasons discussed in Section 4.5. There is a continuum from the large-scale study to the detailed study of an individual case.

Regardless of where the research lies on this continuum, it is important to bear in mind the difficulties of using survey data to disentangle cause and effect relationships. A few years ago I did some research which found a negative correlation (Section 3.7.3) between the time students took to do a maths test and their score in the test. Those who took a shorter time tended to get higher scores. Can we jump from this result to the conclusion that it is the quickness of doing the test which is responsible for the higher scores, and so failing students should be encouraged to work more quickly?

No, of course not. The students who are more skilled will both score more highly and work more quickly, because they are more skilled. The com-parison between those who took a long time to do the test and those who took a short time is not 'fair' because there are likely to be many more good students on the 'short time' side of the comparison.

A similar problem would arise with a study of the relation between spending on health and life expectancy in different countries. The countries spending more on health are likely to be the richer countries, whose citizens live in better conditions and have more to eat, and it may be these factors, not the spending on health, which are responsible for differences in life expectancy (see also Section 3.9).

One response to this difficulty is to try to adjust the results to take account of these extra variables. In Sections 9.4 and 9.7 we saw how multiple regression can be used to separate the effects of several variables, and answer questions about what would happen to one variable if a second is changed while the others remain unchanged. This approach, however, has two problems. First, it can only be used to 'control' for variables on which you have data (Section 9.7). And second, the adjustment depends on a crude model, which is unlikely to be fully realistic (see Section 9.4). A far more powerful way to disentangle cause and effect is to do an experiment.

10.1.3 Interventionist research: experiments and quasi-experiments

The essential feature of this kind of research is that you intervene in the situation and see what happens. There are two main reasons for doing this: to disentangle cause and effect, and to investigate things which would not happen without the experimenter's intervention. Let's look at some examples.

Experiment 1

Suppose you want to find out what happens when the metal sodium is put in water. You could do an experiment: try it and see what happens. You would find it reacts violently with the water to form sodium hydroxide. It would not be possible to find the answer by means of a survey of what happens naturally. Sodium does not occur naturally in its pure metallic form[143] because it is so reactive, so however diligent your search, you would never observe this reaction. As it doesn't happen naturally, you need a contrived experiment to see it happening. Also the result of the experiment is always the same, so you don't need a statistical analysis.

This is a chemistry experiment. Experiments in social sciences generally suffer from the problem that social situations are less easily predicted.

Experiment 2

As part of a research project on problem solving in arithmetic,[144] I wanted to test the hunch that many children were unsuccessful in solving problems because they ploughed in without thinking about what they were doing.

Accordingly, I got a group of children to do a selection of problems under normal (N) conditions without any specific instructions, and then some more problems with the instructions to plan in advance (P), that is, to say how they were going to do the problems before writing anything down or doing any calculations. I wanted to assess the effect of this intervention. The results showed that in a sample of 32 children, 2 were more successful under the N condition, 9 were more successful under the P condition and there was no difference for the other 21 children. (This depends on a clear definition of successful, which need not concern us here.) This experiment obviously has a statistical dimension.

The results seem to indicate that the P condition was more successful than the N condition. Can you see any problems with this conclusion?

There are two difficulties I want to focus on here, although you may well have other concerns. First, the difference may be due to chance. The sample does seem small. Another sample and the luck of the draw may give the advantage to the N condition. The *p* value cited (which takes account of the small sample size) was 3%, which indicates that this chance explanation is not very plausible (see Chapter 8 and Exercise 10.5.1). The second problem is that the P condition always followed the N condition. (It was not practicable to reverse the order.) This raises the possibility that the children improved with practice, or as they became used to the experimental setup, in which case the improvement had nothing to do with asking children to plan in advance. This is obviously a serious difficulty with this experiment.

Experiment 3
To get round this problem, and to get some more convincing evidence for the effectiveness of the P procedure, I organised a further experiment. This was on a much larger scale: it involved two classes of children from each of five different schools. In each school, I put all the children from both classes together in a list, and then divided them into a P group and an N group, at random (see Section 2.5). One of the two teachers was asked to teach the P class, and the other the N class, again, at random. All the pupils were then given a 'pre-test' to measure their initial problem-solving ability. The P groups were then taught by the P method, and the N groups by the N method. After two teaching sessions, all the children did a second test, the 'post-test'.

Teachers teaching the P method were asked to teach their pupils to plan their method in advance: they were given specific instructions about how to do this. This was the 'experimental' group. The N method teachers were simply asked to teach problem solving as they saw fit. The 'treatment'[145] I was interested in evaluating was the P method, and I wanted to show that it was better than all the other possible treatments. This meant that the 'comparison' group (often called the 'control' group) should be taught by the best alternative method. In practice, I did not know what this was, so I told the teachers to teach by whatever method they thought appropriate, but without discussing it with the P teachers.

What do you think of the design of this experiment? In what ways is it better than Experiment 2? What do you think the flaws are?

As with Experiment 2, this raises too many issues to give a complete discussion here. I will just focus on a few points, but you may well have thought of others. This experiment is not open to the same objection as Experiment 2. Each group had the same opportunities to practise and get used to the experiment. This is a much fairer comparison.

One of the key features of this experiment is the fact that the children, and the teachers, were assigned to the P or N groups *at random*. Obviously, there are many differences between individual children, and between individual teachers, but allocating them to the two groups at random is a way of ensuring that the N and P groups are broadly similar, provided that the sample sizes are large enough. 'Random assignment' is a way of controlling for a multitude of unknown factors – sometimes called 'noise' variables – and ensuring that the comparison is fair. The results would be much more convincing than for Experiment 2. Experiments like this are the only rigorous way of getting convincing evidence about causal relationships which are obscured by noise variables.

However, the results of this experiment were not as I had hoped. The mean post-test score for the P group was slightly *lower* than for the N group, after adjusting for the pre-test scores, the influence of sex and differences between the schools.[146] The *p* value was 7.5%, not below the formal limit of 5%, but low enough to suggest that the N group might have had a real advantage. The conclusion was that my hypothesis about the superiority of the P group was wrong.

Experiment 4
A vegetarian diet is often said to be healthier than a non-vegetarian diet. This is based on comparing health statistics for vegetarians and non-vegetarians. The difficulty with this, of course, is that there are likely to be other differences between vegetarians and non-vegetarians besides their diet: perhaps other aspects of their lifestyle, affluence, types of job and so on. It is almost impossible to take account of all these variables, so the obvious approach would be an experiment: get a sample of (say) 1000 people, randomly assign half to a vegetarian group, and the rest to a non-vegetarian group, and monitor the health of the two groups. This should show whether vegetarianism has got health advantages, because the randomisation means that the two groups should be roughly balanced on all variables. Is this experiment practicable?

No. It is impossible to manipulate people in this way and, if it was possible, it would not be ethical. If the intervention required was less ambitious, say trying out a particular dietary supplement, then the experiment may be possible. There are many questions in medicine, education and business, which could be answered by experiments involving interventions that are impossible or unethical. All we can do is use techniques like multiple regression to make allowances for variables which may interfere with the comparison (Sections 9.4 and 9.7).

We've looked at four very different experiments. The first three are investigating things which would happen rarely, if at all, without the experimenter's intervention. Experiment 4 is to investigate a common occurrence (vegetarianism) to determine its effect on health. Experiment 1 does not need statistics; the last three obviously do. The statistical methods in Chapters 6, 7, 8 and 9 can be used to analyse the results of experiments like the last three.

It is often possible to answer a number of subsidiary questions, for example in Experiment 3 we might want to know whether the results for boys were different from the results for girls. One issue would be to look at the *effect* of the sex variable on success in solving problems (do girls do better than boys or vice versa?), another would be to see if there is an *interaction* (Section 9.8) between the treatment used (N or P) and sex (perhaps boys do better with the P treatment, girls with the N?) – see Chapter 9 (especially Section 9.8) for the statistical methods for this sort of problem.

Experiment 2, a comparison of what happened before and after an intervention, would not be considered a 'proper' experiment by many social scientists. It's only a 'quasi-experiment', because it does not use randomisation to control for noise variables. Such before and after comparisons are often the best we can do in situations, like Experiment 4, where a proper experiment is not possible. We might, for example, monitor the health of people who have changed from being carnivorous to being vegetarian or vice versa.

▶ 10.2 The practicalities of doing empirical research

Some brief comments on the practical side of carrying out surveys and experiments are in order here. The first point is also relevant to assessing the credibility of someone else's research, as the sampling strategy is a serious flaw in many studies.

10.2.1 Think long and hard about how you select any samples
The first step in this thinking should always be to clarify the target population, or the wider context you want to research. This is usually easy, but not

always. Take, for example, research to find the relationship between spending on health and life expectancy. Suppose you've got the current data from *all* (or almost all) the countries in the world. What is the target population or the wider context of interest here**?**

At first sight, as you've got data from all the countries, there isn't a sampling problem here. You've got the whole population, so that's it. However, the underlying motivation behind the research is likely to be to see whether increasing spending on health, in any or all the countries, is likely to lead to enhanced life expectancy. In other words, the aim is to research a hypothetical possibility which goes beyond the sample studied. The population metaphor fits uneasily here (what is the population – possible countries?), but if you end up with anything like a confidence interval (Chapter 7), you are presupposing some sort of wider context.

Having sorted out the context to which you want your results to apply, you then need to check that your sample is likely to be representative. The best approach is usually to take a random sample but, as we saw in Section 2.5, there are often problems. The sample may, for example, despite your best efforts, end up biased in the direction of people who are available and willing to answer your questions. And the response rates for many surveys – the proportion of the sample who respond – are often very low. Thirty per cent would be good; less than 10% is common. You can then try bribery (entry into a free draw with a prize) or nagging, but you are unlikely to be fully successful. The question then is whether you can assume that those who don't respond are similar to those who do. The honest answer to this is often 'no', but this is often barely mentioned in many research reports.

Sometimes the sample is a convenience sample: chosen because it is convenient and available, not because it's representative of anything in any systematic sense (the data in Table 3.1 comes from such a sample). Again, you need to think hard about possible biases. Our sample of countries above is, in effect, a convenience sample. We take the countries that exist, as a sample of all the hypothetical countries which might exist. Is it a satisfactory sample? I haven't a clue! But it's all we've got to work with.

10.2.2 Do a pilot study of the data collection, and the analysis, to iron out any difficulties

If you are planning a survey of a thousand people, try it out with, say, six people: get the data, *and analyse it*, then ask your six people for their comments. You should find out whether they can understand the questionnaire, whether you've done anything silly, whether you've got all the information you need, and whether you're collecting anything you don't need. You may be able to use the pilot analysis to assess how large a sample you are likely to want (see Section 7.4).

10.2.3 Coding the data, missing data, outliers and exploring the data

Once you've got the data, you need to key it into your computer. There are some notes on this in Appendix B.1, and two examples of data files on the web, *drink.xls* and *accquest.xls*.

You will need to decide on a coding scheme for each variable, that is, what should be keyed in for each possible answer. The main criterion is convenience: use a coding scheme that sticks in the memory. If you are coding countries, use E for England, F for France, rather than A and B. If you are intending to do any numerical analysis, then it obviously helps to use a numerical code. And if any data is missing, leave the cell blank. It's also a good idea to choose numbers that have a natural interpretation. If you have a five-point scale where one end indicates 'never' and the other 'often', then coding 'never' as 0 and 'often' as 4 means that your results will be far easier to interpret than if you had used (say) 5 for 'never'.

The best coding for yes/no questions is 1 for 'yes' and 0 for 'no'. Similarly, any other category variable which can take one of two values should be coded 1 for one value and 0 for the other. Then the average (mean) represents the proportion of one value, and the variable is coded as a dummy variable in case you should want to bring it into a multiple regression analysis (see Section 9.4 and the variable Sexn in Table 9.1).

If you have a question which asks people to tick all the boxes which apply, you should have one variable (column in your spreadsheet) for each box, and use 1 for a tick (yes). You will need to think about whether unticked boxes represent 'no', in which case they should be coded by 0, or 'no comment', in which case they should be coded by a blank.

Don't forget to check through your data to check for outliers, points outside the pattern of the rest of the data (see Section 3.4.1 for an example). If you find such cases, you then have to decide whether they are credible, or whether they should be removed. You should start the analysis by *exploring* the data, checking it see if it shows the patterns you expected and whether any interesting features catch your eye. SPSS has a procedure specifically for this purpose.[147]

▶ 10.3 Interpreting statistical results and solving problems

In Section 1.6.1 we looked at the different ways in which statistics can be understood. I hope I convinced you of the importance of understanding as much as possible of how a method works, what the answer means and the assumptions on which it rests. Be particularly careful about *p* values, or significance levels (Chapter 8). These are very easy to misunderstand. If you do misinterpret them, you may jump to quite the wrong conclusion.

What should you do if you come across statistical results you do *not* understand? Perhaps they are cited in an article you are reading, perhaps they are part of an SPSS printout for some of your own research, or perhaps you've followed some instructions and worked them out yourself with paper and pencil. What can you do if you feel you don't understand something statistical?

There are a range of tactics available:

- *Ignore it.* Printouts from computer packages almost always include more than you need. The regression Tool on Excel gives you the 't statistic', which is not mentioned in Chapter 9. SPSS is much worse: if you tick the boxes on many of the procedures, you will end up with dozens of co-efficients with strange names. Some may be useful, most won't be, but unless you want to study mathematical statistics for the next ten years, you have no choice but to ignore most of them. Try to focus on really understanding what seems important and ignore the rest.
- *Look it up.* Try the index of this and other books. The manuals for SPSS may be particularly helpful (even if you aren't using SPSS) because these are aimed at giving a user's understanding, instead of a mathematical understanding. There is also a lot on the web which is easily found with a search engine.
- *Remember the building blocks.* Many statistical methods make use of the key ideas of p values (Chapter 8) and 'least squares' models (Chapter 9). The ideas of 'bootstrapping' (Chapter 7) and the 'approximate randomi-sation test' (Section 8.3) are not so standard, but they may also be helpful in making sense of various concepts. The randomisation test, for example, is roughly equivalent to a one-way ANOVA.
- *Try experimenting with small amounts of 'toy' data.* For example, the Excel worksheet `reg2way.xls` will allow you to experiment to see how regression lines work.[148] SPSS is less interactive, but you can still experiment with small data sets. Try to guess what answer you think SPSS will give you, and then check.
- *If all else fails, ask for help.*

If you're conducting your own research, the various chapters of this book should be helpful at different stages (see Section 1.6.3). Some of the approaches we've looked at, particularly those that depend on computer simulation, are not the standard ones. They are, however, perfectly re-spectable methods of analysis, backed up by academic literature.[149]

One 'problem' with the computer simulation of probabilities is that the answer may be different each time you run the simulation. Perhaps this is a good thing, because it emphasises the fact that statistics is an uncertain and variable business. However, if you do want stable results, this can always be achieved simply by running the simulation more times. If you do want to use conventional methods, the section on Similar concepts at the end of most chapters should help. You may be able to use the methods in this book as a sort of mental image to help you visualise what's going on.

Despite all this advice, you may, on occasions, get stuck. You may not be able to work out how to proceed. Exercise 10.5.1 below asks you to work out a *p* value, but does not tell you how to do it. You are expected to work this out for yourself: you have a problem to solve. Many of the other exercises in this book may also have been a problem for you. I could have explained how to do Exercise 10.5.1, but then you wouldn't have got any practice in working things out for yourself, which may be useful to you another time. One of the potential advantages of the non-mathematical methods in this book is that they are simpler, which means you should be able to understand them more thoroughly and be in a better position to work things out by yourself. At least, this is my aim.

The key to solving problems is often to see the right approach. For example, the Monty Hall problem (Exercise 5.8.2) is easy if you look at it in the right way. And it's easy to simulate the lottery (Section 5.4) once you've thought of coding a number you have chosen as 1 and the rest as 0. Unfortunately there is no foolproof way of coming up with these insights, except by suggestions such as:

• try to understand your problem in detail
• experiment with the situation and try out various things
• remember methods that worked with earlier problems.

Fortunately, many of the basic ideas in this book – the two bucket model, bootstrapping, the approximate randomisation test, even the idea of coding yes/no as 1/0 – keep on coming up. They are very general ideas, so there's a reasonable chance they will be useful in your new situation. If all else fails, you could also look at the classic work on 'how to solve it'.[150]

▶ 10.4 Similar concepts

There is far too much written on the logic and practice of research to mention here. Check the literature on research methods in your discipline. On the statistical side, there is a sophisticated mathematical theory of the (statistical) 'design of experiments'. The experiments above involve manipulating just one variable; this more sophisticated theory may be of interest if you want to know the effect of several variables, which may interact with each other. One application of this theory is in industrial quality management: the Japanese quality control expert, Taguchi, has popularised the use of fairly complex experiments to help design industrial processes. These are part of the so-called 'Taguchi methods'.

▶ 10.5 Exercises

10.5.1 Solving a problem: a *p* value for experiment 2

The *p* value for Experiment 2 in Section 10.1.3 was 3% (see Chapter 8 for an explanation of *p* values). This was worked out ignoring the 21 children who did equally well under the P and the N treatments. The null hypothesis was that the each of the 11 remaining children had a 50% chance of doing better under the P treatment, and a 50% chance of doing better under the N treatment. The data showed that 9 of the 11 did better under the P condition. The significance level cited for this was 3%. Can you see how to work this out? (You should be able to use the same method, and the data in Table 3.1 or *drink.xls*, to test the null hypothesis that students, on average, drink the same amount on Saturday as they do on Sunday.)

10.5.2 Investigating the reasons for the riches of the runners

In Section 9.7 four hypotheses are put forward to explain, in causal terms, the tendency on the Isle of Fastmoney for people who can run faster to earn more money (Section 9.1). How would you investigate the truth of each of these hypotheses? Experiments may be worth considering, but would they be possible? Can you manipulate all the variables? And how should the college set about trying to demonstrate that academic qualifications really are useful?

Appendices

▶ **Appendix A. Using spreadsheets (Excel) for statistics**

Spreadsheets are useful for storing tables of data (numbers, words, etc) and performing calculations and producing graphs based on this data. Their strength lies in their flexibility and the ease with which changes can be made.

There are a number of spreadsheets on the market, but the dominant one is Microsoft Excel, so the detailed terminology and formulae in this appendix are based on Excel. However, other spreadsheets work in a very similar way.

As an example, Table 3.1 is a printout of a spreadsheet file – on the web as *drink20.xls* (see Appendix C). It is a rectangular array of cells, known as a *worksheet.* When using Excel, the columns are labelled A, B, C, etc and the rows 1, 2, 3, etc. This means that the cells can then be labelled by the appropriate column and row: eg Cell C2 in Table 3.1 contains the letters FP. It is often useful to put several worksheets together to form a *workbook* (eg *resample.xls* – see Appendix C). If you are not familiar with how spreadsheets work, I would suggest you get the file for Table 3.1 (*drink20.xls*) from the web (see Appendix C) and work through the following suggestions.

To see patterns in the data it is often helpful to sort it. Select (highlight) all the data, and then click on Data – Sort – Sort by and then choose SEX and OK. This will put all the females at the top.

The most flexible way to get a spreadsheet to do calculations is to enter a *formula* in one of the cells. For example, if you key the formula

=(D3+E3+F3)/3

in cell H3 (just to the right of the number 20 in the second row of the *Daycigs* column), and then press Enter, the number 23.3333 will appear in the cell (assuming you haven't sorted the data). The formula is said to *return*, or produce, this number – which is what you get if you add 26, 18 and 26 and divide the total by 3.

Note the use of the = sign to signal to Excel that you are entering a formula, the symbol / to mean divide, and the brackets. The formula

```
=D3+E3+F3/3
```

would not do because only the final number, in cell F3, would be divided by 3. What answer would you get with this formula?

The answer would be 52.66667.

The symbol ∗ is used for multiplication – for example the formula

```
=4∗5
```

would produce 20. Note that you can either have cell references (D3, E3, etc) or numbers, or both, in a formula. You can also give cells names of your own choosing (use Help to find out how to do this).

The original formula above obviously gives you the average number of units of alcohol on the three days, so it makes sense to label the new column by typing *Average units per day* in cell H1.

We would like the averages for the other 19 students in the table, so the next stage is to select cell H3, copy it and paste it to the rest of the column. This works much the same as in any other Windows package – if in doubt click on Help.

If you select the cells you have pasted the formula in one by one, you will see that the formula changes row by row. The fourth row becomes

```
=(D4+E4+F4)/3
```

and so on. This is obviously what we want here. If you don't want cell references to change in this way, you must preface the bits you don't want to change with a $ sign – search for help on Relative vs absolute references.

It is also very easy to produce diagrams based on spreadsheet data. Select the cells containing the data for the diagram, and then use the Chart Wizard – search for Help on charts for more details. However, you need to be careful. Many diagrams are not very useful, and Excel will not help you to distinguish between useful and useless diagrams. In `drink20.xls`, select the Satunits and Sununits columns of data, then choose a Scatter diagram from the menu. This should give you a sensible diagram. (There should be a single series with Satunits as the X-range – if necessary, check this by clicking on the chart with the right mouse button, and using Source data – Series.) Often, you will have to get Excel to calculate the numbers to plot on a diagram: see the notes on producing a histogram below.

You can alter the data, or anything else, very easily and see what effect this will have. If you change the first figure in the *Satunits* column in Table 3.1 from 0 to 30, the average in column H should change from 0 to 10. This is very useful for experimenting to see the effect of changes.

A.1 Functions

As well as formulae based on addition, subtraction, multiplication and division, there are also a large range of built-in *functions*. As an alternative to the formula above you could enter

=average(D3:F3)

and you will get the same answer. You can also copy it down the column in just the same way. To see the full list of functions, click on the function Wizard (f_x on the toolbar). This will also help you enter the cells on which the functions depend. The functions useful for this book include:

average, median, quartile, percentile, max, min, rand, randbetween, stdev, correl, normdist, poisson, if

and many others.

There are also a few extra functions I have written for this book. To use these you will need to install the Add-in, *nms.xla*, as described in Appendix C.

In most cases, what functions do should be obvious. How to use them will also be obvious in some cases; in others you will need to use Help or the function Wizard. *If, randbetween* and *rand* deserve a little more explanation. To see how *if* works, enter

=if(g2>0,1,0)

in Cell I2 (to the right of the top number in the Daycigs column in Table 3.1) of *drink20.xls* and copy it down the rest of the column. This formula checks if G2 is greater than 0, and if it is 1 appears in the cell indicating a smoker, and if it isn't, 0 appears indicating a non-smoker. Click Help for more details.

A.2 Random number functions: generating samples and probabilities

=randbetween(10,15)

will produce a whole (integer) random number between 10 and 15 including both 10 and 15. (This is a part of the Analysis ToolPak so you may need to install this by clicking Tools – Add-ins.) Try pressing F9 repeatedly and watch the numbers you get in the cell to see how this works.

Pressing F9 makes the spreadsheet recalculate everything and produce a different set of random numbers. This will also happen when you change anything else on the spreadsheet. This recalculation can be a nuisance. To stop it, select the cells in question, then click on Edit – Copy and then Edit – Paste special and tick Values. Now the random number formulae will be replaced by particular random numbers, which won't change when you press F9.

If you haven't got the *randbetween* function you can use the *rand* function which produces a random number between 0 and 0.99999. The formula below does exactly the same as the *randbetween* formula above:

=10+int(rand()*(15-10+1))

The *rand* function can also be used to produce values which vary according to specified probabilities.

=if(rand()<0.25,1,0)

will produce 1 with a probability of 0.25 and 0 otherwise. (As *rand()* varies between 0 and 1 there is a chance of 0.25 that it will be less than 0.25.)

=if(rand()<0.5,"Head","Tail")

will simulate the tossing of a coin.

A.3 Statistical procedures

These are accessed from Data Analysis in the Tools menu: if this is not there you will need to install the Analysis ToolPak (Tools Add-ins). These procedures implement a range of statistics methods, including regression (Chapter 9). The Histogram tool, however, has serious weaknesses – an alternative is explained in Section A.7.

A.4 PivotTable reports

These are useful for organising data by subcategories. To see how they work use *drink20.xls*. Click Data – PivotTable, and follow the instructions. In step 2 confirm that the data should be the whole block of data, and in Step 3 click on Layout and then drag (say) Satunits to the Data area, Sex to the Column area, and Course to the Row area. When you see the pivot table you will probably see it set to show the total consumption of units in each category: to change this to the average (mean), click with the right mouse button anywhere in the Data area of the table, choose Field settings, and then Average (Count and Stddev are other options on this menu). If you want to make further changes to the table you can drag more fields to or from the toolbar. If the toolbar disappears retrieve it using Insert – Toolbars.

A.5 The Solver

The best way to see what this does is to try it. Put the number 5 in Cell A1 and the formula =A1*A1-10 in Cell B1. The number 15 (=5*5-10) should appear in Cell B1. Solver is useful if you want to work this backwards: ie find out what should go in A1 to get something in particular in B1. For example, what should go in Cell A1 if you want to get 26 in Cell B1? Or, what is the least possible value we can get in B1?

First check that Solver is installed. It should be on the Tools menu. If it isn't, install it by clicking Tools – Add-in.

Now click Tools – Solver, and then fill in B1 as the Target cell, A1 as the cells to be changed (only one in this case), and specify that you want the target cell set to a particular value: 26. Clicking on OK will find the number you need to put in A1 to make B1 equal to 26. In this case, the answer is obviously 6, but Solver will find answers which are not all obvious. To find the least possible value in Cell B1, you need to tell Solver that you want to find a minimum (the answer is −10).

Solver works by a trial and error process, and is not always completely reliable (it will not find the other possible answer to the first question, −6), although you should have no problems with any of the uses we put it to in this book (see Chapter 9).

A.6 Formatting and rounding numbers

When you get some numerical answers, they are likely to have a large number of decimal places, which makes it hard to see any pattern. To reduce, or standardise, the number of decimal places, use Format – Cells – Number, then highlight Number again and set Decimal places: 0 will round everything off to the nearest whole number.

A.7 Producing a histogram

There is a Histogram tool in the Data analysis menu, but there are a few snags with it. It's better to do it yourself.

To produce a histogram like Figure 3.2, you need to start by adding a column for the estimated weekly total in the file *drink.xls*. Put the formula

=average(D2:F2)*7

in Cell H2 and copy down to H93.

The next step is to create Table 3.2. Put this in the worksheet to the right of the data starting at Cell I1. Enter the first three rows of the *Top of interval* column in Table 3.2, then select the second two of these (10, 20). You should now be able drag the small black rectangle on the bottom right corner – the Fill handle – down to fill in the rest of the column. The range I2:I14 is called the *bin range* by Excel.

A similar trick will do the *Middle* column.

You can now use the *frequency* function to work out the frequencies in the third column. Select *all* the cells in which frequencies will go (ie K2:K15) – this block should extend one row below the bin range. Now enter the array formula:

=frequency(H2:H93,I2:I14)

Because this is an array formula you must press CTRL and Shift and Return to enter this formula.

To create the diagram, select the column of frequencies (K2:K15), then use the Chart Wizard. Choose a Column chart, in Step 2 click on Series and enter the *Middle* column as the Category (X) axis labels, and when the chart is finished, click on the bars of the histogram with the right mouse button and Format the Data series so that the Gap width (under Options) is 0.

Spreadsheets like Excel will do much more than I have mentioned in this brief summary. *If in doubt, click on Help.*

▶ Appendix B. A brief guide to the statistical package, SPSS

SPSS – the *Statistical Package for the Social Sciences* – is one of the software packages available for doing serious statistical analysis. It is widely used by researchers in social sciences and many other areas. These notes are only intended to get you started and give you an idea of what SPSS can be used for. The Help built in to the software is good for helping to find how to do things, but very unhelpful for interpreting answers. For this, you will need to consult one of the many books on SPSS (eg Norusis, 2000).

You do *not* need SPSS to do any of the non-mathematical methods discussed in this book. A spreadsheet is quite adequate. However, SPSS does have two advantages over spreadsheets.

First, if you want tables of standard statistics and diagrams for lots of variables, it is likely to be easier to set this on SPSS than on a spreadsheet. On the other hand, if you have just got a few variables, it may not be worth the effort of getting to grips with SPSS.

Second, as you might expect, SPSS has many more advanced procedures than Excel.

B.1 Data entry

SPSS has facilities for data entry, but I usually enter data on a spreadsheet first, and then transfer it to SPSS. This gives you a chance to do any preliminary analysis with the spreadsheet, and means that you can delay the decision about whether to use SPSS until you have seen what the spreadsheet can do.

Put column (variable/field) headings in the first row, and then enter data for each case (person, company, etc) on successive rows (see Table 3.1 and the files `drink20.xls` and `accquest.xls` for examples of this format). When you transfer to SPSS, tick the box telling SPSS to pick up variable names from the first row.

It is best if the column headings are no more than eight characters and do not include spaces or punctuation marks. If any data is missing, leave the cell blank – do not enter 0 if the data is missing. See Section 10.2.3 for more details.

B.2 Analysis: commonly used methods

In SPSS, after loading your data, use the main menu:

- Analyze – Descriptive statistics for frequencies, means, sds, histograms, etc.
- Analyze – Compare Means – Means to compare means of different groups of cases (like Table 3.5). The dependent variable is the numerical measurement, and the independent variable is the grouping variable.
    To test the hypothesis of no difference between the means by an analysis of variance or a t-test, take the Option of an ANOVA table.
- Analyze – Compare Means – Paired Samples T test to compare the means of two number variables, and test the hypothesis that there is no difference.
- Analyze – Descriptive statistics – Crosstabs for a frequency table of two or more category variables like Table 3.4. To test the hypothesis of no association between the variables, check Statistics is set to Chi Square. For two by two tables, the Fisher exact test gives exact probabilities (significance levels); for larger tables the Pearson Chi square gives an acceptable approximation. It is also a good idea to set the Cell contents so that you get appropriate percentages.
- Analyze – Custom tables to produce tables showing the relationship between several variables – eg Table 3.9.
- Analyze – Correlate – Bivariate for correlation coefficients. You can paste in a list of variables to get a matrix of correlations.
- Graph – Scatter for scatter diagrams.
- Graph – Histogram for histograms.
- Analyze – Regression – Linear for linear regression. For multiple regression, SPSS offers help with choosing which variables to enter in the model. There are several methods, but a good starting point is

stepwise selection – click Method – Stepwise and stick with the default entries.

Sometimes you may need to recode a variable. For example, Table 3.4 requires a variable to tell SPSS which students are smokers. This can be achieved by recoding the Daycigs variable so that any quantity above zero is coded as 1 – all the data will then be 0 for non-smokers, or 1 for smokers. To do this switch to the Data Editor window, and click Transform – Recode and use Old and new values. The old value 0 can be recoded to the new value 0 for non-smokers. Then click Range and set the old range 0.1 to 1000 (say) to the new value 1 for a smoker. (Alternatively use the *if* function in Excel, as described in Appendix A.)

In all cases you will need to explore the statistics and options available.

▶ Appendix C. Data and program files for downloading

These are on the web at www.palgrave.com/studyguides/wood.

Spreadsheet data files
These are the data sets referred to in the book:

- *drink.xls*
- *drink20.xls* (Table 3.1)
- *words.xls*
- *shares.xls*
- *accquest.xls, accdin.txt, accsoc.txt*
- *iofm16.xls* (Table 9.1)
- *iofm.xls*

Spreadsheet data/analysis files
These files are designed to help with, or give you the answer to, some of the exercises and examples in the text:

- *jobs.xls* for the problem of Jenny's jobs in Section 5.3
- *sharesan.xls* some of the analysis of the data in *shares.xls*
- *reg2way.xls* for Exercise 9.9.5

Spreadsheet program files
These are workbooks designed to carry out particular methods. They are all Excel 2000 files, which I have tried to make as simple as possible so that they are relatively easy to change (in case you should want to). None of them, for example, use macros.

They all follow the convention that cells used for inputting data and for-mulae are green. If there's something in a green cell, you can either leave it or change it. Take care if you change any other cell: you may overwrite some formulae and the spreadsheet may not work. You should also avoid using cut and paste in these green cells (copy and paste is OK), because this may change the cells to which formulae in the workbooks refer.

- `resample.xls` for resampling, or the two bucket model, as explained in Section 5.4.
- `resamplenrh.xls` and `resamplenrh-drinkfm.xls` for using a resampling method to test a no relationship hypothesis (the second file includes the data for the example in Section 8.3.1). These both need the add-in described below.
- `pred1var.xls`, `predmvar.xls` for predicting (regression) from 1 vari-able, and many variables (Chapter 9).

Spreadsheet add-in
The file `nms.xla` contains a few extra built-in functions. To install it, down-load it to your computer, and then, in Excel, click on Tools – Add-ins, and then Browse to find the downloaded file. Use the function Wizard (f_x on the toolbar) to find the extra functions and a brief description of what they do. They should be listed under Statistical functions. The extra functions are:

Kendall
Kendall's tau correlation coefficient (see Section 3.7.3). In `drink.xls`

   =Kendall(B2:B93,D2:D93)

will calculate the top entry in Table 3.8. This function, and the next two asso-ciated functions, may be very slow for large ranges: I wouldn't use them for more than 100 pairs of numbers.

Psd
Probability of a same-direction observation (Section 3.7.3).

Pod
Probability of an opposite-direction (reversed-direction) observation (Section 3.7.3).

Rangeofmeans
If you break down a number variable according to subcategory, this function gives the difference between the biggest and smallest means of the subcat-egories. Using `drink20.xls` (Table 3.1), the function

=Rangeofmeans(D2:D21,C2:C21)

will give 8.5 because this is the difference between the mean drunk on Saturday (Column D) by the FB course (the course labels are in Column C), and the mean drunk by the PP course.

Diffofmeans
This works like Rangeofmeans but is designed for two subcategories only. It subtracts the average for the second subcategory from the average for the first subcategory, so the answer may be negative.

PercentileNms
A simpler percentile function than the one built into Excel.

=PercentileNms(D2:D21,0.25)

in *drink20.xls* will give the 25th percentile of the numbers in D2:D21 (1.5).

Numdiffvals
Gives the number of different values in a range.

=Numdiffvals(C2:C21)

will give 3 because there are three different labels in this column.

A standalone program file
The *resample.exe* program does not require any special software to run it. Simply double click on it after downloading it. It saves its results in a file called resample.out in the same folder as the program. There are a few notes on the use of this program in *resample.htm*.

▶ Appendix D. Comments on some of the exercises

2.7.1   (a) 1/13. (b) 22/45 (22 of the 45 two digit even numbers are divisible by 4). (c) 1 (all numbers divisible by 4 are even). (d) Best source here is probably the weather forecast, which will be based on a mixture of empirical data and subjective judgement. (e) Not sure how to estimate this, but the answer would certainly be subjective, in the sense that different people would arrive at different answers.

2.7.3   The best way of choosing the sample of names in the phone book is to use random numbers to choose a page at random, and then to choose a name on the chosen page at random. There are many difficulties with this approach to choosing a sample. Many people will be excluded because they live in households without a name in the phone book (perhaps they all use mobiles?). People who live alone will be 19 times as likely to be in the sample as those living in households of 19 people. People who never answer the phone will be excluded. And so on. This all means that the final sample may be a very untypical group.

3.11.1   The histogram for the academic sociology article has two 'humps': one centred on 2/3 letters, and the other one on 8/9 letters. This suggests there are two distinct types of word in the article. Histograms can be very useful for highlighting points like this.

3.11.2   5% of the employees, or 100 of them, earn more than £40 000. Similarly, 75%, or 1500, earn £25 000 or less. This means that the remaining 1600 earn between these two figures (strictly, this includes £40 000 but excludes £25 000). You haven't got the information to answer the last two questions.

3.11.3   The Kendall coefficient is −0.7. This suggests that the two subjects involve different abilities and that there is a tendency for people who are good at one to be poor at the other. The different standard deviations reflect the fact that marks in mathematics are far more spread out than those in English. This means that adding the marks would give an (unfair?) advantage to those good at mathematics.

   Halving the mathematics marks halves the standard deviation, but subtracting 30 makes no difference. Neither has any impact on the correlation coefficient. The standard deviations of the final two sets of marks are 11.5 and 0. All these answers should be obvious without any calculation.

3.11.5   The sd shows how much the returns varied from day to day. This is often taken as a measure of the riskiness of the share – on the assumption that the past pattern will continue into the future. The correlation between two of the share returns tells you whether there's a tendency for one to go up when the other goes up. The file *sharesan.xls* shows these statistics, and also some histograms. (The analysis ignores dividends and a few other complications.)

5.8.2   You should change your choice. If you do this your chances of winning are 2/3. If you stick with the original choice your chances are 1/3.

   The easiest way of arriving at this conclusion is to imagine the situation after you have made your original choice, but before Monty gives you his clue. The probability that you have guessed right is 1/3. If you stick with this choice, nothing changes, so the final probability is still 1/3. Now think of the three possibilities – the car is either behind the door you have chosen (probability 1/3), or behind one of the other two (probability 2/3). But if it's behind either one of these other two, Monty's clue means you will certainly find it (because he tells you which door it's not behind so you can choose the other). This means that if you change your mind, you will get the car if it's behind *either* of these two doors – so the probability of success becomes 2/3.

5.8.3   The probability of getting the first ball is 6/49. If you get this the probability of getting the second too is 5/48. And so on. Multiplying the six probabilities together gives 1 in 13 983 816. You can't increase your chance of winning a prize, but you can increase the amount you will win if you win the jackpot by avoiding numbers that others are likely to choose – eg 1, 2, 3, 4, 5, 6 is an obvious choice, so don't choose it.

5.8.5   Using resampling, or the Excel hypergeometric distribution, the probability is about 35% for a batch containing 6 defectives. This is rather low, given their desire to reject batches with this level of defectives. If they decided to reject the batch if they found any defectives in the sample (instead of allowing one), the probability of rejecting the batch would be 75%. To do better than this, they need a bigger sample, which may be expensive.

5.8.6   According to the Poisson function in Excel, they can be 99% sure that there will be no more than 12 patients in an hour, and 99.99% sure that there will be no more than 17 – which seems good enough. The difficulty with this is that it assumes arrivals are independent of each other (think of how we set the football simulation up in Section 5.5). If there is an accident with multiple casualties, this estimate will not apply. So it should be treated with caution.

The average should be 4.3 lottery winners; no winners should have happened about once; more than 50 winners should not have happened. This shows that some numbers are more popular than others: avoid obvious combinations like 1, 2, 3, 4, 5, 6!

5.8.7   According to the normal distribution, 1.3% of boys were shorter than the average girl, and only 0.5% of girls were taller than the average boy. Both answers are smaller than I expected! (The percentiles given are roughly consistent with the normal distribution, but the distribution may not be normal outside these two percentiles.)

5.8.8   Making what I consider reasonable assumptions, the probability is somewhere between 50% and 75%.

6.7.1 (b) Posterior probabilities are 19% (0% world), 27% (50% world) and 54% (100% world).

(c) The probability I got, using *resample.exe*, was 0.7%. This is a small probability; she would be very lucky to achieve this by chance. But I can't tell you what you should conclude from this.

To get this, you need to simulate the null hypothesis – see Section 5.4. In the first bucket – the sample – I would put a one to represent a correct guess, and 51 zeros to represent incorrect guesses. Then you need to find the probability of her getting three, or more, right in 20 attempts.

6.7.2 It's about 50 times more likely that the patient does *not* have disease.

6.7.3 There are likely to be four people with a matching sample of whom James is one – so the probability of his guilt is about 25%. Notice how different this is from the 99.99% of the prosecutor's fallacy.

6.7.4 I simulated Pearce's experiments 5000 times under the null hypothesis assumption that he was guessing. The highest result I got was 1750 hits – just 135 better than the chance score. Pearce's actual score was 1434 better than chance! This is obviously too good to be explained by chance, but could it be cheating? He convinced Rhine, but perhaps Rhine wanted to be convinced?

7.8.1 Batch 2 should have the wider confidence intervals. The 95% intervals should be wider than the corresponding 50% intervals.

7.8.4 It obviously doesn't make much sense. The world record (currently 223.13 seconds) is obviously *less* than the fastest time in the sample! You can't assume that the sample minimum is equally likely to be bigger or smaller than the world record: it's definitely not smaller. You will need to adjust the argument in Section 7.2 bearing this in mind. A good starting point is the fact that a resample minimum of 310 seconds is 60 seconds *more* than the guessed population minimum. If the sample minimum – 250 – was also 60 seconds more than the world record, the world record would be 190, 60 seconds *less* than the sample minimum.

8.9.4 The results are very similar to what would be expected if the reviewers were not reading the papers, and tossing a coin to decide whether a paper gets a good or a bad review. The p value would be very high (approaching 100%) and the result statistically *insignificant*. This is obviously very significant in other ways, because it implies that the review process is a complete waste of time.

9.9.1 (a) Slope is 0.44, intercept is –3.0, MSE is 8.37, R squared is 0.83, 95% interval for slope 0.40–0.48. The slope and intercept are very similar to the values in the text based on 16 values. In general you should expect the confidence intervals for the larger sample to be narrower, indicating a more reliable answer.

(c) R squared is 0.56 and the slope for the run time is −2.25 with a 95% confidence interval from −2.7 to −1.8. This means you can be confident that there is a genuine negative relationship here. This slope means that if you could run 5 minutes faster (*reduce* your time by 5 minutes), you would expect to earn about 11 thousand euros (2.25 × 5) *more* – if nothing else changed.

9.9.3   The fact that the regression coefficient is negative means that, on average, a share with a level of returns above the mean for the last four years would produce an expected return *below* the mean over the next four years. On the other hand, if the returns over the previous four years were below the mean, the expected return over the next four years would be slightly above the mean.

For example, suppose you had the choice of two shares – A produced a return of −5% over the last four years (a loss), and B produced +5%. The difference between the two returns is 10% and the regression slope is −0.112, which means that the prediction is for the return from B to be 1.12% *less* than A. (It may help to sketch a scatter diagram.)

Needless to say, these are averages over a large number of companies and time periods; the R^2 value quoted (0.0413) suggests that this prediction is extremely unreliable. However, this negative regression coefficient does show that there is a very weak tendency for shares which have done well over the last four years to do badly over the next four years, and vice versa. This provides support for the hypothesis of 'investor overreaction', and suggests it may be worth buying shares which have done *badly* in the past.

10.5.1   The null hypothesis is like tossing a coin – heads for P and tails for N – 11 times. You can simulate it with `resample.xls` or `resample.exe` as described in Section 5.6. The *p* value is the probability of getting 9 or more Ps. This method is known as the 'sign test' because the results can be recorded as + or −.

Notes

1. Pedants often insist that data is plural, so the grammar of this sentence is wrong. My dictionary allows the word's use in the singular, or the plural.
2. UK Meteorological Office website (www.met-office.gov.uk/) accessed on 10 January 2000.
3. Based on *Formulae and tables for actuarial examinations*. Institute of Actuaries and Faculty of Actuaries, 1980, p. 22.
4. BBC News at 1 pm, 4 January 2000.
5. Doll, S. R. (1987). Major epidemics of the 20th century: from coronary thrombosis to AIDS. *Journal of the Royal Statistical Society Series A*, **150**(4): 373–95.
6. Statisticians like the figure 95%, I'm not sure why this number is chosen.
7. The standard text on this is Huff (1973).
8. Supposedly said by the nineteenth-century prime minister, Disraeli.
9. *Formulae and tables for actuarial examinations*. Institute of Actuaries and Faculty of Actuaries, 1980, p. 21. To be honest, there is another source of distortion in the figure of 33 years: when I saw the answer derived from the tables, I didn't like it, so I changed it. This is the crudest form of distortion.
10. The main difference is that the lottery probability refers to the individual ticket, whereas the asteroid probability refers to the whole earth. If the remote chance of a substantial asteroid impact were to occur, then millions of people would suffer from the one event. On the other hand, if a lottery ticket wins, there is just one winner. Another problem is that the asteroid probability refers to a whole lifetime, whereas the lottery probability refers to a single lottery ticket. And there's the obvious point that taking precautions against asteroids is difficult: is there actually anything you can do? For all these reasons a direct comparison of the probabilities is not really meaningful.
11. Urquhart, J. (1987). Deadly clusters, the *Guardian*, 20 March.
12. The *Observer*, 2 February 2003, p. 19; www.sallyclark.org.uk/AppealStats.html.
13. I am grateful to David MacKay for pointing this out.
14. For further examples see Matthews, R., Lies, damned lies and the public image of the RSS, *Royal Statistical Society News*, **30**(2) October, 2002, 1–2.
15. The idea of what mathematics is, implicit in this definition of what it is not, is one which some mathematicians may not accept. If mathematics is defined in terms of the generality or rigour of its arguments, then the approach here is mathematical. I am using the term non-mathematical in what I take to be the layman's sense.
16. In the spreadsheet Excel, the formula =int(rand()*365+1) copied to 50 cells will do the trick. Alternatively, use the randbetween function, if this is available. Pressing the function key F9 regenerates the random numbers, which generates another audience. You may think this is rather hard work. For each new audience, you've got to check the numbers carefully. You could get round this by teaching Excel to recognise if there are two people with the same birthday automatically. I have done

this: you will need to install the add-in `nms.xla` and use the function =numdiff-vals(A1:A50) (assuming the 50 numbers are in these cells). This gives the number of different birthdays, so the number to watch for is 50. Press F9 and see how often this appears.

17. The pros and cons are discussed in Wood, M. (2001). The case for crunchy methods in practical mathematics. *Philosophy of Mathematics Education Journal* (a web journal at http://www.ex.ac.uk/~PErnest/), *14*.

18. Negative numbers behave in obvious ways, except (perhaps) when you multiply two of them together. The answer is positive. To see why, imagine yourself driving north from a motorway service area at 50 miles per hour (mph). After 4 hours you will be $4 \times 50 = 200$ miles north. Now –50 mph would mean you're driving south at 50 mph, and –4 hours would mean 4 hours in the past. So $(-4) \times (-50)$ represents where you were 4 hours ago if you are driving south at 50 mph. This must be 200 miles north, so $(-4) \times (-50) = +200$.

19. Squared means multiplied by itself. So five squared is 25 because 5×5 is 25. The phrase presumably derives from the fact that the area of a square of side 5 units is 25 square units. The square root of a number is the number which, when squared, gets you back to the original number. So the square root of 25 is 5, and of 20 is 4.47. (You will need a calculator or spreadsheet function to work out the last one.)

20. Because the proportion 15/100 is the same as 3/20.

21. There is some evidence that people tend to exaggerate their degree of certainty, see Clemen, R. (1996), *Making hard decisions* (2nd edn), Belmont, CA: Duxbury Press, p. 284.

22. I can't think of any other obvious, general term for what the buckets represent. This is an important reason for using the bucket and ball image.

23. Pedants may insist that the singular form of dice is die. My dictionary permits either: I have not used 'die' because it is rarely used in everyday language.

24. For a discussion of this see Goodwin, P. and Wright, G. (1998). *Decision Analysis for Management Judgement* (2nd edn). Chichester: Wiley.

25. Based on estimates in Lomborg, B. *The skeptical environmentalist* (Cambridge: CUP, 2001, p. 337) with a few additional assumptions. I am also ignoring the 1 in 2 000 000 chance of dying from cancer caused by cosmic radiation which is an additional (small) hazard of flying.

26. Copy the formula =randbetween(1,40000000) or =1+int(rand()*40000000) to as many cells as you need.

27. Put some random numbers in a column by the side of your list using the function =rand(). Now select the block containing your list and the random numbers, and use Data – Sort.

28. Smith, A. Presidential address to the Royal Statistical Society, 1996. The data is based on the years 1986–90.

29. In the Excel file `drink.xls` put the formula =average(D2:F2)*7 in Cell H2 and copy down to H3:H93.

30. There is a Histogram tool built into Excel (search for Help on this), but there are a few snags with it. An alternative approach is explained in Appendix A.7.

31. Click on Analyze – Descriptive statistics – Frequencies, or Graphs – Histogram.

32. In Excel there are the built-in functions average (mean) and median. In SPSS use Analyze – Descriptive statistics.

33. The functions are median, percentile, quartile. There is also an extra function, PercentileNms, in the add-in `Nms.xla`: this uses the 'midway' method in the text. Check the function Wizard (f_x on the toolbar) and experiment to see how they work.

34. Use Analyze – Descriptive statistics.

35. Gregory, J. and Lowe, S. *National diet and nutrition survey: young people aged 4 to 18 years*, Vol 1. London: Stationery Office; 2000, p. 350.
36. Squared means multiplied by itself. So five squared is 25 because 5 × 5 is 25. Going the other way, the square root of 25 is 5.
37. You can easily calculate the range and interquartile range from the functions max, min and quartile. The mean deviation is avedev. There are two different functions for standard deviation: the one which mirrors the method here is stdevp. The reason for the other function, stdev, is explained in the Similar concepts section.
38. The function =countif(D2:D93, "<3") will count the number of drinks.
39. You need to recode the Daycigs variable, and then use Crosstabs – see Appendix B.
40. In Excel you first need to add an extra column to show if an individual is a smoker. Enter =if(g2>0,1,0) in Cell H2 and copy it down the rest of the column. This formula uses the if function. It checks if G2 is greater than 0, and if it is 1 appears in the cell, and if it isn't, 0 appears.

    Next you need to use a Pivot Table (use Help or see Appendix A.4). When you get to Layout, drag Sex to the Column area, Smoker to the Column area, and Sex again to the Data area. (You could put Smoker instead of the Sex in the Data area, although this is a little less convenient for the next step – try it to see the difference.)

    To change the table to row percentages, right click on the Data area, then choose Field settings, then Options and click the box for Show data as. Finally, use Format – Cells – Number – Percentage to set the number of decimal places to 0.
41. Use a Pivot Table (use Help or see Appendix A.4). After clicking Layout, put Sex in the Column area, and Satunits and Sex in the Data area.
42. Use Graphs – Scatter and then search for Help on Showing sunflowers.
43. In SPSS use Analyze – Correlate – Bivariate. If you paste in a list of variables you will get a whole matrix of correlations, like Table 3.8.
44. There is no built-in Excel function for the Kendall's tau, so I have included one in the add-in *nms.xla*. In *drink.xls* the function =Kendall(B2:B93,D2:D93) will calculate the first correlation in Table 3.8. There are two other related functions, psd (probability of same-direction) and pod (probability of opposite-direction): =Psd(B2:B93,D2:D93) will produce the answer 0.39.
45. Analyze – Custom tables – Basic table and click on Statistics to include the mean, count, quartiles (25th and 75th percentiles) and, if you want, other statistics.
46. Use Graphs – Bar – Clustered in SPSS. In Excel, use the Chart Wizard to draw a clustered bar chart from the Pivot Table output.
47. For example Smithson (2000).
48. Argyle, M. and Henderson, M. *The anatomy of relationships*. Harmondsworth: Penguin; 1985, p. 22.
49. Lomborg, B. *The skeptical environmentalist*. Cambridge: CUP; 2001, p. 11.
50. Einstein's famous equation for the energy equivalent (E) of a mass m kilograms (c being the speed of light). This tells us (for example) that if I were to be completely converted to energy, I would keep a 100 watt bulb burning for about two and a quarter million million years.
51. For a review of alternatives to probability see Smithson, M. (1989). *Ignorance and uncertainty: emerging paradigms*. New York: Springer-Verlag.
52. Clemen, Robert T. *Making hard decisions* (2nd edn). Belmont, CA: Duxbury Press; 1996, p. 281.
53. Some prostitutes in Nairobi, according to the CNN website accessed on 23 July 2002.
54. Wood, M. and Christy, R. Sampling for possibilities. *Quality & Quantity*, 33. 1999: 185–202.

55. Kosko (1994).
56. Stewart (1990).
57. Enter the starting £1250 in Cells B2:D2. You now need a formula in B3. For step 1 the formula would be =b2/1000. Applying step 2 to this formula, it becomes =b2/1000–1; with step 3 it becomes =(b2/1000–1)*(b2/1000–1) and with step 4 it is (for Account 1) =(b2/1000–1)*(b2/1000–1)*500.

    Now copy this formula across to C3:D3, and change the 500 in this formula to 1750 in C3 and 2000 in D3. To round off balances to the nearest whole number, you will need to format the cells (Appendix A.6). Finally, copy all three formulae down Columns B:D.
58. This term is due to Edward Lorenz.
59. The so-called 'random' numbers generated by computers are often called 'pseudo-random' numbers, because they are actually based on explicit arithmetical rules – similar in type to the rule on which the first three columns of Table 4.1 are based, but obviously more complex. Computers cannot behave randomly, so chaos is used to simulate randomness. (The 'random' Account 4 in Table 4.1 is actually chaotic.) This means that there may be hidden patterns in computer-generated random numbers, which may distort results. This is rarely a problem in practice, but it is a possibility of which you should be aware. The reason why the same sequence of random numbers is not produced on every occasion is that the time is used as an initial condition to 'seed' the rule for generating the 'random' numbers.
60. For an accessible introduction see Stewart (1990) or Gleick (1998).
61. Historically, one of the oddities of probability theory is the fact that it did not emerge until the seventeenth century, despite the fact that games of chance are far older. The Greeks, for example, did not formalise probability in the same way that they formalised geometry. Ian Hacking (*The emergence of probability*. Cambridge University Press, 1975, Chapter 1) suggests various possible explanations for this.
62. Or, using a calculator to change fractions to decimals, 0.0588 times 0.0769 which is 0.0045.
63. The *Observer*, 2 February, 2003, p. 19.
64. Copy the first three rows from Table 5.1 putting each entry in a different cell. 'Any offer' will be in Cell E1, 'Probabilities' in Cell D2, and 0.5 will be in Cell B3. Then enter these Excel formulae:

In cell B4:	=if(rand()<B$3,1,0)
In cell E4:	=if(sum(B4:D4)>=1,1,0)
In cell E1004:	=average($E$4.$E$1003)

These are the only formulae you have to key in. The rest are copied: copy cell B4 to C4 and D4, and then B4 to E4 to the next 999 rows. The easiest way to put the numbers in the first column is to use the Fill handle (check Help on Fill handle). The formulae in Cell B4:D1003 use random numbers to generate probabilistic events. Press F9 to generate another set of random numbers. The method is explained in Appendix A.2.
65. The Read me sheet in the workbook explains how to do this example.
66. The sample comprises six 1s and 43 0s, and you want the *sum* of resamples of size 6 *without* replacement (as each ball is not replaced in the lottery machine after it is drawn out). There is some further help in *resample.htm*.
67. You will need to install *nms.xla* and use the function numdiffvals as described in Appendix C. You also need to use resampling *with* replacement, as described in

Section 5.5. A simulation of this problem is described in terms of *three* buckets in Section 1.5. From the point of view of `resample.xls`, the middle bucket – the audience – does not count as a bucket!

68. Named after a French statistician called Poisson.

69. Like many statements on which statistical models are based, this is a half-truth. There is some evidence that goals are about 50% more likely towards the end of a match than they are at the beginning (Morris, D. *The soccer tribe*. London, Jonathan Cape; 1981). And goals may also come at a faster rate against weaker teams. However, the assumption that goals are equally likely at all stages of all matches is good enough to build a useful model. You don't need the whole truth in statistics, in fact, if you have the whole truth, you don't need statistics.

70. In the sample (Bucket 1) sheet, you need to put a single 1 and 42 0s in the column for Variable 1. It doesn't matter where you put the one as they will all be mixed up by the resampling process. The sample size of 43 should appear at the top.

    Now on the Single resample sheet you need to tell the spreadsheet the resample size and the statistic to calculate. The resample size is 90, because each match is 90 minutes. The formula for the statistic is =sum(F7.F96). This will find the total number of goals scored. Note that it is based on the block which is sampled *with replacement*.

    Finally, on the Lots of resamples (Bucket 2) sheet you need to enter the Values of interest – the possible numbers of goals – 0, 1, 2, 3, and so on. Then press F9 and let the spreadsheet calculate the probabilities. On the left-hand side of the worksheet, you will see the scores for each individual match being simulated – 2, 1, 2, 4 . . . on my computer. Each of the 200 scores represents one simulated match.

71. Either use `resample.exe` (10 000 simulated matches would be no problem), or adjust the spreadsheet as described – click on the tab for the Read this worksheet.

72. But quite possible if you adjust the maximum sample and resample size as described on the Read this sheet.

73. To get the probability of Manchester United scoring four goals, for example, enter the formula =Poisson(4,2.1,false) and the value 9.9% will appear. False in the for-mulae tells the spreadsheet that you do *not* want a *cumulative* probability, that is, the probability of any number of goals up to and including four. Use Help for more detail.

74. Except that the probability of having a girl is slightly less than 50%: boys are slightly commoner. This is nature's way of compensating for the frailty of the male. I'll ignore this for now.

75. Using `resample.xls`, put 100 in for the resample size, and =SUM(F7.F106) in as the resample statistic.

76. You won't manage to simulate this number with `resample.xls`. Figure 5.3 is a printout from `resample.exe`: when you are asked if you want Manual or Auto-matic scaling on the histogram, go for Manual with the bottom bar equal to 3 and the width equal to 5.

77. Gregory, J. and Lowe, S. *National diet and nutrition survey: young people aged 4 to 18 years*, Vol 1. London: Stationery Office; 2000.

78. The standard deviation is a measure of how spread out a group of numbers are; see Section 3.4.4.

79. As each resample is the total of 100 draws from Bucket 1, the average of the two balls in Bucket 1 has to be 178/100 or 1.78. The bigger number will obviously be a certain amount above this, and the smaller number the same amount below it. In the Bucket 1 from which Figure 5.3 was derived, the average was 0.5, and this amount above and below was also 0.5 (as 1 = 0.5 + 0.5). The standard deviation of

Figure 5.3 is 5 (not obvious from the figure but you can get the answer from the software), whereas the standard deviation we want is larger, 6.7. This suggests that the height distribution needs to be 6.7/5 times as spread out as Figure 5.3, that is, the amount above or below should be 0.5 × (6.7/5) or 0.67. The two numbers are 1.78 + 0.67 and 1.78 − 0.67. But all this doesn't matter much. All I want to show is that it can be done.

80. Use the function Wizard (f_x) on the toolbar. X should be 190, and Cumulative should be set to true since you want the cumulative probability all the way up to 190.

81. There are two reasons for discrepancies: the size of each resample and the number of resamples. The larger you make both of these, the closer the simulation will approach the normal probabilities produced by the Excel functions. If you drew a ball from Bucket 1 1000 times instead of 100 (this will mean the numbers 1.11 and 2.45 need to be changed), and put 1000 balls instead of 200 in Bucket 2, the answers would be closer.

82. The formula =norminv(rand(),178,6.7) will produce a random value from a normal distribution with a mean of 178 and an sd of 6.7. One thousand copies of this formula will produce 1000 values from this distribution.

83. From Palisade: www.palisade.com.

84. Gregory, J. and Lowe, S. *National diet and nutrition survey: young people aged 4 to 18 years* Vol 1. London: Stationery Office; 2000.

85. In this case, of course, the chances would have misled us.

86. This is not actually true. But please imagine it is.

87. Rhine, J. B. (1997). *Extra-sensory perception*. Boston: Branden.

88. Hansel, C. E. M. (1966). *ESP: a scientific evaluation*. London: MacGibbon & Kee.

89 O'Hagan, T., 'Maintaining Bayes's tomb', *RSS News* (the newsletter of the Royal Statistical Society), April 1999.

90. Except for errors produced by rounding numbers. These errors can be reduced by putting more balls in the bucket, for example 100 000 instead of 1000 in the example which follows.

91. Strictly, confidence intervals based on Bayes' principle are called 'credible intervals'.

92. The word 'confidence' is used instead of 'chance' or probability, because many statisticians are uncomfortable about referring to the probability of the 'true' proportion of voters lying in a particular range. According to this attitude, either it does or it doesn't, and it's meaningless to give it a probability (see also Section 6.4.1). However, in my view, this attitude is rather confused, and not worth worrying about.

93. The term is due to Bradley Efron, and reflects the idea that the method is like pulling yourself up by your own bootstraps – I'll leave you to judge if this is accurate when you've seen how it works.

94. This data is genuine. It is on the web in *accquest.xls*.

95. It's worth choosing a coding scheme with a natural interpretation. If, for example, 'not at all' had been coded as 5, it would be difficult to interpret the results without constant reference to the key. Perhaps coding 'strongly' as 100%, and 'not at all' as 0 again would be the best scheme, because then the figures range from 0 to 100%, a range with which people are familiar.

96. You may ask why. I haven't a clue: it is just a very widespread convention. In practice an 80% confidence interval may often seem good enough, although on other occasions, when greater confidence is called for, we may insist on 99% or even 99.9%.

97. The data is in the file *accsoc.txt* in a suitable format for *resample.exe*. You can, if you prefer, use *resample.xls* (see the example in the Read this sheet),

in which case you can paste the data from `accquest.xls`. I have used `resample.exe` in most of this chapter, because it is easier to simulate large numbers of resamples. Using either program, you want the mean of resamples of 98, *without replacement*.

98. This data is in `accquest.xls`, and also in `accdin.txt` in a format suitable for `resample.exe`.

99. Put the two variables in the Sample worksheet, and then use the correl or kendall (in the add-in `nms.xla`) function in Cell B4 of the Single resample worksheet.

100. Diaconis and Efron (1983).

101. You could try this using one 1 and 99 0s in your sample, and a resample size of 82.

102. Use Analyze – Descriptive statistics – Explore and click on Statistics. Or use Help.

103. Although the function confidence is not very helpful and badly explained. I don't recommend it.

104. It's easier to use `resample.exe` with this sample size. When keying the data in, you are given the option of taking the previously keyed in number as a default. If you do this, you can start by keying in 1, then keep your hand on the Enter key until 350 1s have been entered, and then do the same for the 650 0s.

105. The minimum is the 0th percentile.

106. Frankel, S., Sterne, J. and Smith, G. D. (2000). Mortality variations as a measure of general practitioner performance: implications of the Shipman case. *British Medical Journal*, 320: 189. They conclude, for a variety of reasons, that 'routine monitoring of mortality . . . would have limited benefit . . .'.

107. The Excel Poisson formula for, say, 30 deaths is =poisson(30,40,false). To use `resample.xls`, enter one 1 and 89 0s in the Sample sheet to simulate the 1 in 90 (1.1%) death rate. You will then need to extend the Single resample sheet to accommodate a resample size of 3600 to simulate Shipman's 3600 patients; click on the Read this sheet to see how to do this. This may make the workbook rather slow to calculate all the random numbers.

108. The formula is =1-poisson(50,40,true), check Help for more detail.

109. It's also 'normal' in the statistical sense (Section 5.6).

110. Noreen, E. W. *Computer intensive methods for testing hypotheses*. Chichester: Wiley; 1989.

111. We could do this shuffling process replacing each ball after it is drawn. This would be resampling *with replacement*, which is a way of simulating samples drawn from a large guessed population. The underlying rationale is explained in Section 7.2. I think it makes good sense here, but in practice it makes little difference to the answer.

112. I have set up this example in the file `resamplenrh-drinkfm.xls`; you will need to follow the instructions in the Read this sheet carefully. Alternatively, use the general workbook `resamplenrh.xls`, and put the data in yourself.

113. To run this on Excel, start from `resamplenrh-drinkfm.xls`. You now need to paste in the data from the Course variable instead of Sex, and change the function in the Data and Single resample sheets to rangeofmeans. This is also in the add-in `nms.xla`, so this must be installed (see Appendix C).

114. Using `resamplenrh.xls`, paste the Satunits data in as Variable 1, and Daycigs as Variable 2 in the Sample sheet. Then the resampling process will shuffle the two variables and simulate the hypothesis that there is no relation between them. The function you paste into Cell B4 should be kendall or correl. (The kendall function is a bit slow.)

115. Using `resample.xls`, paste the values of the Sex variable in the Variable 1 column. Variable 2 needs to be a new variable, coded as 1 for a smoker, and 0 for a non-

smoker (see Section 3.5). In the Single resample sheet, the resample size should be 92, and the resample statistic is =diffofmeans(G7:G98,F7:F98). This is one of the functions in the add-in *nms.xla*, so you need to install this – see Appendix C for more details.

116. Using *resample.xls* again (see previous note). The function kendall is rather slow, so it may be better to use the other correlation coefficient (the function correl).

117. In *resample.xls* enter 0 as the 'cut value' in the Lots of resamples sheet.

118. Probabilities of 0% produced by simulation should be treated with caution. The probability will often creep up slightly with a larger number of resamples. In statistics, very few probabilities are exactly zero. Few things are impossible, just very unlikely.

119. You can set up a 95% confidence interval which has a clear relationship with a 5% significance level (Section 8.4). But the 95% confidence applies to this interval, not to the alternative to the null hypothesis.

120. *Clinical evidence*, BMJ Publishing Group, June 1999, p. xiv.

121. This example is fictitious, but it mirrors a problem in many published studies.

122. Gardner, M. and Altman, D. G. Confidence intervals rather than P values: estimation rather than hypothesis testing. *British Medical Journal*. 1986 Mar 15; 292: 746–50.

123. The null hypothesis for the randomisation test is defined in terms of shuffling the data, and for the conventional tests in terms of probability patterns in a wider population. There are two important differences here. First the conventional tests are mainly 'parametric' in that they assume particular probability distributions (usually the normal distribution); the randomisation test is 'non-parametric' in that no such assumptions are necessary. Second, there is a strong argument that the conventional tests are appropriate for inferences about populations, whereas the randomisation test is appropriate for inferences about causation (Lunneborg, 2000: 551–6; see also Section 3.9). However, in practice, this distinction is usually ignored.

124. See any textbook on quality control or total quality management.

125. For example, many scientists spend their time measuring things. There is an extensive literature on the philosophy of science, which deals with questions about what science is and what scientists do.

126. See, for example, Popper, K. R. *The logic of scientific discovery*. London: Hutchinson; 1980. You will also find many commentaries on Popper's ideas by other authors.

127. Wood, M. and Roberts, M. (2002). The reliability of peer reviews of papers submitted to the 2001 UKAIS Conference: implications for academic knowledge management. In B. Howell and G. Orange (eds) *Information systems research, teaching and practice: proceedings of the 7th annual UKAIS conference, Leeds* (pp. 261–6). Leeds Metropolitan University.

128. The advantage of stratified samples over random samples is that the sampling error (Section 7.1) should be less because the sample is fixed so that the male/female balance is exactly right. This advantage, however, is usually very slight.

129. Key or paste in the data, then click on the Model sheet, and enter 0.5 as the slope and 0 as the intercept.

130. See Appendix A.5 for a brief introduction. In *pred1var.xls* I have set up the relevant details in the Solver box: click Tools – Solver and then OK.

131. The term comes from the idea of 'regression to the mean': the fact that the predicted values tend to cluster closer to their mean than the dependent data. Don't worry if you don't follow this; it's not important.

132. Use the function Wizard (f_x) to see how these work. The known ys are the values

of the dependent variable (for example the earnings data), the known xs are the values of the independent variable (for example the run time data), and x (in the forecast function) is the value from which you are trying to predict. In *iofm16.xls*, keying =forecast(50,$G$2:$G$17,$F$2:$F$17) will give the predicted cycle time corresponding to a run of 50 minutes.

133. The Excel function we want here is varp. The other function var incorporates the correction explained in Section 3.10 in relation to the standard deviation. SPSS produces the corrected function as a matter of course.

134. According to mathematical statistics this is only roughly right for small samples. But it's good enough for a rough estimate, particularly with large samples.

135. Put the run data in as Variable 1, and the earnings data as Variable 2. The re-sample size will be 16, and the resample formula is =slope(G7:G22,F7:F22). (You need to use the Excel formula for the slope instead of the Solver method, because you can't enter the Solver results in a formula.)

136. The resample size should be 17, and the resample statistic =G23-forecast (F23,G7:G22,F7:F22).

137. See a more detailed text on regression, for example Lewis-Beck (1993).

138. Remember that two negative numbers multiplied together are positive – see Note 18.

139. The problem is that the slope and forecast functions do not work for more than one independent variable.

140. You can use the approximate randomisation test (Section 8.3) to derive these *p* values, although *resamplenrh.xls* will only deal with a single variable regression. The relationship statistic to test the whole model should be R squared, the square of the correlation.

141. Dissanaike, G. (1999). Long term stock price reversals in the UK: evidence from regression tests. *British Accounting Review*, 31, 373–85.

142. Edit the formula in Cell F8 on the Model sheet: change *E8^2* to *ABS(E8)*. Then copy it to other cells in the column. Also change the labels referring to squares and MSE.

143. It occurs in compounds such as sodium chloride (salt).

144. Wood, M. Unpublished D. Phil thesis, University of Oxford Department of Educational Studies, 1984, p. 132.

145. The jargon is based on agricultural experiments, where a treatment might be a fertiliser, and drug trials, where a treatment might be a course of a new drug.

146. The analysis used an analysis of covariance, a type of analysis of variance which includes covariates (see Section 9.8).

147. Analyze – Descriptive statistics – Explore.

148. Try changing the numbers in the green cells. The lines on the graph should make sense as sensible predictions. For more details, see Chapter 9.

149. For example Noreen (1989), Simon (1997), Lunneborg (2000), and also see www.statistics.com.

150. Polya, G. (1973). *How to solve it: a new aspect of mathematical method*, Princeton University Press.

References

This only includes publications, referred to in the text, notes or appendices, which are of general relevance to the theme of this book. I have not included works cited in the notes to sources of information, and other specific issues.

Diaconis, P. and Efron, B. (1983) Computer intensive methods in statistics. *Scientific American*: May, 96–108.

Gleick, J. (1998) *Chaos: making a new science*. London: Vintage.

Huff, D. (1973) *How to lie with statistics*. Harmondsworth: Penguin.

Kosko, B. (1994) *Fuzzy thinking*. London: HarperCollins.

Lewis-Beck, M. S. (1993) *Regression analysis* (*International Handbooks of Quantitative Applications in the Social Sciences*, volume 2). London: Sage.

Lunneborg, C. E. (2000) *Data analysis by resampling: concepts and applications*. Pacific Grove: Duxbury.

Noreen, E. W. (1989) *Computer intensive methods for testing hypotheses*. Chichester: Wiley.

Norusis, M. (2000) *SPSS 10.0 Guide to data analysis*. Englewood Cliffs, NJ: Prentice Hall.

Simon, J. L. (1997) *Resampling: the new statistics*. Arlington, VA: Resampling Stats.

Smithson, M. (2000) *Statistics with confidence*. London: Sage.

Stewart, I. (1990) *Does God play dice?* London: Penguin.

Index